The One Year Book
OF
Proverbs

THE ONE YEAR®

Book of

Proverbs

DEVOTIONALS BY

Neil S. Wilson

Tyndale House Publishers, Inc.
Wheaton, Illinois

Visit Tyndale's exciting Web site at www.tyndale.com

The One Year Book of Proverbs devotionals copyright © 2002 by The Livingstone Corporation. All rights reserved.

Scripture quotations are taken from the *Holy Bible*, New Living Translation, copyright © 1996. Used by permission of Tyndale House Publishers, Inc., Wheaton, Illinois 60189. All rights reserved.

Cover photograph © 2002 by Ira Spring. All rights reserved.

Spine photograph © 2002 by Richard Cummins/Corbis Images. All rights reserved.

Designed by Timothy R. Botts

Library of Congress Cataloging-in-Publication Data

Wilson, Neil S., date.
  The one year book of Proverbs : devotionals / by Neil S. Wilson.
    p. cm.
Includes indexes.
  ISBN 0-8423-5607-X
  1. Bible. O.T. Proverbs—Meditations. 2. Christian life—Meditations. 3. Devotional calendars. I. Title.
BS1465.54 .W55 2002
242'.2—dc21   2002007130

Printed in Italy

06 05 04 03 02
7   6   5   4   3   2   1

INTRODUCTION

Welcome to *The One Year Book of Proverbs!*

The book of Proverbs in the Bible is one of the most difficult to read. It includes no stories and few explanations. It lacks flow. In fact, Proverbs wasn't collected for reading, but for savoring.

In the book of Proverbs, God provides us with a training ground for biblical meditation. Most verses in Proverbs can stand alone. They are bite-sized portions of deep wisdom. Individual proverbs allow us to wrap our minds around a single profound idea and explore it through meditation. That is crucial. If we don't move beyond reading, Proverbs will never accomplish the mind-shaping and life-changing effect God intended it to have on us.

So, what is biblical meditation?

Years ago, Billy Graham and others promoted a wonderful idea for developing systematic Bible reading. As part of a larger plan of study, Mr. Graham pointed to the happy coincidence between the thirty-one chapters of Proverbs and the number of days in a month. He revealed a personal practice of reading each day the chapter of Proverbs that corresponded to that particular day of the month. Thousands have discovered the wisdom of that approach. It creates a familiarity with the book of Proverbs that leads to meditation and application.

Biblical mediation begins when the Scriptures have taken residence in our minds. We can meditate on what we have just read, but we can meditate more productively if we have read a passage enough times that we have memorized it. Once you have meditated once on a passage of God's Word you have only begun to delve into the depths you will eventually discover if you persist. Meditation improves with repeated exposure!

The One Year Book of Proverbs allows you to practice this discipline. It assumes that you will read the chapter of Proverbs for the day. Then, each day, a single proverb will be lifted for closer examination.

As a way of broadening the scope of your thinking, we have also included a

"Sabbath proverb" every seven days. These will be proverbs spoken by Jesus and others in Scripture that deserve our special attention. Think of them as an occasional change of pace. They are not "Sabbath" readings because they fall on Sunday (most months they won't). Rather, they are a way of learning and meditating on proverbial sayings that can be found throughout Scripture.

The principle of repetition in meditation will be illustrated on the second "Sabbath" reading of each month, which will focus on the same passage, Mark 12:29-31. Twelve visits to the same verses will still not exhaust the wealth of spiritual riches in what could be called "The Greatest Proverb."

If *The One Year Book of Proverbs* has the desired effect, you will have an increased sense of confidence as you meditate on God's Word. And if God's Word has its desired effect on you as a result, your life will be transformed. May you discover the truth of Psalm 1:2 and become a person whose life demonstrates the components of joyful living: "But they delight in doing everything the LORD wants; day and night they think about his law."

How to get the most out of *The One Year Book of Proverbs*

- If you skipped the Introduction, go back and read it!
- Keep this book with your Bible, so you can read the chapter of Proverbs for the day. You should know that the quoted proverbs in *The One Year Book of Proverbs* come from the New Living Translation of the Bible.
- Keep a notebook with this book so you can record insights that come as you meditate on individual proverbs throughout the year.
- Note in your Bible individual proverbs that have struck you on particular days. Some have found it helpful to put the date in the margin next to the proverb and two or three words to jog their memories about the personal significance of that proverb.
- Don't beat yourself up if you miss a day of reading occasionally. Don't try to catch up; just pick up at the current day's reading. Persistence will develop into a habit.

JANUARY

January 1

**Read
Proverbs 1**

✳

WISDOM IN ACTION

*Through these
proverbs, people will
receive instruction in
discipline, good
conduct, and doing
what is right, just,
and fair.*
Proverbs 1:3

How would a wiser version of you look and act differently? The book of Proverbs promises to provide wisdom. The first six verses list at least fifteen aspects of wise living that can be gained through a continuous exposure to the book. Today's highlight verse aims at three areas of instruction: discipline, good conduct, and actions characterized as right, just, and fair.

The three areas of instruction have to do primarily with outward behavior. Discipline involves positive trained habits that demonstrate self-control. Good conduct covers those situations in which we work with others, making sure our participation promotes goodness. Wisdom also learns to manage the fine balance between right, just, and fair actions.

We must be instructed into wisdom. It does not come naturally. That is why the quality of our wisdom will always depend on the source of our wisdom. If God has instructed us, our wisdom will be genuine.

WISE WAYS How seriously do you want to be a wise person? To what degree are you open to God's wise instruction?

Dear Lord, help me to recognize that you are the ultimate source of all wisdom and that I can count on you to instruct me.

January 2

Kids mimic. One of the unavoidable realities of raising children involves seeing ourselves in their actions. They pick up words, tones, and habits from us. What parents haven't experienced the shock of hearing a familiar expression or seeing a certain mannerism from their children only to realize that the children are mimicking them!

Unfortunately, children don't always choose the most flattering characteristics to mimic. We want them to do as we say, not as we do. They will tend to do what we do rather than what we say, and at the worst possible times. They have an uncanny way of publicizing our contradictions by imitating what we want to hide.

We live wisely before our children when what we do matches what we say. If our doing and our saying are the same and good, it doesn't matter which one they mimic. When we are inconsistent, forcing our children to choose whether to imitate our words or our actions, we do them a great disservice. We can't really expect them to treasure what we don't think is valuable enough to demonstrate by our lives.

WISE WAYS   Live so your children won't have to edit their heritage.

Dear Lord, help me to be an example of consistency before others so that even my failures become good lessons for them as I depend on you for forgiveness.

**Read
Proverbs 2**

WISE HERITAGE

My child, listen to me and treasure my instructions. Tune your ears to wisdom, and concentrate on understanding.
Proverbs 2:1-2

January 3

Read
Proverbs 3

✸

MORE THAN SKIN-DEEP

Never let loyalty and kindness get away from you! Wear them like a necklace; write them deep within your heart.
Proverbs 3:3

What connection can we find between loyalty and kindness that would cause them to be the subject of Solomon's solemn thought? They are qualities that require both internal (heart) and external (necklace) evidence in order to be true. Loyalty and kindness may be faked—for a while. The context indicates that Solomon was thinking of character traits that create a solid relationship between a person and God as well as between that person and others. The very next proverb says, "Then you will find favor with both God and people, and you will gain a good reputation" (3:4). A good way to remember the principle of this proverb relies on a version of an old saying: When it comes to loyalty and kindness, you may be able to fool people part of the time, but you will fool God none of the time.

The phrase "get away from you" also deserves attention. Neither kindness nor loyalty fits as an automatic or permanent trait. They are hard-won and easily lost. Both require continual practice with people and before God.

WISE WAYS If you want to wear loyalty and kindness inside and out, you will have to put them on every day.

Dear Lord, help me see the opportunities you offer me to keep loyalty and kindness fresh in my life today.

January 4

Businesses that want to survive and succeed must invest in research and development. Money, personnel, and time make up that investment. A company unwilling to improve on even good products will quickly find that others will eagerly step in to profit from making better versions of the same things.

Daily life tests wisdom. Yesterday's insight may help face the first of today's problems but fall short on the second. Every day allows us to apply what we have already learned and to engage in fresh research and development for tomorrow. We "learn to be wise" and "develop good judgment" as we acknowledge our lack of wisdom and our poor judgments. Part of each day's investment will involve the mistakes and errors that lead to wisdom. That wisdom grows as we remember and don't turn away from God's words. We love wisdom when we realize she always has more to teach us.

WISE WAYS The continual exposure to God's wise words in Proverbs will greatly improve the pattern of wise ways in your life.

Dear Lord, help me to love your Word today as I seek to practice wisdom.

**Read
Proverbs 4**

WISDOM R & D

Learn to be wise, and develop good judgment. Don't forget or turn away from my words. Don't turn your back on wisdom, for she will protect you. Love her, and she will guard you.
Proverbs 4:5-6

January 5

**Read
Proverbs 5**

THIN ICE!

*The lips of an
immoral woman are
as sweet as honey,
and her mouth is
smoother than oil.
But the result is as
bitter as poison,
sharp as a double-
edged sword.*
Proverbs 5:3-4

Appearances offer tempting deceptions. Whether
they come in the form of a thin coating of ice on a
deep pond or an enticing cover on a book, what we
see often doesn't turn out to be what we get. The
first few steps may seem secure enough and the first
pages may seem harmless, but the end results chill
the body and soul. The writer of this proverb
understood that character counts more than
appearance.

Proverbs offers truth without subtlety. The sweetest
kiss can't make up for a dark heart. Sweetness and
smoothness tend to be temporary—poisons and
swords cause permanent damage. The poison of
immorality leaves relationships ruined and trust
severed. Those who cannot see beyond their momentary needs and wants will discover the painful consequences of their shortsighted decisions.

WISE WAYS The danger behind immediate gratification includes delayed but extended consequences
that are seldom good.

*Dear Lord, help me to think twice about your truth rather than
looking twice at temptation.*

January 6

Scams, disappointments, and financial ruin often begin with misplaced trust. What does the requirement of a cosigner or guarantor indicate right away? It tells you that someone who handles money for a living doesn't consider the primary signer fully able or willing to pay the debt. They need a third person to share the risk—and if you sign on the dotted line, then you are putting yourself at risk. If the person for whom you co-sign a debt defaults on the loan, then you become responsible for that person's debt. Have you anticipated what it will take to pay the debt yourself? The proverb recognizes how easy it is to fall into these commitments. Better to avoid them—at all costs!

In other words, if you would hesitate or be unable to give or loan this "friend" the money, then why would you want to place yourself in a position of being responsible for the debt by cosigning? A genuine friendship represents too valuable an item ever to be equated with money or real estate. Those who trade on your friendship do not have your best interest in mind.

WISE WAYS Demonstrate genuine friendship by being willing to say no to a risky proposition.

Dear Lord, if a friend has a genuine need, give me wisdom to help him/her find a responsible way to meet that need.

**Read
Proverbs 6**

HANDCUFFS

My child, if you co-sign a loan for a friend or guarantee the debt of someone you hardly know . . . quick, get out of it if you possibly can!

Proverbs 6:1-3

January 7

SABBATH

**Read
Proverbs 7**

UNHEALTHY DISCRIMINATION

You have heard that the law of Moses says, "Love your neighbor" and hate your enemy. But I say, love your enemies! Pray for those who persecute you!

Matthew 5:43-44

The decision to follow Jesus may begin as a simple choice, but following the Lord daily will not be easy. He never said it would be. In fact, Jesus' statements often show us how far we have to go. For example, we seldom succeed in loving our neighbors, which Jesus took as the expected starting point from which to love our enemies. We ask: "Lord, how can I even call them enemies and love them?" To which God answers: "Now you get my point!"

Forget about differentiating between neighbors and enemies. Simply start next door. Who lives there? How well do you know them? What are their needs? What specific action could you take (have them over for a meal, help them with a project, pray for them, return with gratitude something you've borrowed for too long, etc.) that would be an expression of love for them? Carry out that action in the next several days.

WISE WAYS   Property lines can represent imposing barriers or be the greatest opportunities to practice obedience to God's instructions.

Dear Lord, help me love my neighbor, _____, in some specific way this week.

January 8

First, to whose "words" does this proverb refer?
This chapter is one of the few in Proverbs dedicated
entirely to one specific theme. Wisdom speaks
throughout the chapter. She states the case for her
own trustworthiness.

This particular proverb offers two healthy
perspectives on wisdom. One of them belongs to
people who have already gained wisdom (understanding). The more wisdom they gain, the more
wisdom seems plain—the plain truth. The other
positive view of wisdom grows in those who genuinely "want to learn."

This could be called the before-and-after experience of wisdom. The desire for wisdom leads to
greater understanding. As understanding grows,
further wisdom stands out in plain sight. A passion
for wisdom leads to wisdom, which in turn leads to
even more wisdom.

Wisdom advertises results. She challenges people
to take her up on her promise.

WISE WAYS One of the clearest marks of a wise,
or soon to be wise, person is an insatiable desire to
learn.

Dear Lord, fill me with that unquenchable thirst to know you, the
source of all wisdom.

Read
Proverbs 8

CRYSTAL CLEAR

My words are plain
to anyone with
understanding, clear
to those who want
to learn.

Proverbs 8:9

January 9

UNDER CONSTRUCTION

*Wisdom has built her
spacious house with
seven pillars.*
Proverbs 9:1

This is just the kind of parable that provokes a meditation question: Why seven pillars? Do they represent seven principles, or seven characteristics of wisdom? Throughout history there have been numerous and ingenious efforts to identify each of the seven pillars. Though interesting, the explanations haven't been persuasive.

The proverb itself offers few clues. Other proverbs that mention numbers usually do so to introduce a list. See for example 6:16-19; 30:15-16, 18-19, 21-23. The verses that immediately follow 9:1 include other actions that Wisdom has set into motion: prepared a feast (v. 2); sent servants to invite and broadcast the same invitation over the city (v. 3). Clearly, the writer was using figurative language.

The tone of this proverb conveys the idea that Wisdom is an expansive host. Her house is "spacious" and complete. The only thing she lacks is enough guests to take advantage of her invitation. How often have you visited Wisdom's house?

WISE WAYS   Wisdom is an inexhaustible commodity. No matter how much you use, you will never find the end of its source—God.

Dear Lord, allow me to make good use of the wisdom you have already provided to me, and keep me alert for more.

January 10

The people in Old Testament times had a high regard for the value of a person's name. Names carried with them special significance. In a culture of verbal agreements, where a promise given carried the weight of a binding contract, a person's name represented his character.

Certain names remind us of people long dead who have left an indelible mark on history, or on us. Other names receive mention only when they serve to illustrate a negative lesson. The first group seems to grow in value over the years, but the second seems to fade, or as the text says, "rot away." The application of this proverb becomes a pointed question about life: What will the mention of our names bring to people's minds after we have died?

WISE WAYS The best personal models for life are people who have left a lasting impression.

Dear Lord, thank you for the people who give me happy memories. Allow me to keep their example in mind as I live my life.

**Read
Proverbs 10**

BIODEGRADABLE REPUTATION

We all have happy memories of the godly, but the name of a wicked person rots away.

Proverbs 10:7

January 11

Read
Proverbs 11

✳

GOD DELIGHTS

The LORD hates cheating, but he delights in honesty.
Proverbs 11:1

We tend to think of God as a reactor rather than a responder. Because God is good, he reacts to anything that disturbs his normal pattern. However, this view of God seriously diminishes our capacity to appreciate God's divine delight over good.

We know God delights because we know he delights in his own work. After each day's worth of the creation masterpieces, God didn't summarize his effort with the resounding declaration, "This is normal!" No, God's delight must have reverberated through every fiber of his expanding creation when he thundered, "This is good!" Six times in the first chapter of Genesis we are told that God saw his creation as good. By the end of the sixth day, God concluded that his work was "excellent in every way" (Genesis 1:31). God responds to good with delight.

God desires to delight in us. He does this partly, this proverb tells us, when we practice honesty. The test of honesty comes when we are tempted to think what we do doesn't matter because no one is watching. But we always have an audience. Does God delight in what we do?

WISE WAYS God does not observe you with the intent of noticing evil, but with the desire to delight in the good he finds!

Dear Lord, help me live this day with a constant recognition that you enjoy the good in my life even more than I do.

January 12

In one sense, this proverb describes two different types of people: those who learn, and those who refuse to learn. The first, the learners, understand and accept the necessity of discipline as part of the learning process. The second, the refusers, ignore and reject correction. The learners decide to love discipline; the refusers decide to hate anything and everything that might offer a good lesson. The learners grow in wisdom; the refusers sink into stupidity.

Both types of people may be dealing with the same experience, for discipline and correction often take the same form. For example, both the learners and those who refuse to learn can make the same mistake. When it is pointed out to the first, they appreciate the correction and adjust their actions. Meanwhile, the second resent the correction and often refuse to change their ways.

Love or hatred for discipline can be claimed anytime, but the proof comes when discipline occurs. How we respond demonstrates whether we have made the wise choice to learn or the wrong choice to remain foolish.

WISE WAYS   Anticipate inevitable mistakes. Prepare your attitude to respond with appreciation for the opportunity to learn.

Dear Lord, please remind me today that when I make my next mistake I have also created a good opportunity to learn. Help me love that!

**Read
Proverbs 12**

THANKS!
I NEEDED THAT

*To learn,
you must love
discipline;
it is stupid
to hate
correction.*
Proverbs 12:1

January 13

✳

WELCOMED DISCIPLINE

A wise child accepts a parent's discipline; a young mocker refuses to listen.

Proverbs 13:1

Adults who know how to practice loving discipline are grown-up versions of children who have been wisely trained. The cycle or process begins with an adult. Until discipline is offered, a child has no choice between acceptance and refusal. The earlier in life that loving discipline is offered, the greater a child's opportunity to develop wisdom.

Both the wise child and the mocker are the products of training. Mockery is a form of disrespect that must be confronted early in life. Someone who is young and a mocker has not benefited from early discipline. Perhaps the child's capacity to make fun of others was considered cute. Eventually that skill becomes an ingrained habit. Such a youth has gotten so accustomed to disrespecting others through mockery that he or she finds it almost impossible to listen.

Children aren't born wise. It takes loving and courageous discipline to teach them wisdom. When that isn't given, mockery and other natural evidences of sin take over. Wise parents seek help from God and his Word every step of this process.

WISE WAYS Wise parents look for ways to challenge disrespect and encourage wisdom in their children from the earliest age.

Dear Lord, forgive my own parent's failures and thank you for their successes. Help me to benefit from all the past by learning and applying wisdom.

January 14

SABBATH

What really matters? What's up? What's the bottom line? When all is said and done, what has to be said and done? The questions may sound different, but they all express in one way or another the common, deep-rooted desire in people to know that their lives mean something.

Jesus had an answer for the man who asked him the question. It had two parts, or dimensions: the vertical (our love for God) and the horizontal (our love for people, including ourselves). Every other true rule for living falls under the summary Jesus gave.

Because it is the central proverb and the key commandment, we will return to it on the second Sabbath reflection of each month. If Jesus said something was the most important statement of wisdom, we can expect to gain great benefit from giving it our repeated attention.

WISE WAYS God's directions for living are not complicated—just challenging. They can be summarized and pursued. They can be accomplished with God's help.

Dear Lord, teach me to consider important what you consider important. Keep me from distractions that focus my attention on what is not important.

**Read
Proverbs 14**

BOTTOM LINE

Jesus replied, "The most important commandment is this: 'Hear, O Israel! The Lord our God is the one and only Lord. And you must love the Lord your God with all your heart, all your soul, all your mind, and all your strength.' The second is equally important: 'Love your neighbor as yourself.' No other commandment is greater than these."

Mark 12:29-31

January 15

**Read
Proverbs 15**

✳

DEFLECTING
RESPONSE

*A gentle answer turns
away wrath, but
harsh words stir
up anger.*
Proverbs 15:1

The wisdom in this proverb can be found in the
volume and the tone of our responses to anger. We
know that some of the harshest, anger-provoking
words can be spoken very quietly. Sometimes it takes
a shouted "I love you!" to move an argument in a
better direction. The tone, or character, of our
responses—more than their volume—determines the
outcome of a tense exchange.

Wise listeners pay attention to both words and
tone. Sometimes a person's angry words and tone
are justified. The gentleness of an answer doesn't
necessarily eliminate the anger; it deflects it so that
truth can be discovered. Meanwhile, harsh or
thoughtless words not only create angry responses;
they often intensify anger that is already present.

Godly wisdom seeks to respond gently because it
places a higher value on truth than on the particular
wrapping of words and tone. Gentleness unwraps
the feelings and expressions to find the truth.

WISE WAYS Ask God to make you aware of situations that will train and improve your capacity to
respond with gentle wisdom.

*Dear Lord, help me learn to affect people for you by listening to both
their words and their tone and by answering them gently.*

January 16

One of the exciting evidences of a personal relationship with God occurs when he supplies us with an answer we know didn't originate with us. Preparation, or gathering our thoughts, puts us in the best position to recognize God's answers. But preparation does not eliminate our need for God to supply answers. The value of good preparation comes from the way it disciplines our heart and mind to respond to God's direction.

There are two challenges behind this proverb. The first involves our willingness to do our best at preparation. The second involves our willingness to rely on God before, during, and after we have prepared. The discipline of studying these proverbs day by day represents significant preparation for wise living. But the appropriate application of that wisdom comes with God's help. We must not forget the stunning truth that the wise collector of these sayings failed in many ways to rely on God. Solomon received many right answers, but he didn't put some of them into practice. Gathering wisdom doesn't automatically mean we are living wisely.

WISE WAYS Those who fill their minds with God's Word and act on the answers God provides experience wise living.

Dear Lord, please allow me to put into practice today a wise insight you have supplied in your Word.

Read
Proverbs 16

BEYOND
PREPARATION

We can gather our thoughts, but the LORD gives the right answer.
Proverbs 16:1

January 17

Read
Proverbs 17

✳

BENEFICIAL
MELTDOWN

*Fire tests the purity
of silver and gold,
but the LORD tests
the heart.*
Proverbs 17:3

Impurities cannot be removed from silver and gold until the costly metal has been melted. Heat causes the liquid state that allows the impurities to rise to the surface, where they can be skimmed off. When the precious metal has been purified, *tried* and *tested* are some of the terms used to describe it.

So, how does God test a heart? He melts it. He allows it to suffer unprovoked difficulties, as well as the consequences of poor decisions, in order to bring "heat" into our lives.

The smelting process provides an excellent illustration of the word *repentance*. Repentant people have a molten heart. Repentance brings the impurities of the heart to the surface where they can be confessed and burned away by forgiveness. At the same time, a molten heart can be re-formed. A repentant attitude describes people whose central motivations reach a state that allows God to continually reshape them so they will be useful for God's kingdom. Effective repentance eventually leads to humility. Genuine humility describes a person continually willing to be cleansed and reshaped by God.

WISE WAYS Recognize that the tests of life can accomplish much that is good in your life and help eliminate much that is bad.

Dear Lord, I give you permission to melt down those parts of my heart that are hard, so that I can be more purely yours.

January 18

Did Jesus have this proverb in mind as he watched the woman approach the well in Samaria (John 4:6)? Perhaps. He told her that his words were life-giving water (John 4:14). Did Jesus' conversation with the woman at the well have the refreshing effect promised in this proverb? It certainly did.

What a transformation! The woman went from being the town outcast to being an outspoken evangelist. Her message? "Come and meet a man who told me everything I ever did! Can this be the Messiah?" (John 4:29). Jesus' words had shown her that he really knew her and her needs. They also conveyed his care and his ability to meet her needs. She became a bubbling brook that drew others to taste Jesus' life-giving water (John 4:39-42). We can have the same effect on others as we experience daily intimacy with Jesus.

WISE WAYS   If you can think of someone whose needs might be met by a soft word or gesture from you, then perhaps today is the day to offer some living water.

Dear Lord, I know that my words will not have a life-giving and refreshing effect on others unless they come from you. Please fill me with such words.

**Read
Proverbs 18**

VERBAL REFRESHMENT

A person's words can be life-giving water; words of true wisdom are as refreshing as a bubbling brook.
Proverbs 18:4

January 19

Read
Proverbs 19

WORSE THAN POVERTY

It is better to be poor and honest than to be a fool and dishonest.

Proverbs 19:1

The comparison in this proverb may catch the reader by surprise. Why doesn't the second line read "rich and dishonest"? Good question! Although we might tend to jump to the conclusion that riches and poverty automatically sit at opposite ends of any spectrum, the truth resides in the fact that wealth and poverty can be the companions of any number of character traits. For everyone who is rich and dishonest, there is probably someone who is poor and dishonest.

This proverb points out that poverty and honesty are not inseparable. Someone who is poor and honest is wealthy by comparison to someone who is a fool and dishonest, for the latter does not appreciate the depth of his poverty. Dishonest fools, whether rich or poor, are good for little more than to serve as negative examples. Meanwhile, the poor who are honest offer some of the best examples of genuine wisdom to the world. They accomplish a lot with little, and often work their way right out of poverty.

WISE WAYS In what ways have you experienced the wisdom of honest poverty in your life? (For some possibilities, see the devotional for January 28.)

Dear Lord, help me to see and be honest about areas of poverty in my life. I desire to experience how you supply where I lack. Thank you!

January 20

This proverb does not deny the fact that conflict may be necessary. Rather, it challenges those who go out of their way to create conflict. It also turns upside down the typical attitude that honor is best defended by eagerness to fight. Honor doesn't need to prove itself by "insisting on quarreling."

The wise person pictured in this proverb learns to see a fight coming. Such a person knows that a fight may demonstrate who is stronger more often than it demonstrates who is right. Thus, fighting may not move the parties any closer to a resolution. Hostilities may bury the truth more deeply. It is better, and more honorable, to seek the truth before a fight breaks out.

Quarreling usually turns out to be an attempt to verbally defeat an opponent by superior volume, threat, or insult. Rarely does quarreling have to do with the truth. Therefore, those who readily resort to quarreling reveal their foolishness; even if those doing so happen to be us!

WISE WAYS The temptation to quarrel is often an indication that you have lost sight of the truth and are more interested in "winning." The wise resist such temptations.

Dear Lord, I admit I can be foolish and quarrelsome. I need your help to recognize this temptation when it appears in my life.

**Read
Proverbs 20**

PICKING FIGHTS
OR PICKING
YOUR FIGHTS

*Avoiding a fight is a
mark of honor;
only fools insist on
quarreling.*
Proverbs 20:3

January 21

SABBATH

**Read
Proverbs 21**

UNPACKING FOR THE JOURNEY

Then Jesus said to the disciples, "If any of you wants to be my follower, you must put aside your selfish ambition, shoulder your cross, and follow me."
Matthew 16:24

Jesus never hesitated to add sobering warnings to shocking announcements. In the preceding verses, he had informed his disciples plainly of his approaching execution and resurrection. Because they couldn't imagine what he meant by describing his own death, they didn't even consider what he meant by his prediction to be raised the third day.

Quickly rejecting Peter's insistence that Jesus' outlook was unacceptable, the Lord turned his attention to the disciples with the challenge in today's proverb. Note that his audience (the disciples) probably assumed that they were already his followers, but His words questioned that assumption. Jesus noted four characteristics of genuine disciples: (1) a disciple desires to follow; (2) a disciple sets aside self-centered plans, expectations, and schedules; (3) a disciple accepts (takes up, shoulders) the burdens associated with following Christ; and (4) a disciple actually does follow Christ.

WISE WAYS   In what ways would a stranger spending this day with you discover that you are a follower of Jesus?

Dear Lord, point out to me anything on my schedule today that is nothing more than selfish ambition. Please give me courage to put that aside and follow you.

January 22

Today's proverb offers us one practical application of yesterday's wise saying. Jesus spoke of the dangers of selfish ambition and challenged his disciples to have a godly ambition that intentionally seeks to please God, even to the point of bearing a cross (Matthew 16:24).

Here, godly ambition makes the choice between a good reputation and great riches. Both can be pursued, but only one has lasting value. Only one will prove itself ours beyond this life. Riches will stay behind, no matter what we sacrificed to gain them. Why should we choose what we will have to leave behind when we can choose something of eternal value?

Godly ambition aims high. Godly ambition sets its sights on living the kind of life that will create a good reputation with God. If that can be accomplished, everything else will fall into place. Ultimately, this great purpose in life becomes possible when we realize that God will actually help us gain his high esteem.

WISE WAYS How often do you appraise your ambition? What are the top three objectives you are pursuing in life?

Dear Lord, help me to intentionally seek to make choices that please you. I want to have a good reputation with you!

**Read
Proverbs 22**

REPUTATION
APPRAISAL

*Choose a good
reputation over great
riches, for being held
in high esteem is
better than having
silver or gold.*

Proverbs 22:1

January 23

Read
Proverbs 23

❋

BANKRUPT
EFFORT

*Don't weary yourself
trying to get rich.
Why waste your
time? For riches can
disappear as though
they had the wings of
a bird!*

Proverbs 23:4-5

The writer advises us not to weary ourselves trying to get rich because those riches have a way of disappearing. Like birds that fly to the bird feeder and just as quickly are gone, so money has a way of disappearing with a whisper of wings.

Who has not deposited the paycheck in the bank, only to wonder—a day later—where it all went? Even a windfall of wealth has the wings of a bird. Or we get that pay raise, but immediately raise our standard of living so that we still never have enough money. It seems to fly away.

The focus of life should never be riches, for that is a desire that will never be satisfied. Who ever says, "I have enough money; I don't need any more"? But if we can learn contentment with what we have, we will not be wearying ourselves going after riches only to watch them fly away.

WISE WAYS   What is the focus of your life? How high on your list of priorities is the pursuit of wealth?

Dear Lord, help me not to focus on the wrong priorities but to learn contentment in you.

January 24

Sometimes evil does seem to triumph over good. Sometimes bad people win. Sometimes good guys finish last. Sometimes the wicked prosper while the good wonder. The implication of this proverb is that evil people may indeed have what we desire.

Unfortunately, the word *discrimination* has been twisted to carry primarily negative connotations. But discrimination has to do with our capacity to judge or weigh people and situations before entrusting ourselves to them. We may discriminate for the wrong reasons, but that doesn't invalidate the importance of that ability. We don't want our children to discriminate against people because of skin color, but we certainly want their capacity to discriminate in full force when a drug-pusher or a peddler of immorality approaches them. Wise discrimination sizes up people for the right reasons. Wise discrimination allows us to spot people of character and make a point to associate with them. And wise discrimination warns us when to be cautious of certain people and avoid their company.

WISE WAYS You can resist the temptation to envy evil people and their earthly wealth by remembering the priceless eternal treasures you have in Christ.

Dear Lord, I know how easy it is to envy those I shouldn't. Help me to wisely discriminate where I rest my emotions and desires.

**Read
Proverbs 24**

WISE
DISCRIMINATION

*Don't envy evil
people; don't desire
their company.*
Proverbs 24:1

January 25

**Read
Proverbs 25**

✳

PERFECT DELIVERY

*Timely advice is as
lovely as golden
apples in a
silver basket.*

Proverbs 25:11

Timing is almost as important as truth when it comes to advice. Hindsight may have the reputation for perfect vision, but it arrives too late to prevent a disaster. Even the best advice, given at the wrong time, may not be recognized. Timely advice is a lovely package with contents that we really need.

Effective counsel arrives at the right time. It is neither so early that it is forgotten when needed nor does it arrive too late to be useful. The timing of advice is as much the evidence of wisdom as the contents of advice. Anyone can say, "Be careful," after their friend has already stubbed his toe. Timely advice says, "The last time I traveled this path there were some roots that tripped me up. Let's be careful." Both statements are good advice, but timing makes the second one lovely.

WISE WAYS Much of God's wisdom is available to you in his Word. But wisdom in timely application comes from experience with God.

Dear Lord, I know that learning your wisdom is my responsibility, but I want to consciously depend on you for timing when I share it with anyone else.

January 26

Fools, summer, and harvest represent the givens in this proverb. Each one comes with a set of characteristics or expectations. In summer, we expect heat; at the harvest, cool weather. Snows don't fit with summer, and rains make a mess out of harvest. Likewise, when it comes to fools, honor is always out of season.

So what are the traits that accompany fools? To use the terms of this proverb, dishonor summarizes a foolish profile. Dishonor describes people who don't take responsibility for their decisions ahead of time so they can make them carefully, nor do they take responsibility for their mistakes and failures once they occur. Whenever we find ourselves surrounded by thoughtless decisions and excessive blaming, we can safely assume that a crop of fools has sprouted. The last thing we expect to find there is honor. And if we expect to be people of honor ourselves, we won't go with them.

WISE WAYS List the people in your life that are your clearest examples of honor. Thank God for them and imitate their lives.

Dear Lord, I give you permission to expose the foolishness in my life. Help me be a person in season when it comes to honor.

**Read
Proverbs 26**

SEASONS

Honor doesn't go with fools any more than snow with summer or rain with harvest.
Proverbs 26:1

January 27

**Read
Proverbs 27**

FUTILE
FORECAST

*Don't brag about
tomorrow, since you
don't know what the
day will bring.*
Proverbs 27:1

James, the brother of Jesus, penned one of the finest comments on the truth of this passage: "Look here, you people who say, 'Today or tomorrow we are going to a certain town and will stay there a year. We will do business there and make a profit.' How do you know what will happen tomorrow? For your life is like the morning fog—it's here a little while, then it's gone. What you ought to say is, 'If the Lord wants us to, we will live and do this or that.' Otherwise you will be boasting about your own plans, and all such boasting is evil. Remember, it is sin to know what you ought to do and then not do it" (James 4:13-17).

According to James, we don't ignore tomorrow. But we don't take it for granted either. Because God holds the future, we make plans based on his over-riding will and wisdom. We don't know what will happen tomorrow, but we know and trust someone who does!

WISE WAYS When was the last time you placed your dreams, goals, and plans before God and asked for his wisdom and blessing?

Dear Lord, it is easy to presume on tomorrow—even on the rest of today. Help me to treasure each moment as a gift from you.

January 28

SABBATH

On the fourth "Sabbath" of each month, we will highlight a beatitude. Most of them are found in the opening verses of the Sermon on the Mount (Matthew 5–7). For the purposes of these reflections, beatitudes are promises given by Jesus that attach God's blessing to a specific action or attitude on our part.

The sequence of the Beatitudes in the Sermon on the Mount describes the process of transformation that people experience when they pass from darkness to light, death to life, and from separation from God to union with God.

The first beatitude describes those at the starting point: people who realize their need for God. They have stopped wondering if they need God; they know they do. They freely and honestly admit their deep spiritual poverty. There is no clearer, more life-changing moment of truth than when we acknowledge before God our utter spiritual bankruptcy and accept his grace. God blesses that conviction with a gift—the kingdom of Heaven!

WISE WAYS   In what specific ways have you acknowledged your need for God? How are you practicing that dependence in a consistent way?

Dear Lord, today I acknowledge my poverty of spirit in the following ways: ____. Thank you for the freedom to approach you with my needs.

Read
Proverbs 28

THE BEGINNING OF GOD'S BLESSINGS

God blesses those who realize their need for him, for the kingdom of Heaven is given to them.
Matthew 5:3

January 29

CHEERS

*Evil people are
trapped by sin, but
the righteous escape,
shouting for joy.*
Proverbs 29:6

This proverb offers a healthy alternative to the drab
life too many Christians take for granted. We avoid
sin's traps too seldom and rejoice too little over our
occasional escapes. We give far too much attention
to discovering how close to sinful living we can come
without becoming trapped. Meanwhile, we don't
give nearly enough attention to the ways of escape
that God has pledged to provide when we are
tempted (I Corinthians 10:12-13).

When was the last time you understood the danger
of sin so clearly that you shouted for joy because you
escaped? Have you cheered over today's close calls?
Until avoiding sin becomes at least as exciting and
thrilling as temptation itself, we won't know we are
making much real progress toward righteousness.

WISE WAYS   Take a moment to rejoice over a
recent escape from sin that God provided for you.

*Dear Lord, remind me to be more expressive over the victories you
help me win when I escape one of sin's traps.*

January 30

When people understand events clearly, we often say that they "see the big picture." Today's highlighted proverb makes the point that the clearest view of the "big picture" will always include God. The sequence of rhetorical questions helps us consider the awesome identity and capacity of God. Much like the litany of questions that God showered on Job (Job 38:1–41:34), these push us toward humble and silent worship.

Agur was feeling overwhelmed (30:1), insignificant (30:2), and limited (30:3). But when he turned away from his own smallness to contemplate God's greatness, an atmosphere of confidence filled the rest of the chapter. He began with a little picture, no bigger than himself, but he soon looked at the big picture and forgot that he was weary and worn out. God gave him a new and refreshing point of view.

WISE WAYS   One of the best remedies for a weary and tired spirit is to contemplate the majesty and greatness of God. How have you found that to be true?

Dear Lord, when I look at all you have made, I know it makes me feel smaller, but it also fills me with wonder over how great you are! I worship you.

Read
Proverbs 30

IMPRESSIVE PANORAMA

Who but God goes up to heaven and comes back down? Who holds the wind in his fists? Who wraps up the oceans in his cloak? Who has created the whole wide world? What is his name—and his son's name? Tell me if you know!

Proverbs 30:4

January 31

**Read
Proverbs 31**

A TIME FOR SPEAKING UP

*Speak up for those
who cannot speak for
themselves; ensure
justice for those who
are perishing. Yes,
speak up for the poor
and helpless, and
see that they
get justice.*

Proverbs 31:8-9

This proverb states a strong biblical antidote to the prevailing "mind your own business" mentality that cripples righteous living today. Yes, there are situations in which we shouldn't meddle. Those who can speak or fend for themselves do not necessarily want our help. Yet most of us are aware of children and others who cannot speak for themselves but are suffering injustice while those who could help do nothing. The size of the problem does not excuse our silence.

Twice this proverb directs us to "speak up." The problem for most Christians is not that we can't see things that are wrong or that we can't speak up. The problem is that we won't speak up. Why? We're intimidated, ashamed, or simply disobedient. If we're unwilling even to speak up, it is practically certain that we will also be unwilling to "see that they get justice." A warning from James that we read several days ago applies here just as well: "Remember, it is sin to know what you ought to do and then not do it" (James 4:17).

WISE WAYS   The defenseless offer the clearest opportunity to practice the "golden rule"—treat others as you would want to be treated if your situations were reversed (see Matthew 7:12).

Dear Lord, I realize my heart needs to be opened more than my eyes do. Help me speak up for those who can't defend themselves.

✳ FEBRUARY

February 1

Read
Proverbs 1

A GOOD BEGINNING

*Fear of the LORD is
the beginning of
knowledge. Only
fools despise wisdom
and discipline.*

Proverbs 1:7

The Bible makes it clear that God is sovereign. In other words, he has total and complete authority. We, his creations, should indeed "fear" him—for he has ultimate power. Yet we also know from the Bible that God is loving, merciful, and compassionate. So we are not afraid of God; instead, our "fear" should be reverence and awe that an all-powerful, sovereign God would care to reach out to us. When we fear the Lord, we are beginning to have knowledge about what really matters for our lives, which creates an attitude open to wisdom.

Those who would turn away at the possibility of having true wisdom are called "fools." Such people despise what matters most, and therefore their lives are spent focusing on all the wrong priorities. God promises to give wisdom to all who ask (James 1:5). Let us fear the Lord so that he can teach us and make us wise.

WISE WAYS   In what ways do you show your reverence and awe of God?

Today, Lord, may I seek wisdom from you, knowing that you are the ultimate source of all wisdom and knowledge.

February 2

Some things are worth searching for, waiting for, and working for. If we lost a hundred dollar bill, we would probably turn the house upside down trying to find it. We would retrace our steps until we remembered where we had put it. In adventure stories, there is often a hidden treasure that both the good guys and the bad guys are intently seeking—even to the point of death. Most of the time, they don't know what the treasure holds, they just know something is there and they want to be the first to find it.

It is with such passion that we should search for "insight and understanding." These are as valuable as hidden treasure. Life is a mystery; so much is unclear. Our sovereign God will not give us all the answers, but he does promise a certain amount of insight and understanding that will help us through. To find him is to find the greatest treasure of all.

WISE WAYS   In what area of your life do you need extra insight and understanding? God promises to give it to you if you ask him.

Today, Lord, may I seek you and the insight and understanding you give as I deal with the difficult and confusing situations in my life.

**Read
Proverbs 2**

TREASURE
HUNTING

Cry out for insight and understanding. Search for them as you would for lost money or hidden treasure.

Proverbs 2:3-4

February 3

**Read
Proverbs 3**

✳

WITH ALL YOUR HEART

*Trust in the LORD
with all your heart;
do not depend on
your own
understanding.*
Proverbs 3:5

How much do we trust God, really? Do we relegate him only to the huge crises in our life, not wanting to bother him with the mundane problems? Or do we do the opposite—relegating him to the little problems, while we work through the big decisions on our own? What keeps us from trusting God with all our heart in all our situations?

To trust God with all our heart means to turn everything over to him so that he can guide us and direct our paths (3:6). Of course, we can still work through our problems logically. We have been told in Proverbs to cry out for understanding (2:3), so we do need it, but ultimately we do not depend on that understanding. Instead, we depend on God. When we trust in him, we have the final authority— the one who sees the big picture—helping us to take the next step along the path of life.

WISE WAYS   In how many of your life decisions do you depend on your own understanding, and in how many do you trust in the Lord? What needs to change in order for you to trust in the Lord with all your heart?

Today, Lord, teach me how to trust in you with all my heart.

February 4

Jesus certainly had a way of boiling things down to the basics. He was surrounded with people who were experts at finding loopholes and exceptions in the law. They were skilled at the art of overlooking the obvious, as Jesus pointed out a number of times. His description of people straining out gnats while swallowing camels (Matthew 23:23-24) may strike us as hilarious until we gag on the truth that he is talking about people like us.

The mouthful of reality in Jesus' joke points out our tendency to see ourselves as the exception. We want others to treat us as we deserve to be treated, but we balk at treating them the same way. We know what we want others to do for us, but doing the same for them is too much trouble. They might not reciprocate. The principle in this proverb, of course, is the risk involved in following Jesus. Common sense might tell us to see how others treat us so we will then know how to treat them. Jesus rejects that approach. He tells those who want to be his disciples that they must actively pursue treating people as they themselves want to be treated.

WISE WAYS   Doing what is right often boils down to doing what seems risky.

Today, Lord, remind me not to wait until others do for me; help me do for them first.

Read
Proverbs 4

RISKING
KINDNESS

Do for others what you would like them to do for you. This is a summary of all that is taught in the law and the prophets.
Matthew 7:12

February 5

**Read
Proverbs 5**

✳

A CROOKED
PATH

*[The immoral
woman's] feet go
down to death; her
steps lead straight to
the grave. For she
does not care about
the path to life. She
staggers down a
crooked trail and
doesn't even realize
where it leads.*

Proverbs 5:5-6

The immoral woman is a person who has turned from godly paths toward pleasure, passion, and lust. How apt is this chapter for today, for we don't need to go much farther than the local newsstand or a few clicks on the Internet to find plenty of immoral women and men. The Bible is clear that to follow these people's ways is a path to death, footsteps to destruction. And so many people are tempted onto that path—some who should know better, many who don't.

God created sex within the confines of marriage as intimate and beautiful. Satan knew what he was doing when he made illicit sex so exciting. But against the "no one gets hurt" thinking stand millions of broken families, diseased bodies, and lonely people. Immorality is a path to death. Believers who have been tempted onto the path need to consider the consequences and turn around before it is too late.

WISE WAYS Are you involved in (or thinking of being involved in) any form of immorality? How are you trying to rationalize it? Does your rationale stand up against what God says in his Word?

Today, Lord, help me to be strong against temptation to immorality. Help me to run from temptation, and guide me in your paths.

February 6

Who doesn't want to hit the snooze button when that blaring alarm wakes us out of our slumber? Fortunately, this proverb doesn't mean that using the snooze button every morning is going to send us onto the streets, homeless. Nor does it mean that a bit of rest from our labors will ruin us. Indeed, the Bible even talks about God resting from his labors (Genesis 2:2), and Jesus and his disciples went away to rest (Mark 6:31). These should not be considered the workaholic's life verses, for they are not meant that way.

These verses are talking about a habit of laziness. Lazy people always have an excuse for not being productive with the gifts and talents God has given them. Laziness will have its consequences, often leading to poverty and scarcity, as these verses predict.

God calls us to work, support ourselves and our families, and be productive for his kingdom. God has little use for lazy laborers other than graciously to transform them into productive ones.

WISE WAYS   What is your attitude toward your work? Are you being as productive as you should be?

Today, Lord, help me to work hard and well at the tasks you have placed before me.

Read
Proverbs 6

LAZY LABORERS

A little extra sleep, a little more slumber, a little folding of the hands to rest—and poverty will pounce on you like a bandit; scarcity will attack you like an armed robber.

Proverbs 6:10-11

February 7

Read
Proverbs 7

✳

PRECIOUS OBEDIENCE

Obey [my commands] and live! Guard my teachings as your most precious possession. Tie them on your fingers as a reminder. Write them deep within your heart.
Proverbs 7:2-3

Many people look at the Bible as a long list of dos and don'ts. They think that God gives all kinds of laws in order to keep people from having any fun or pleasure in life. They might look at these verses and say, "See? All God wants is for people to obey!"

But they have it wrong. Yes, God does command obedience, but not because he is some tyrant who needs to have people be subject to his every whim. Instead, God requires obedience because he knows that obedience is best for us. Obedience to God's laws helps us to live life to all its fullness—protected from foolish mistakes and able to make wise choices. That's why the writer tells us to guard these teachings like precious possessions, tied on our fingers, written in our hearts so we can never forget.

WISE WAYS Do you allow obedience to God's laws to guide you every step of the way through every day? Are his laws your most precious possession?

Today, Lord, help me to remember your commands so that I might truly live for you.

February 8

Silver, gold, rubies—sounds like the standard fare of royalty. Who among us does not strive for a certain amount of wealth, comfort, and security? We may not have precious metals and jewels on our wish lists, but we all set goals and strive to achieve certain standards of success. While gold, silver, and jewels are fine in themselves, they should never be our ultimate goal, nor should they be obtained in wrongful ways. The writer says that we should choose instruction, knowledge, and wisdom far above anything else in this life.

The trappings of success are nothing without wisdom and understanding to go along with them. We all know very rich people who have acted foolishly in business or in their family lives. They may have it all, but they are the most unhappy and bitter people around. Ultimately, a person who has nothing but wisdom is by far the richest person of all.

WISE WAYS What are your goals in life? How does your search for wisdom rank compared to your striving for other things? What can you do to change your priorities, if needed?

Today, Lord, show me where my priorities are wrong so that I will be striving for the right things in the right way.

**Read
Proverbs 8**

WISE ACCOUNTING

Choose my instruction rather than silver, and knowledge over pure gold. For wisdom is far more valuable than rubies. Nothing you desire can be compared with it.
Proverbs 8:10-11

February 9

**Read
Proverbs 9**

✳

THE WIDEST
INVITATION

*[Wisdom] has sent
her servants to invite
everyone to come.
She calls out from the
heights overlooking
the city.*
Proverbs 9:3

Wisdom does not hold exclusive parties. She is not
seeking only the brightest, or the best-looking, or
the most likely to succeed. She does not keep anyone
who desires to come from taking part in her festivi-
ties. In other words, wisdom is available to anyone
who asks for it!

In this picture of wisdom as a woman inviting
people to her spacious home, we see a picture of the
grace of our great and loving God. In the Garden of
Eden, Eve thought that eating the fruit would make
her "so wise" (Genesis 3:6). She thought that God
was keeping something from her, and so she
disobeyed. She failed to realize that God had given
her all that she needed to know. So she and Adam
turned their backs on wisdom and welcomed the
ultimate foolishness of sin. Although we all now exist
under the curse of sin, God seeks to give us the
wisdom that we need in order to have a relationship
with him. What grace! Wisdom is calling. Have we
answered?

WISE WAYS   God wants to give you wisdom; all
you need to do is ask. Have you sent your RSVP to
Wisdom's invitation?

Today, Lord, may I respond to the invitation to find your wisdom.

February 10

Some people are very good liars. They can make up all kinds of stories and fabrications of events in order to keep themselves from being incriminated. What often happens, however, is that they can't keep all their lies straight.

By contrast, when we speak only the truth, we have only one story to remember—the true one. No trying to remember to whom we told what, or which lie we told in what way. In other words, as the verse says, with integrity, we have firm footing. We stand on a solid foundation, the truth—even if that truth is difficult to have to tell. Being a liar, however, sends us on crooked paths where we slip and fall.

People of true integrity are difficult to stereotype. Often they seem a bit unreal, because so much of what they do is clearly right. Their "firm footing," however, makes them people we know we can trust. They show us that when we speak and live the truth, we walk with sure footsteps into and through every situation.

WISE WAYS Would people say you are a person of integrity? In what areas do you need to improve?

Today, Lord, may I be truthful and trustworthy, may I build a reputation for integrity so that I may have firm footing.

**Read
Proverbs 10**

WORTHY EXAMPLES

People with integrity have firm footing, but those who follow crooked paths will slip and fall.

Proverbs 10:9

February 11

SABBATH

**Read
Proverbs 11**

FAMILIARITY

*Jesus replied, "The
most important
commandment is this:
'Hear, O Israel! The
Lord our God is the
one and only Lord.
And you must love the
Lord Your God with
all your heart, all your
soul, all your mind,
and all your strength.'
The second is equally
important: 'Love
your neighbor as
yourself.' No other
commandment is
greater than these."*

Mark 12:29-31

The man who asked Jesus the question that brought this profound response received something as familiar as his own name. As a devout Jew, in accordance with Deuteronomy 6:4-9, he had probably said those very words as he left his home that morning. He said them every day. They were a spiritual verbal habit, as ingrained as wiping his feet before entering the house. Now he heard them from Jesus as the central commandment from God. He had no trouble agreeing with Jesus, and he said so (Mark 12:32). He knew the right answer when he heard it, even though it was familiar.

Jesus' response to the man's agreement makes a stunning point: "You are not far from the kingdom of God" (Mark 12:33). He was close because he knew; now he just had to go and do! He wasn't in yet. But Jesus let him know he definitely had the right idea. We know Jesus' words silenced the crowd; we don't know if the man entered the kingdom or settled for being close. His predicament invites us to consider where we have settled: not far from the kingdom of God, or in it?

WISE WAYS Knowing the right answer doesn't mean you have applied it.

Lord, I affirm my trust in you as the one who declares me a citizen of your kingdom by grace. Help me practice the love life of the kingdom today.

February 12

Proverbs has much to say about wives and husbands. This one offers a glimpse of the way spouses have a deep influence on one another. This has nothing to do with the perfection of the husband, for no husband can be perfect. Nor does it refer to a wife being no more than a doormat or a trophy on display. Instead, this verse is referring to a loving relationship in which both husband and wife honor each other. And it reveals the power a wife has in a relationship.

When a wife builds up and supports her husband, when she is faithful and loving, then she is like a crown on his head and she brings him joy. But when she hurts and shames him by her actions or words, she can ruin him. Husbands and wives need to work together to build a relationship in which they are "worthy" for each other. Then they will find great joy in their marriage.

WISE WAYS Are you a worthy husband or wife? Regardless of the flaws you see in your spouse, what can you do to be the best husband or wife you can be?

Today, Lord, may I be a joy to my husband (wife), helping him (her) to be the best he (she) can be for you.

Read
Proverbs 12

HOME TREASURE

A worthy wife is her husband's joy and crown; a shameful wife saps his strength.
Proverbs 12:4

February 13

SPEECH
CONTROL

*Those who control
their tongue will have
a long life; a quick
retort can ruin
everything.*
Proverbs 13:3

In the New Testament, James wrote, "The tongue is a flame of fire. It is full of wickedness that can ruin your whole life" (James 3:6).

How true are these words! Who has not spoken words in a fit of anger, only to regret them immediately? The tongue can run away with us sometimes, and we say things that are better left unsaid. And once those words have escaped our lips, there is no way to get them back. They can indeed "ruin" everything—or at least cause devastating damage that may take many years to repair.

How much better for us to control our tongue, to think before we speak, to measure our words carefully. Then we will say what we mean in the best way possible. We will be clear, concise, and concerned for the welfare of the listener. And we will show self-control, for we will be in control of our tongue.

WISE WAYS   How well do you control your tongue? Are you careful with the words you say and how you say them? Do you need to apologize to someone for your uncontrolled tongue?

Today, Lord, may I think before I speak, learning from your Holy Spirit the self-control I need in order to control my tongue.

February 14

In Proverbs 12:4 we read how a woman can build up or destroy her husband by her actions and words; the same holds true for her household. Like it or not, the woman of the house—the wife and/or mom—has a huge influence over her family. She literally has the power to build or tear down her home with her own hands.

How does a wise woman "build" her house? Consider other proverbs to get a bigger picture. She cares for her husband and family (31:27); she has discretion (11:22); she builds up with her words and does not constantly nag or complain (19:13; 21:19); she is understanding (19:14); she is a great treasure (18:22). She is trustworthy, and so is capable of enriching her husband and children's lives (31:10-12). The opposite characteristics would obviously "tear down" a woman's home. Women have great influence and the responsibility from God to live wisely.

WISE WAYS Are you building your home, or are you tearing it down bit by bit? What can you do to make your home a positive and enriching place?

Today, Lord, help me to take the steps needed to "build" my home into the place you want it to be.

**Read
Proverbs 14**

CONSTRUCTION SITE

*A wise woman builds her house;
a foolish woman tears hers down with her own hands.*

Proverbs 14:1

February 15

**Read
Proverbs 15**

✳

GOD'S DELIGHT

*The LORD hates the
sacrifice of the
wicked, but he
delights in the prayers
of the upright.*
Proverbs 15:8

The teaching in this verse occurs in various forms
throughout Scripture (see 1 Samuel 15:22; Hosea
6:6; Micah 6:6-8; Matthew 12:7; Hebrews 10:8-9).
The point is that God does not delight in people
who go through the motions of faith without allowing it to make any difference in their hearts or
minds. In Old Testament terms, it would be like
bringing an animal to sacrifice only because the law
required it, not in order to be cleansed from sin. In
today's language it would be like attending church,
and even serving there, without allowing God to
penetrate one's heart and life. That is the "sacrifice
of the wicked," and the Lord hates it.

God delights, however, in the prayers of his
followers. He longs to hear from his people who are
open and listening—seeking to grow and change in
order to please him. We delight God when we, his
children, come to him in prayer because we love and
need him.

WISE WAYS Do you have a personal relationship
with God so that he delights in you, or are you just
going through the motions?

*Today, Lord, may I delight you by my devotion, my life, and my
prayers.*

February 16

People can justify anything. We human beings have an amazing capability to rationalize our actions and so remain "pure" in our own eyes. Many subscribe to the adage that "the end justifies the means," and they will explain away all manner of wrong behavior if they think it will bring them to the desired "end."

However, while we may be fooling everyone around us, we are not fooling God. He sees right through us, down to our basest desires and motivations. No matter how "pure" we may think we are, a God's-eye view will quickly show us otherwise.

If we have felt God's touch on our conscience regarding our motives in a particular situation, we need to ask forgiveness. Then we need to ask God to help us straighten out our thinking so that we are following his commands every step of the way. His Word provides a faithful mirror.

WISE WAYS Are you acting wrongly and then attempting to justify those actions? God sees your true motivations, and he has another way for you to go.

Today, Lord, examine my motives and show me how to act in accordance with your will.

Read
Proverbs 16

FAITHFUL MIRROR

People may be pure in their own eyes, but the Lord examines their motives.
Proverbs 16:2

February 17

Read Proverbs 17

THE REMEDY FOR MOCKERY

Those who mock the poor insult their Maker; those who rejoice at the misfortune of others will be punished.

Proverbs 17:5

It is difficult to imagine the type of person who would mock the poor or rejoice at the misfortune of others. But in our own little ways, we may do just that without realizing it. Do we turn up our nose at the poorly dressed—and perhaps a bit fragrant—person at church who obviously has very little? Do we suppose that people with financial difficulties have probably caused their own problems and don't deserve our concern? Do we walk away, thanking God that we are not poor like them?

God makes it clear that he created all people—rich and poor alike (22:2). The rich have nothing that God has not given them; therefore, they have no reason to be arrogant. Jesus told a parable about this very topic in Luke 16:19-31. We ought to be compassionate to those less fortunate, seeking God's wisdom for how we can help.

WISE WAYS   Do you thank God for everything you have that has been given to you? How do you act toward those less fortunate?

Today, Lord, thank you for all the blessings you have given me. Show me how to be compassionate toward others.

February 18

SABBATH

Clearly, discipleship has little to do with how we feel and almost everything to do with how we obey Jesus Christ. In other words, since there is no feeling to which disciples are immune, it is possible to experience almost any feeling and remain a faithful disciple of Jesus. The central question for the disciple of Jesus is not "How do I feel right now?" but "Am I continuing to obey?"

Note that Jesus did not promise an "obey-feel good, obey-feel good" kind of instant gratification cycle to his disciples. His standard of faithfulness covers those who "keep obeying." If there is a cycle in Jesus' proverb, it might be described in this way: Those who keep obeying find in their persistent obedience a deeper awareness of what is true, which leads in turn to a greater sense of freedom to continue to obey.

WISE WAYS   Knowing precedes obedience. In order to keep obeying Jesus' teachings, you must make it a point to know them. Get to know the Gospels well.

Lord, keep me aware throughout the day that I want to be an obedient disciple of yours for the long run of life.

Read
Proverbs 18

DISCIPLESHIP MARATHON

Jesus said to the people who believed in him, "You are truly my disciples if you keep obeying my teachings. And you will know the truth, and the truth will set you free."
John 8:31

February 19

**Read
Proverbs 19**

✳

MISPLACED ANGER

*People ruin their
lives by their own
foolishness and
then are angry at
the LORD.*

Proverbs 19:3

Many people thumb their noses at God and his laws
for living. They refuse to be hemmed in by his
"restrictive" commands. Instead they decide to have
sex before marriage, commit adultery, gamble, drink
heavily, use drugs, lie, cheat, and steal. Then come
the consequences from those actions—unplanned
pregnancy and a total change in life plans, a ruined
marriage and family, loss of jobs and finances, even
jail. Though they have done all these things against
God's laws, they get mad at God for their awful situation. What's wrong with this picture?

Certainly there are many times when people
suffer for no known reason—for example, look at
Job. However, if we are honest with ourselves, our
suffering is usually caused by our own foolishness.
God can still bring good out of it; but he will not
erase the consequences. When we stop being angry
at God, we can learn the lessons he has for us.

WISE WAYS   Are you blaming God for a situation
that you have caused? Can you stop being angry and
trust God to bring good from the bad?

*Today, Lord, may I accept the consequences for my own actions,
trusting that you can still work miracles in my life.*

February 20

What better motivations exist for us to be people of integrity than that our children will be blessed for it! Parents who are godly, who live with integrity and truthfulness, are wonderful examples to their children. Granted, this does not always guarantee that children will turn out perfectly, but children will nevertheless receive a great blessing from having such parents.

So what does it mean to "walk with integrity"? It means that we "walk the talk." In other words, plenty of people know the right thing to do, but when the right time comes, they don't do it. They know they should tell the truth, for example, but if telling the truth will hurt, they opt for a lie instead. Children learn best from models they see and hear, but if they learn to bend the truth whenever needed, they set themselves up for problems in life. But if they learn to follow God and walk their faith, then they will have been greatly blessed.

WISE WAYS Are you walking with integrity in front of your children or those over whom you have influence? What kinds of blessings will they have from following your example?

Today, Lord, help me to walk with integrity so as to be a good example to others.

**Read
Proverbs 20**

A HERITAGE OF BLESSINGS

The godly walk with integrity; blessed are their children after them.

Proverbs 20:7

February 21

**Read
Proverbs 21**

ROYAL
AQUEDUCT

*The king's heart is
like a stream of water
directed by the LORD;
he turns it wherever
he pleases.*

Proverbs 21:1

God rules his creation. Nothing is outside his authority—not even the leaders of the nations and kingdoms of this world. No person is placed in a position of power outside of God's will. This can be a great comfort when we see leaders take over in various places, especially leaders with whom we do not agree.

So what does this mean for the cruel tyrants of the world? It means that they too are under God's authority. Satan may author their evil acts, but their wrongdoing can only occur within the boundaries God sets. Why those boundaries are where they are for some nations is a question only God can answer. But we can rest assured that no power is in authority outside of God's plan. God always accomplishes his will, even through the most wicked leaders. God is always the final authority.

WISE WAYS   How will you pray today for the leaders of your country, as well as for leaders around the world?

Today, Lord, may I trust that you are the sovereign authority over all that happens in my nation. May I trust you, even as I work on your behalf.

February 22

In the minds of most people throughout history, riches have been the sign of God's blessing while poverty reveals God's curse. According to Solomon, however, the rich and poor are on equal footing before God because God made them both. The wealth of rich people cannot get them any closer to God than poor people. The poor person's poverty is not a free ride to heaven. The thing that matters is the state of a person's heart. In fact, Jesus explained that it is actually harder for the rich to enter God's kingdom because they have a more difficult time understanding their need (Matthew 19:23).

Because God created both the rich and the poor, and because both have been infected by the curse of sinfulness on humanity, they both need the Savior. We are not to show favoritism either way but are to look on both the rich and poor as people whom Christ died to save.

WISE WAYS In what ways are you training yourself to be able to look at all people, whether rich or poor, as people God loves and died to save?

Today, Lord, give me sensitivity to all people, regardless of their status, so that I might be able to tell them about you.

**Read
Proverbs 22**

EQUAL VALUE

*The rich and the poor
have this in common:
The LORD made
them both.*

Proverbs 22:2

February 23

Read
Proverbs 23

✳

INEVITABLE
JUDGE

*Don't steal the land of
defenseless orphans by
moving the ancient
boundary markers,
for their Redeemer is
strong. He himself
will bring their
charges against you.*
Proverbs 23:10-11

The word Redeemer has two very distinct applications in this proverb. Within the culture of Israel,
orphans and widows were the responsibility of their
extended family, represented by the closest relative
who was called a "redeemer." An excellent example
of how this worked can be seen in the book of Ruth.

From the perspective of God's purposes in
composing Scripture, the Old Testament redeemers
were built into the culture so that we could understand the role and wonder of the great Redeemer,
Jesus. His life, death, and resurrection declare the
divine strength behind God's plan.

Whatever the temporary successes of evil or injustice in this world, God has the final judgment. Whatever boundaries are violated or property or dignity
stolen, God will make things right in his time.

WISE WAYS   Those learning and practicing
wisdom make it their goal to defend those whom
God has declared are under his special protection.

*Today, Lord, help me be especially aware of those who feel
defenseless. Please guide my words and actions on their behalf.*

February 24

Substitute any number of words for "house" in this proverb, and you will get the idea of the writer's intent. Consider how we build our "home," our "life," our "business," our "church," how we set our "goals," make our "decisions." In others words, anything we build in this life should be based on a foundation of wisdom, good sense, and knowledge. We build wisely by understanding God's direction and guidance. We develop good sense when we use our mind and experiences to think through our options.

Through accumulated knowledge, God helps us take what we have learned about the particular situation or decision and avoid others' mistakes. When we make use of these God-given directions, we can build a home, life, business, etc., that is valuable to all—but mostly to God, for it will then be able to accomplish his will in the world. When God is the master builder, we can be sure what we are building is part of eternity.

WISE WAYS What is the foundation for the "buildings" in your life? Who is your master builder?

Today, Lord, as the architect of my life, take the plans I've tried to make and become my master builder.

**Read
Proverbs 24**

BUILDING PLANS

A house is built by wisdom and becomes strong through good sense. Through knowledge its rooms are filled with all sorts of precious riches and valuables.
Proverbs 24:3-4

February 25

Read
Proverbs 25

GODLY SORROW

God blesses those who mourn, for they will be comforted.

Matthew 5:4

This second beatitude, like the first (January 28), concerns the internal remodeling of the soul of a disciple. Those who come to realize they are spiritually bankrupt (poor in spirit) must then move on to repentance (mourning)—a genuine, deep sadness over sin to the point of real change. Those who acknowledge they are lost in sin and take full responsibility for their condition will receive God's comfort.

Just as grieving over the loss of a loved one can take different forms and require varied amounts of time, so the spiritual mourning that God blesses may have an ongoing effect throughout a Christian's life. While it touches the whole person, it will not touch everyone the same way. For instance, we tend to equate mourning with tears. Unfortunately, most of us know people who shed tears of repentance but return immediately to the same sin. Others give amazing evidence of spiritual transformation without shedding a tear. Spiritual mourning is necessary but personal. As it occurs, God promises to bless in a comforting way.

WISE WAYS Do you understand your own need for a grieving process over sin in your life? To what degree has it occurred?

Today, Lord, give me one lesson or reminder that helps me understand the importance of allowing the things that break your heart to break my heart.

February 26

Proverbs is certainly not a book for the faint of heart or weak of stomach! It confronts adultery, sin, and folly in no uncertain terms and with vivid images. Here we have a graphic picture of the type of person who makes a mistake and then makes it again. This person, here called a "fool," has not learned from the foolish mistake and so is doomed to repeat it. This is as disgusting as the habit of a dog that goes back to its own vomit.

Everyone makes mistakes—even foolish ones. If we desire to be wise, our mistakes can become beneficial. Many times we have said things we now regret, spent money we should not have, acted in ways that now embarrass us, or faced severe consequences for a foolish mistake. But most of us learn from those mistakes and put those hard lessons to use so that we do not make those mistakes again. That is the path of wisdom.

WISE WAYS What mistakes have you made in the past? What current practices or habits do you have that demonstrate what you have learned from your mistakes?

Today, Lord, help me remember and learn from my past mistakes so that I don't have to repeat them.

Read
Proverbs 26

SICKENING PICTURE

As a dog returns to its vomit, so a fool repeats his folly.
Proverbs 26:11

February 27

Read
Proverbs 27

✳

WORTHWHILE
PRAISE

Don't praise yourself;
let others do it!
Proverbs 27:2

How simple, yet how profound! We all know people who, often to cover their insecurities, are quick to tell us all their accomplishments. Such people rarely receive words of praise from us, for we resist praising someone who is always praising himself or herself.

On the other hand, many people who certainly deserve praise humbly refuse to shower themselves with kudos. We are often surprised to discover the depth of such people, and the breadth of their accomplishments. We give praise so that others can know about them as well. What a joy it is to give well-deserved praise to someone who hasn't sought it!

We should strive to be humble people. When we don't draw attention to ourselves with self-centered praise, we allow others to do it for us. But even if no one notices our efforts or accomplishments, we know that God sees and is pleased with our hard work for him. Ultimately, his praise is the most important of all.

WISE WAYS Are you upset at something you have done that has gone unnoticed and/or unpraised? Ask God to help you understand the value of his praise.

Today, Lord, may I do your work patiently, not seeking praise but knowing that you are pleased.

February 28

Justice means righteousness, lawfulness, and moral rightness, the quality of being true or correct, the moral principle determining just conduct. So justice has a moral quality. It contains a concept of what is right and, therefore, must also have a concept of what is wrong. Only people who understand these concepts of right and wrong can understand and administer justice. By extension, only those who follow the Lord can understand justice. Why? Because they subscribe to the foundational laws of the one who created them.

Thus, as this proverb points out, evil people don't understand justice. Because they refuse to subscribe to justice's moral underpinnings given by God in his Word, they are left to discover their own truths. As a result, many conclude that there is no truth. Others conclude that everyone can have different truths. Both perspectives are hopelessly doomed. And as a building without a foundation will crumble, so justice can never be served without the foundation of right and wrong as given by God in his Word.

WISE WAYS   What are you using for your foundation? Where do you get your concept of truth, of right and wrong?

Today, Lord, teach me the foundational truths about life that are given in your Word.

**Read
Proverbs 28**

AWARENESS OF JUSTICE

Evil people don't understand justice, but those who follow the Lord understand completely.
Proverbs 28:5

MARCH

March 1

**Read
Proverbs 1**

LIFE'S PASSAGES

*Listen, my child, to
what your father
teaches you. Don't
neglect your mother's
teaching.*
Proverbs 1:8

Why should we listen to our parents? Especially as we grow older, we might think this proverb no longer applies to us. However, listening to our parents' teaching is a way of honoring them, and numerous passages in the Bible connect honoring our parents with living a long and blessed life (see the fifth commandment, Exodus 20:12). This naturally raises questions about how God connects longevity with parental honor.

When we honor our parents by listening to them, we gain wisdom to avoid the hard lessons our parents had to learn. Even more, we have an amazing chance to develop a positive view of aging. If we respect our parents, we are more likely to embrace our own process of aging as a blessing.

As your parents give you advice, put yourself in their position. When you are their age, would you rather be treated as a constant burden or respected as a blessing to the family?

WISE WAYS   The next time an older person offers instruction, turn down your pride and really listen.

Lord, you created the stages of life. Help me to respect my parents as I will want to be respected.

March 2

How can someone become wise? Many people think that wisdom comes only through education or experience. But the truth is that wisdom is also a remarkable gift from God. That's right—it's a gift. God does not discriminate in bestowing wisdom on the young and the old, the scholar and the servant. In fact, God takes special joy in giving wisdom to those whom society considers unworthy.

On the other hand, God views the world's idea of wisdom as foolishness. Since God is the ultimate source of wisdom, those who try to become wise on their own will not succeed.

If you want wisdom, first seek the creator of wisdom. The Lord grants wisdom because he wants you to be confident of the hope that is within you. So continue to question and search out the answers! He waits patiently to offer you the meat of his Word. If you seek him, he will pour out understanding.

WISE WAYS   Ask yourself whether you would be able to tell your neighbor what and why you believe.

Lord, give me an understanding of who you are so that I may confidently stand for you.

**Read
Proverbs 2**

TAKING WISDOM FOR GRANTED

For the LORD grants wisdom! From his mouth come knowledge and understanding.
Proverbs 2:6

March 3

Read Proverbs 3

✳

WISDOM IN ACTION

Don't be impressed with your own wisdom. Instead, fear the LORD and turn your back on evil.

Proverbs 3:7

If anyone could have been impressed with himself, it was Solomon. God made him the wisest man alive. Yet, despite Solomon's great wisdom, he still made many poor choices that eventually led him away from God.

Solomon's life illustrates a valuable lesson: Wisdom becomes useless if it is not applied. We can know what is right, but if we do not do what is right, our knowledge lacks value. Searching for wisdom does not put us on the wrong track, for we are told to search for it. However, the proverb points to something far beyond the search for wisdom. It tells us to fear the Lord and obey him. Fearing the Lord means giving God a proper place in our life. When we respect God in humility, we are more likely to turn from evil to obedience.

WISE WAYS   What are some behaviors or attitudes to which you consistently yield, although you know they are wrong? Take steps today to combine wisdom with obedience.

Lord, help me not only to know your path, but also to walk that path in obedience.

March 4

SABBATH

God commanded us to love. It would have been easier if God had just said, "Run a mile each day," or given us some other physical task. Then we wouldn't have to think about it. We could create a routine of basic action. But God speaks of love as an action that requires our whole selves.

Why must we love God? In the divine plan for those creatures called human, loving God is as essential as breathing is to our physical life. We must breathe. We can make ourselves unable to breathe, or we can refuse to breathe—but not without consequences. We must love God because the alternative, though possible, is unthinkable and unbearable. How tragic that many choose to give "lip service" rather than "lung service" to this basic law of spiritual life. Take a deep breath and ask yourself what specific opportunities you will have today to demonstrate your love for God.

WISE WAYS Think of some specific ways you could demonstrate your love for God in your neighborhood.

Lord, teach me to love you with my whole being and share this love with others.

Read Proverbs 4

WHOLE LOVE

Jesus replied, "The most important commandment is this: 'Hear, O Israel! The Lord our God is the one and only Lord. And you must love the Lord your God with all your heart, all your soul, all your mind, and all your strength.' The second is equally important: 'Love your neighbor as yourself.' No other commandment is greater than these."
Mark 12:29-31

March 5

**Read
Proverbs 5**

RUN!

*Run from [an
immoral woman]!
Don't go near the
door of her house!*
Proverbs 5:8

"DANGER! Bridge out ahead!" This proverb screams out like a yellow warning sign along the side of the road. And that's what it is supposed to be—a two-part warning about temptation.

The first part of the proverb gives us directions about sin that seeks us. It tells us to run away! Just look at Joseph in Genesis 39. He ran away when Potiphar's wife propositioned him to have an affair with her. If you find yourself in a similar situation, don't try to be brave. Just get out of there!

The second part shows us what to do when we are tempted to seek out sin. Stay away! Translated into today's society, this verse might suggest driving a different route home from work to avoid passing an adult bookstore.

You can't control the actions of other people, but you can ask God to help you control your own behavior.

WISE WAYS   Honestly identify a temptation that you faced today and make a plan on how you will run from or resist that temptation in the future.

Lord, give me the strength to run away from sin. Help me to stay on your path day by day.

March 6

Hate is a strong word. In fact, it almost seems out of character for God to hate. Isn't he supposed to be a God of love? We might use the word "hate" lightly when we speak, but the thought of God's hatred conveys a very frightening concept. This view of God helps us think more seriously about his response to our actions.

Notice the things that God hates—pride, dishonesty, and impurity. Interestingly, each phrase connects these sins with a part of the body. Now, our physical bodies are not bad in themselves. God created us in his image to perform great acts. Our bodies are his masterpiece. Yet, the greatest gifts of a human can become the most evil when they are twisted for evil purposes.

Each day you have an opportunity to use your body for good deeds or for wickedness. Choose today to honor God with your body. Avoid corrupting yourself with the things God hates.

WISE WAYS Whom could you encourage with your mouth today or help with your hands?

Lord, I am fearfully and wonderfully made! Help me to use each part of my body to uplift others.

**Read
Proverbs 6**

WHAT GOD HATES

There are six things the LORD hates— no, seven things he detests: haughty eyes, a lying tongue, hands that kill the innocent, a heart that plots evil, feet that race to do wrong, a false witness who pours out lies, a person who sows discord among brothers.
Proverbs 6:16-19

March 7

**Read
Proverbs 7**

✳

A SISTER'S WISDOM

*Love wisdom like a
sister; make insight a
beloved member of
your family. Let them
hold you back from
an affair with an
immoral woman,
from listening to the
flattery of an
adulterous woman.*
Proverbs 7:4-5

Whether biological or spiritual, our sisters and
other family members remain in a unique position
in our lives. When we are blinded by our temptations, they can step in and say, "Open your eyes.
You don't want that." While often painful, our
family's honesty may help us to wake up. This
honesty directly confronts the seductive lies of our
temptations.

In this same way, wisdom acts as a sister, guarding
us from our temptations. Wisdom and insight lose
their effectiveness, however, when we stubbornly
refuse to listen. Notice the wording: we must let
them hold us back. To overcome temptation, we
must first be willing to listen. Wisdom, like our
family members, often reveals to us that which we
are unable to see. When we are willing to listen,
God's wisdom will guide us along the correct path.

WISE WAYS   The next time you are offered advice
from a family member, or brother or sister in
Christ, listen carefully with an open and humble
heart.

*Lord, help me to open my ears to your wisdom, so that I may open
my eyes to temptation.*

March 8

Wisdom, good judgment, knowledge, and discernment all apparently live in the same neighborhood. For the purposes of meditation and practice, these terms may be used interchangeably. Within this proverb, though, wisdom clearly takes the chief position. The other three terms seem to indicate aspects or components of wisdom. Good judgment has to do with decision-making. Knowledge has to do with gathering and organizing facts. Discernment describes a capacity for understanding people or events in subtle ways.

Those who seek wisdom from God will find along the way that they are also discovering and growing in good judgment, knowledge, and discernment. Your commitment not only to read Proverbs daily, but also to concentrate on a single proverb for meditation means that you are spending time every day in Wisdom's neighborhood. Good things will come out of that time investment.

WISE WAYS Would people say you are a person of discernment and good judgment? Why or why not?

Lord, please continue to lead me into Wisdom and the good companions that come with her. Guide me to use wisdom in your service.

Read Proverbs 8

WISDOM'S PARTNERS

I, Wisdom, live together with good judgment. I know where to discover knowledge and discernment.

Proverbs 8:12

March 9

**Read
Proverbs 9**

A SPECIAL
INVITATION

*"Come home with
me," [Wisdom]
urges the simple. To
those without good
judgment, she says,
"Come, eat my food,
and drink the wine
I have mixed."*

Proverbs 9:4-5

An invitation has arrived in the mail. The whole town has been invited to a huge banquet! We excitedly rush to get dressed in our best clothes. At the last minute, we call our best friend or loved one to check on the time. To our dismay, he tells us he is too busy—he isn't going to the banquet!

In this same way, God has prepared a banquet for each one of us. If we choose to go, God offers us food unlike any other—his wisdom. And God's wisdom nourishes us completely. However, some of us never take the time to reply to his generous invitation.

Don't let any other pursuit in your life cause you to ignore the invitation of wisdom God has for you. All that God requires is a response.

WISE WAYS   Think about your spiritual life. If you feel you are lacking in a certain area, pray that God would help you grow through his wisdom.

Lord, I desire your wisdom. Help me follow your will and make good choices today.

March 10

The world's way of promoting peace differs remarkably from God's way. We would rather let everyone do as they please—just "wink" and mind our own business when we see others sin. This sort of practice, however, does not work. As humans, our life is unavoidably tied to and affected by those around us.

On the other hand, God's way of promoting peace begins when we hold his truth as of utmost importance. This means we have the responsibility to bring back, gently but sternly, those who stray from the truth.

The process of confronting others might be uncomfortable, but peace does not appear when all our problems disappear. We will always have struggles! Peace comes when problems and sin within relationships are dealt with correctly and humbly.

WISE WAYS Is there a friend or loved one in your life that you have seen fall gradually into a particular sin? Begin to pray for that person and then humbly confront that person in love.

Lord, help me to stand boldly when others seek to compromise your truth.

**Read
Proverbs 10**

PROMOTING
PEACE

People who wink at wrong cause trouble, but a bold reproof promotes peace.
Proverbs 10:10

March 11

Read Proverbs 11

✳

SLAVERY TO SALARY

No one can serve two masters. For you will hate one and love the other, or be devoted to one and despise the other. You cannot serve both God and money.

Matthew 6:24

How do we serve money? Workaholism, bondage to debt, living above our means, the "I have to have it" attitude—these are all signs that point to a faulty system of priorities. These behaviors enslave us to money because they consume all our thoughts and time.

Jesus asked some hard questions of the people who desired to follow him. Jesus told one wealthy man to give all his possessions away before becoming a follower (Matthew 19:21-22). Sadly, the man ended up walking away. Jesus knew the man loved money more than he loved God.

If we want the Lord to be first in our life, we first must examine our attitudes. Are we working and living for money or for God?

WISE WAYS What in your life would you not be able to give away? If you're thinking mostly of material objects, pray for a more heavenly perspective.

Father, help me to examine my perspective. May my life be dedicated to you and not to making money.

March 12

This proverb compares the lives of two types of people: those who have no foundation, and those who choose God as their foundation. What kind of foundation have you chosen for your life? How clearly have you communicated it to your family? If we choose to live our lives without God, or even refuse to pass down our faith to our children, we deprive them of a firm foundation. After we are gone, they will have nothing upon which to stand.

On the other hand, by developing godliness in our own lives, we benefit not only ourselves but also the generations that come after us. Today's proverb demonstrates this truth by describing the godly through their children. When we pass on a heritage of faith, we create a firm foundation for our kids' lives. Then, when we are no longer with them, they will have the grounding to continue to grow and rely on God.

WISE WAYS Take a trip with your children to a Christian bookstore. Pick out a children's book you can read together and discuss.

Lord, help me to grow in godliness, so I may pass your truth on to my children.

**Read
Proverbs 12**

A FIRM
FOUNDATION

The wicked perish and are gone, but the children of the godly stand firm.

Proverbs 12:7

March 13

**Read
Proverbs 13**

✳

TRUE SUCCESS

*Godliness
helps people
all through life,
while the evil are
destroyed by their
wickedness.*
Proverbs 13:6

What describes godly living? We develop godliness when we seek to make choices in accordance with God's will. These good decisions help us live successful lives. This is true even when the good results do not occur obviously or immediately.

Sometimes it may seem that poor choices will actually prosper us more than godly ones. Isn't it easier to cheat and steal than it is to work hard?

While these choices may tempt us with their short-term benefits, they set in motion a series of events that eventually will destroy us. For instance, people who step on others to get to the top will find that they have no support when they finally get there.

When we choose to make honest decisions and follow God's will for us, he will lead us into true success. The success wrought through godliness completely surpasses any temporary accomplishment gained through dishonesty. That's what God calls a "whole-life" kind of success, and it lasts for eternity.

WISE WAYS Take time to ask God to help you accomplish goals in a way that pleases him. But be prepared for changes! God has a plan for your life greater than anything you could imagine.

Today, Lord, show me how to make godly decisions in my work and at home with my family.

March 14

Wouldn't it be great to see into the future? To have the ability to bypass future mistakes? In a way, Christians have this ability. God has given us a precious gift—the gift of sight.

This "sight" is not like the false sight of fortune-tellers or magicians. It is the spiritual ability to see who is in the future, instead of merely what is in the future. So, we no longer blindly grope around in this life as those who are lost. Christ is our future and our hope.

Just as a successful marathon runner knows the location of the finish line before setting goals for the race, we identify Christ as our finish line. This great knowledge allows us to set daily goals for wise living. In the end each day of our lives may be lived victoriously if we remember our final outcome. The Christian's race is already won through Christ's victory on the cross. And when we cross the finish line of life, we will be in Christ's presence.

WISE WAYS The next time you feel fear or persecution regarding your faith, remember that Christ has already won the victory!

Lord, help me to look ahead to you so that I may live victoriously.

Read
Proverbs 14

VICTORIOUS FORESIGHT

The wise look ahead to see what is coming, but fools deceive themselves.

Proverbs 14:8

March 15

Read Proverbs 15

✳

MATTERS OF THE HEART

Even the depths of Death and Destruction are known by the LORD. How much more does he know the human heart!

Proverbs 15:11

We humans have a knack for forgetting the true knowledge of God. Just look at Adam after he sinned. He thought he could hide from God! Like Adam, we often hide what we truly feel in our hearts. Perhaps we think we are too evil, or that we've let God down. In the midst of our trials, we hide from God. We forget that God knows us down to our deepest motives!

This thought can be very frightening. It can also be extremely comforting. God knows us as we are right now—and he wants us as we are right now. So unlike any other relationship, we can let down our guard with God.

We can forget about trying to conquer that one temptation before coming to God. We can forget about dressing up and putting on a good face. God knows what's in our hearts, and nothing we feel is too terrible for him to handle.

WISE WAYS   Is there something about yourself you are afraid to show God? Take a step and open your heart. God is waiting with loving arms.

Lord, give me the courage to come to you honestly, so that I may be healed.

March 16

If we are serious about our work, we probably have specific vocational goals already laid out. Perhaps we want to expand our industry, or advance to a certain position by a particular date. It's easy to get into a mode where we rarely think about work and God simultaneously. Anyway, we might think, What business does God have in my business?

Note the proverb's progression: Our plans will succeed after we commit our work to the Lord. Committing our work to God does not imply that we can't make a profit. It means that God wants to be Lord over every part of our lives, including our daily work. It also means that God desires to be pleased with the way we do our work because we are doing it for him.

There's no task too mundane or ordinary for God. He will bless us if we seek his guidance in our work. His power does not stop when we begin our work day.

WISE WAYS Think about a specific goal you are working toward right now. Ask God to guide you in achieving that goal.

Lord, help me to have balance in my daily life as I work my hardest yet trust you for success.

**Read
Proverbs 16**

GOD'S BUSINESS

Commit your work to the LORD, and then your plans will succeed.

Proverbs 16:3

March 17

Read
Proverbs 17

✳

THE POWER OF WORDS

Eloquent speech is not fitting for a fool; even less are lies fitting for a ruler.

Proverbs 17:7

Have you ever been drawn into watching an infomercial on TV? After what seems like a few minutes, you realize you've just spent an hour hearing about a kitchen utensil. This illustrates the power of persuasive words. These words catch our attention. They cause us to believe.

Now this might not be harmful if we're just listening to infomercials. However, some of the most eloquent and powerful speakers (Adolf Hitler, for example) have been able to convince people to believe atrocious things.

As Christians, we need to guard against mistaking powerful, persuasive speech for the truth. Moreover, we also need to be careful not to mistake eloquent speech for wisdom. Throughout the Bible God used people with poor speaking ability, such as Moses and the apostle Paul, to spread his Word. In the end, a person's character, not her position, should be used to judge the value of her words.

WISE WAYS   Can you think of someone in your life who influences you into sin? Identify the words he or she uses to persuade you, and be aware of those persuasive words the next time.

Lord Jesus, help me to distinguish between persuasive lies and your truth.

March 18

Jesus used childlikeness to describe people who are real citizens of the Kingdom of Heaven. This proverb begins with the act of repentance ("turn from your sins") and then describes a process with the word *become.* In fact, the word *become* is used twice to indicate that this is an ongoing experience of learning and growing.

So what did Jesus find so compelling about childlikeness? He specifically mentioned humility. How are children humble? They exhibit a trusting curiosity. They are full of questions for which they really want answers. Their questions don't hide an unwillingness to believe. They want to learn! As a child trusts a loving parent, so a citizen in the Kingdom of Heaven deeply trusts the heavenly Father.

From the moment we turn from our sins, we begin the lifelong learning experience of growing in deep trust of our heavenly Father.

WISE WAYS   The next chance you get, watch a child playing or talking with a loving parent. Use your observations to think about your relationship with your heavenly Father.

Lord, becoming like a trusting little child in your presence will develop a humility that pleases you. Help me become more childlike.

**Read
Proverbs 18**

WISE CHILDLIKENESS

I assure you, unless you turn from your sins and become as little children, you will never get into the Kingdom of Heaven. Therefore, anyone who becomes as humble as this little child is the greatest in the Kingdom of Heaven.
Matthew 18:3-4

March 19

✳

TO FESTER OR FORGIVE

People with good sense restrain their anger; they earn esteem by overlooking wrongs.
Proverbs 19:11

Anger is an emotion that double crosses us when we least expect it. When we are angry with someone, we often think that our anger is hurting that person. We fume and rage internally, but gradually the bitterness begins to eat away at our own spirits. In the end, our anger actually hurts us!

So how can we restrain our anger? Restraining anger does not entail stuffing our emotions deep inside to fester. Instead, the proverb couples restraint with the action of overlooking wrongs. Instead of festering, we are given a tool to lessen our anger when it begins.

At the point when we start to get angry, we can make a choice to overlook wrongs. In other words, we can choose to release our anger through forgiveness. We will never have control over other people's actions, but we do have control over our own. If we must express anger, it should be done early rather than late, with a calm sense of self-control and restraint. That itself is a mark of spiritual maturity.

WISE WAYS Each time your anger starts to rise, remind yourself that you have control over your emotions, not the other way around.

Lord, give me a forgiving spirit so that I will be able to let go of my anger toward others.

March 20

How often do we see the evil around us and pray for God's justice? We wonder, Why does God allow all this evil to go on! This kind of thinking leads to two of the most common double standards: (1) judging others more harshly than we judge ourselves, and (2) believing God should judge others but remain lenient with us.

The Lord despises double standards because they elevate one person at the expense of others. These man-made standards also lack the mercy of God.

In our cry for fairness, we should not forget the frightening consequences of justice. As sinners, God could justly destroy each one of us today for missing the mark of perfection. When we remember that God's patience and mercy block his judgment towards us, we will be more likely to show others patience and mercy.

WISE WAYS Before you rush to judge another person, ask yourself whether you would be able to endure the same standard.

Today, Lord, give me the strength to replace judgment with mercy.

**Read
Proverbs 20**

GOD'S MEASURE

The LORD despises double standards of every kind.
Proverbs 20:10

March 21

Read
Proverbs 21

✳

SECRET MOTIVES

*People may think
they are doing what is
right, but the LORD
examines the heart.*
Proverbs 21:2

At first glance, this proverb seems to be contradicting itself. How can our heads tell us one thing while our hearts tell God another? Yet exactly that often happens. We can talk ourselves into believing that we are acting correctly because we can rationalize our behavior. Our feelings (heart), however, often show the reality no matter what we say.

Perhaps outwardly we do nothing wrong, but the proverb reveals that God is more concerned about our secret motives. For example, by tithing each week we act in obedience. Yet if we tithe with bitter resentment in our hearts, we might fool our neighbors, but we will not fool God.

So even "good" deeds lose their value if we lack the right heart. Ultimately, our motives should be to please God. Our actions become worthless if we only seek to please ourselves or impress others.

WISE WAYS   You should be alerted if you feel guilt over a specific behavior. Ask God to renew your heart with pure motives so that you will please him.

Lord, examine my heart and remove any unclean motives.

March 22

Interestingly, this proverb expects that dangerous situations will arise in our lives. If these situations are indeed inevitable, then we should plan a course of action. For some people taking action means devising endless preventive measures. Still others feel that taking precautions implies that they are not living in faith. Neither of these solutions displays a balanced trust in God.

We must examine where our confidence lies. Are we really trusting in God? Trusting does not mean that we should purposely step into pitfalls. If we see ourselves heading for danger, we can take precautions to avoid the situation. We lack faith when we feel that we alone possess the strength to conquer any temptation. Humbly anticipating our weaknesses will allow us to bypass harsh consequences.

WISE WAYS   Is there a specific temptation you face continually during the week? Take steps to avoid situations that foster that behavior before you come to them.

Lord, help me to live wisely by knowing my weaknesses and anticipating dangerous situations.

**Read
Proverbs 22**

ANTICIPATING DANGER

A prudent person foresees the danger ahead and takes precautions; the simpleton goes blindly on and suffers the consequences.
Proverbs 22:3

March 23

Read Proverbs 23

✳

TUNING IN TO GOD

Commit yourself to instruction; attune your ears to hear words of knowledge.
Proverbs 23:12

Have you ever used walkie-talkies to communicate with friends? If you have, then you know that both people have to tune in to the same frequency, otherwise they can't hear each other. This is a great picture of how communication works between God and us.

We must "tune in" if we want to hear God's instructions. Listening to God becomes difficult if we're too busy doing our own thing. So how can we tune in to God? First, the proverb tells us to commit ourselves to instruction. This could mean setting a spiritual goal and then relying on God to help us accomplish that goal.

Once we've made a commitment, then it's time to attune our ears. This means focusing our lives on listening to God's instruction. Our continued attention to the book of Proverbs will accomplish a significant amount of "tuning" in our lives.

WISE WAYS Write down some short-term and long-term spiritual goals you could accomplish in the next year. Commit to reading them every week.

Today, Lord, help me to attune my heart to your instruction.

March 24

Muscular strength usually comes to mind when we hear words like "power" and "might." Through self-discipline, this kind of strength may be achieved, but it has real limits. Although physical exercise is a good habit, the proverb stresses the importance of exercising the mind. Building our bodies provides us with endurance in a battle or competition. Nevertheless, neglecting strategy only allows an opponent with more cunning to defeat us.

The verse following this proverb aptly refers to victory during war. As Christians, we are warriors in an ongoing spiritual war. If we think we are strong enough alone, without the guidance of others, we will surely falter. By gaining God's wisdom and direction, we will be able to overcome challenges that appear too great for us.

WISE WAYS Think about how you divide up your time during the week. How much time, if any, do you spend exercising your mind in God's Word?

Today, Lord, help me to take time to grow in wisdom and strength through your Word.

**Read
Proverbs 24**

TRUE STRENGTH

A wise man is mightier than a strong man, and a man of knowledge is more powerful than a strong man.
Proverbs 24:5

March 25

**Read
Proverbs 25**

MEEKNESS

*God blesses those
who are gentle and
lowly, for the whole
earth will belong
to them.*
Matthew 5:5

Older translations of this beatitude have often used the word *meek* to name the character trait Jesus had in mind. In Matthew 11:29, Jesus used almost the identical term to describe himself: "Take my yoke upon you. Let me teach you, because I am humble and gentle, and you will find rest for your souls."

If *meekness* is an unfamiliar term to us, perhaps *gentle* and *lowly* are a little too familiar. They don't capture the underlying fierceness that seems to hide within meekness. A meek person is not a weak person. A meek person is a person of immense character and, often, physical strength. What makes a person meek is the fact that, although he or she could exert power or overwhelming ability at any time, he or she actively chooses not to do so.

In order to meditate on meekness, picture the largest, strongest man that you know carrying his little daughter in his arms. Spiritual meekness depends on God's strength and power, choosing not to rely on obvious personal strength.

WISE WAYS Those whose faith and life rest fully on God don't have to conquer the world; it already belongs to them.

Lord, to the degree that I can turn away from self-reliance and independence, grow me into a meek person. Teach me about being gentle and lowly.

March 26

Throughout history, people have made huge blunders by believing what they thought to be the right answer. Just look at the thousands of years that people believed the earth was flat. It didn't matter how much they believed they were right; they were still wrong!

For this reason, we should always be willing to examine what we hear, and especially what we believe. The people of Berea understood this principle (Acts 17:10-12). They made sure everything Paul preached to them could be found in the Scriptures. We would be wise to follow their example.

If we think we are too smart to make a mistake, we inevitably will do just that! We must continue to humbly scrutinize our beliefs against the Word of God. God will honor us more for admitting when we are wrong than for claiming that we know everything.

WISE WAYS   The next time you hear a sermon, make sure it can be backed up with Scripture. If you have any questions, ask until you find the answers.

Lord, give me the humility to inspect my beliefs and continue to search for your truth.

Read
Proverbs 26

HUMBLE
WISDOM

*There is more hope
for fools than for
people who think
they are wise.*
Proverbs 26:12

March 27

**Read
Proverbs 27**

✳

TAKE A
LOAD OFF

*A stone is heavy and
sand is weighty, but
the resentment
caused by a fool is
heavier than both.*
Proverbs 27:3

When someone hurts or annoys us, our immediate reaction is to focus on the offense. In our resentment, the focal point remains on the other person, not us. The proverb reverses this progression. It chooses not to detail the fool's specific actions, but instead to describe the effects of resentment in our own lives.

Resentment, or bitterness, weighs us down. Once we've chosen to resent someone's actions, consuming anger becomes our only alternative. Ironically, we often feel we're teaching our opposition a lesson or hurting them in our bitterness. The opposite is true. We only end up oppressing ourselves.

When we're angry, forgiveness might seem like condoning bad behavior. However, forgiveness really means letting go of our own bitterness—essentially, taking a load off. From this beginning, God's hand can begin to mend the relationship.

WISE WAYS Can you think of a relationship that you have let diminish because of resentment? Ask God for grace to forgive that person.

Lord, when I am tempted to hold on to my resentment, help me to release it in forgiveness.

March 28

Each of us has probably raised, known, or been a teenager who befriended certain people just to spite his or her parents. As parents, what kinds of emotions do we feel when this happens? Shame? Anger? Worry?

Parenting allows us to uniquely understand God's role as our heavenly Father. When we ourselves seek out worthless companions, we bring shame to God. And just like our response at our children's disobedience, God's anger builds when we intentionally sin against him.

As members of God's family, we represent him wherever we go. Many times our example will be one of the only pictures of God others will see. As Christians we have the opportunity to reinforce Christ's reputation or undermine it. Obeying God's law not only builds up God's family, but also brings glory to God himself.

WISE WAYS Examine the kind of picture you present of Christ in your daily life. Would others be able to easily identify you as a believer?

Today, Lord, give me ways to show others your love through my obedience.

**Read
Proverbs 28**

GOD'S REPRESENTATIVES

Young people who obey the law are wise; those who seek out worthless companions bring shame to their parents.
Proverbs 28:7

March 29

Read
Proverbs 29

DISCIPLINED WISDOM

To discipline and reprimand a child produces wisdom, but a mother is disgraced by an undisciplined child.

Proverbs 29:15

In today's world, the lines between discipline and abuse have grown exceedingly blurry. Many parents, frightened to be labeled as abusers, have abandoned disciplining their children altogether. The message of the Bible offers us a different alternative.

A good model of discipline arises from Hebrews 12:6, which states, "The Lord disciplines those he loves." Thus, love and wisdom are integrally tied to God's discipline. God allows us to face some of the consequences of our sins. Through this painful process we begin to judge between good and evil on our own.

Likewise, we should discipline our children because we love them and want them to succeed. Success comes through self-discipline. If we truly desire our children to be self-disciplined adults, we must lovingly discipline them as children. Later they will be wise enough to avoid serious mistakes by first pondering the consequences on their own.

WISE WAYS   Tell your kids you love them, especially after you discipline them. Later, sit down and discuss why discipline is necessary.

Lord, give me the strength to discipline my children in love and to accept your discipline myself.

March 30

The truth of God's Word usually becomes painfully obvious as soon as we cease to follow it. When our plans crumble, we realize that God's Word does, in fact, show us the good way. In this aspect our very lives prove the truth of God's Word.

But what about telling others about God's truth? Confrontation and debate still spark fear in the minds of many believers. We fear that we will be trapped if we step up to defend our faith in God. Ironically, the proverb reveals that it is God who defends us.

If every word of God is true, he has said some pretty amazing things. For instance, Jesus said, "I will never leave you, nor forsake you." When faced with disbelief and cynicism, God remains with us to give us the right words and the courage to speak them.

WISE WAYS   In a conversation with an unbeliever, ask God to give you the right words to say. However, always be ready to give an answer for what you believe and why you believe it.

Today, Lord, help me to rely on you as my Defender and Protector.

Read
Proverbs 30

THE BEST
DEFENSE

Every word of God
proves true.
He defends all
who come to him
for protection.
Proverbs 30:5

March 31

ESTABLISHING VIRTUE

*Who can find a
virtuous and capable
wife? She is worth
more than precious
rubies. Her husband
can trust her, and she
will greatly enrich his
life. She will not
hinder him but help
him all her life.*

Proverbs 31:10-12

From this proverb, we see the qualities of a virtuous woman: strong, trustworthy, and supportive of her husband. Next, we may reasonably ask, "How did she acquire this virtue?" Wives who take after this model spend time developing their relationship with God. Virtue flows naturally from their lives as a result of this personal time in prayer and God's Word.

Accordingly, we gain insight into the health of our marriages by examining the level of intimacy we share with God. Strength and trust must first be developed with God before they can be fully demonstrated with our spouses.

Many times, when our relationship with our spouse begins to falter, we have really wavered in our dedication to God. We then fight an uphill battle to save our marriage. By first valuing our relationship with God, we acquire tools to maintain our relationship with our spouse.

WISE WAYS Make a weekly goal of how much time you want to spend alone with God. Ask your spouse to keep you accountable for your goal.

Today, Lord, may my devotion to my spouse reflect my devotion to you.

✴

APRIL

April 1

Read
Proverbs 1

VESSELS
OF MERCY

*If you forgive those
who sin against you,
your heavenly Father
will forgive you. But
if you refuse to
forgive others, your
Father will not
forgive your sins.*
Matthew 6:14-15

The Bible seems to speak of forgiveness in at least
two different ways. In an ultimate sense, forgiveness
refers to God's eternal pardon of all our sins when
we look to Christ as the only one who can make us
right with God (John 5:24; Romans 8:1; Ephesians
1:7). No actions on our part can make this happen.
This is the mystery of grace—God's undeserved favor
to sinful men (Ephesians 2:8-9). Theologians call
this "justification." Fully forgiven, we enter into
relationship with a holy God.

Another kind of forgiveness mentioned in the Bible
is the ongoing cleansing we need in order to maintain
daily intimacy with God (1 John 1:9). It is this second
kind of forgiveness that Jesus speaks of in the verses
above. If we refuse to show mercy to those who have
wronged us, we distance ourselves from God and will
cease to experience and appreciate his wonderful love.

As you come to God to receive mercy for daily
wrongs, ask yourself, "Have I forgiven all those who
have wronged me?"

WISE WAYS   Against what person or people in
your life do you find yourself nursing an old grudge?

*Today, Lord, remind me of the shocking way in which you canceled my
debt of sin, and let that undeserved mercy move me to treat others with
similar mercy.*

April 2

Treasure. What a "rich" word! It makes most folks daydream about pirates, dragons, or genies. Lost in thought, we imagine all we might do if we found a chest full of priceless gems and precious metals.

God offers treasure of a different kind. It is the richness of "good sense." This kind of rare wisdom is not about IQ or intellect; no, it's actually a moral matter of the heart. The idea here is "skill in living"— a treasure enjoyed only by the godly, by those who take God seriously in their daily lives. But not only that. Look closer at today's proverb. Those who live consistent, morally upright lives receive another priceless benefit: They are protected. Almighty God acts as their shield.

The insight to know how to live in a perverse and confusing world and protection as you live for God— can you think of a more valuable find than this?

WISE WAYS   If you knew there were a treasure chest buried somewhere on your property, how diligently would you seek it? Why don't you pursue God's wisdom in the same way?

Today, Lord, increase my hunger for the "good sense" that only you can give. Teach me how to walk with integrity.

**Read
Proverbs 2**

GOD'S TREASURE CHEST

*[The Lord] grants a treasure of good sense to the godly.
He is their shield, protecting those who walk with integrity.*
Proverbs 2:7

April 3

**Read
Proverbs 3**

ETERNAL INVESTMENT

*Honor the LORD with
your wealth and with
the best part of
everything your land
produces. Then he
will fill your barns
with grain, and your
vats will overflow
with the finest wine.*

Proverbs 3:9-10

"Get all you can, can all you get, and sit on your can." In many ways this quip is an accurate picture of modern materialism. We in the West seek to accumulate wealth and to use it largely for ourselves. How easy it is to forget that all we have is from God . . . and should be used for him (Colossians 1:16).

By giving the first and best portion of their harvest back to God, the ancient Israelites acknowledged his goodness and their dependence (Deuteronomy 26). Such humble gratitude served as a continual reminder that God is the source of all material blessings. In exchange for this honor, God promised to continue to provide abundantly for the needs of his people.

Of course, both Scripture and experience provide us with exceptions to this "piety guarantees prosperity" rule. Sometimes generous people don't reap a big financial return. But, as Jesus assured us, there is always great blessing and joy in giving (Acts 20:35).

WISE WAYS On a scale of one to ten (with one being "almost never" and ten representing "almost always"), how often do you think of God when you are making financial decisions?

Today, Lord, I want to keep in mind that everything I have is from you. Help me learn to hold my possessions loosely. Make me a godly giver.

April 4

We go to great lengths to "get" things. Some will arise early and drive all over town to find bargains and "get" great deals at garage or estate sales. Others work long hours to "get" a promotion or a big contract. Still others sweat and strain day after day to "get" in shape. More often than not, these determined efforts pay off.

According to today's proverb, the most significant thing we can ever "get" is wisdom. And "get" this: the implication of this verse is that such wisdom is available not just to the smartest person or to the lucky person who "gets" all the breaks, but to the person who decides to go for it. In other words, a wise life begins with the decision, "I will do whatever it takes to 'get' godly insight." You "get" wisdom when you make the choice to pursue it above all else.

WISE WAYS Would a stranger, after examining your life, conclude that you are serious about "getting" wisdom? What is one thing you need to begin doing/stop doing in order to acquire good judgment?

Today, Lord, show me where my priorities are wrong. Bring wise people into my life so I can have role models to follow.

Read
Proverbs 4

GO FOR IT!

Getting wisdom is the most important thing you can do! And whatever else you do, get good judgment.
Proverbs 4:7

April 5

THE MORNING AFTER

Afterward you will groan in anguish when disease consumes your body, and you will say, "How I hated discipline! If only I had not demanded my own way!"
Proverbs 5:11-12

Regret is our anguished wishing to be able turn back the clock and undo foolish choices . . . and the haunting realization that we cannot. Few things in life are more devastating than a heart filled with bitter remorse.

In Proverbs 5 it is the adulterer who groans in anguish. Following the sweet, short-term pleasures of illicit sex, the foolish person is left to wallow in the bitter, long-term consequences of his sin—including disease. What a timeless passage! Talk to anyone who has lost spouse, family, reputation, health, and/or spiritual vitality because of sexual misconduct, and you'll find a person overflowing with regret. Contrast this with the wise person who lives a disciplined life and submits to God's ways rather than his/her own passions.

"If only I had not . . ." is a sad statement made all the more tragic by the realization that we brought this nightmare upon ourselves.

WISE WAYS In our sexually permissive age, it makes sense to have an accountability partner who will ask you hard questions and keep you on track. Do you have such a person in your life? If not, can you think of someone who would be appropriate?

Today, Lord, I pray for the grace to avoid sexual sin. Father, keep me pure, for your glory and for my own health.

April 6

Our culture has a list for everything—the worst-dressed celebrities, the safest cars, the best places to live, the highest paid athletes, the top colleges. Lists are always informative, often fascinating, and occasionally disturbing.

The Bible also has its share of lists. The Ten Commandments (Exodus 20) and the Beatitudes of Christ (Matthew 5:1-12) are the most famous. And then there's the lesser-known list of things God hates in Proverbs 6.

It is not intended to be an exhaustive list, but it is intended to give us pause. The primary idea is to show that people of corrupt character naturally live in a way that dishonors God. They live for self, giving little or no thought to their Creator and his standards. Check your own attitudes, thoughts, speech, and actions. Are you engaged in a lifestyle that the Lord says he detests?

WISE WAYS   Write out the specific sins mentioned in this passage. Then ask the Spirit of God to search your heart. If you become aware of these "hateful" things in your life, confess and accept the forgiveness available in Christ (1 John 1:9).

Today, Lord, I want to do what you love—the things that please you, not the things that you hate. Make me self-aware, vigilant, and desirous of doing good.

Read
Proverbs 6

THE SINFUL SEVEN

There are six things the LORD hates—no, seven things he detests . . . a heart that plots evil, feet that race to do wrong . . .
Proverbs 6:16, 18

April 7

Read
Proverbs 7

DRESSED TO KILL

*The woman
approached him,
dressed seductively
and sly of heart.*

Proverbs 7:10

The mantra on Madison Avenue is, and seemingly
always has been, "sex sells." Take your product—
makeup, milk, even mufflers—and showcase it with
gorgeous models in sensual settings. The formula
works like a charm. Like moths to the flame, we are
foolishly attracted. Hey, this isn't rocket science—
seductive things are meant to seduce!

In Proverbs 7, Solomon tells the sad story of a
young man who encounters a seductive woman. She
is attractive, alluring, and dressed (literally) to kill.
This temptress is the epitome of style and fashion.
She has "the look."

Because this man is "simpleminded"—he lacks the
wisdom to look beyond the surface or see beyond the
moment—he ends up as willing prey in the trap of
this adulterous woman—"like a trapped stag . . . like
a bird flying into a snare." And our fate is likely the
same whenever we become enamored with eroticism.

WISE WAYS Do you find yourself drawn to
popular commercials or TV shows that feature
"pretty people" involved in behavior that God calls
ugly? How is this mental diet affecting your attitudes
and actions?

*Today, Lord, I need to be careful about the images I see and dwell
upon. Grant me the wisdom to see beneath the surface and beyond
the moment.*

April 8

"Boil it down for me, Jesus," the Jewish scribe essentially asked. "Of all the laws on the books, which one should I focus upon?" In so many words, this is the great dilemma of the ages: What is the point of life? Is there a succinct philosophy or world view that spells out why we are here and how we are to live?

Jesus not only summarized over six hundred Jewish laws in a handful of short sentences, he also revealed the only way to a rich existence full of meaning and purpose.

Life is all about relationships, Jesus stated. Knowing God (and loving him with all that we are, in all that we do) is foremost. Hand in hand with this is our God-given responsibility to care for others and to look out for their interests (Philippians 2:3-4). When our passion and purpose in life is to please the living God and bless others, then (and only then) we will find the simplicity, freedom, and joy that eludes most people.

WISE WAYS Can you think of one or two specific behaviors in your life that violate Jesus' command to love God completely and love others compassionately? What do you need to do?

Today, Lord, I want to love more fully. Ignite within me a passion for you and a compassion for others.

**Read
Proverbs 8**

BOILING IT DOWN

Jesus replied, "The most important commandment is this: 'Hear, O Israel! The Lord our God is the one and only Lord. And you must love the Lord your God with all your heart, all your soul, all your mind, and all your strength.' The second is equally important: 'Love your neighbor as yourself.' No other commandment is greater than these."
Mark 12:29-31

April 9

THE TEST OF CRITICISM

*Anyone who rebukes
a mocker will get a
smart retort. Anyone
who rebukes the
wicked will get hurt.*

Proverbs 9:7

One of the first lessons every lifeguard learns is that it is extremely dangerous to try to save a struggling, thrashing person in danger of drowning. Such people, desperate and unable to think clearly, often lash out and pull their would-be rescuers under with them.

In many ways, this is a good example of today's proverb. A wise, discerning person notices someone making foolish, perhaps even dangerous, choices. The wise person moves in to warn of danger. Instead of quietly and humbly taking this verbal rope (and letting himself be pulled to safety), the endangered one lashes back with angry, even personal, insults. He is unteachable and—barring a miraculous change—unreachable.

We can pray for the stubborn and foolish, but in truth, we really can't help them until they are willing to quit fighting and listen to what God says.

WISE WAYS   How do you handle constructive criticism? Do you get defensive? Do you attack your critics? Why or why not?

Today, Lord, grant me the wisdom to hear the truth in any criticism I receive, and please show me when I need to try to intervene in the lives of others.

April 10

Some people didn't just wake up on the wrong side of the bed, it almost seems they were born there! Mad at the world, they pick fights, agitate, and cause problems—as a way of life.

In stark contrast are those who live by love. They make it their goal to create an atmosphere where confession, confrontation, forgiveness, and contentment lead to peace. The Hebrew verb translated "covers" doesn't mean "conceals." It means "forgives." The idea is that love has no desire to rub someone's nose in his or her mistakes (1 Corinthians 13:5; James 5:20). The goal of love is to resolve and retire offenses and problems. Once love covers an issue, it's over!

When conflicts arise, do you keep them stirred up or do you work toward a resolution? God always knows our true intentions. We need his supernatural help in order to succeed at loving and forgiving.

WISE WAYS Think of an ongoing conflict in your life. What hateful attitudes or actions on your part have stirred up the situation, making it worse? What is God telling you to do?

Today, Lord, I want to be an instrument of peace and healing. Keep me from bitterness, and enable me to forgive and to love.

Read
Proverbs 10

TROUBLEMAKER OR PEACEMAKER?

Hatred stirs up quarrels, but love covers all offenses.
Proverbs 10:12

April 11

**Read
Proverbs 11**

FULL OF SELF?

*Pride leads to
disgrace, but with
humility comes
wisdom.*

Proverbs 11:2

In his classic book *Mere Christianity*, C. S. Lewis wrote extensively about pride. He called it "the great sin," noting that it was through pride that the devil became the devil! As long as we are prideful, he argued, always looking down on everything and everyone, we cannot see the God who is above us.

In today's proverb, the word for pride comes from a Hebrew verb meaning "to boil up." The picture is of a kind of "bubbling arrogance" that seeks to dominate others and promote self. Note the result of this kind of mind-set and lifestyle. Those with inflated egos will soon be deflated!

God's way is the way of wisdom, which goes hand-in-hand with humility. This is the quiet, modest, trusting approach to life (Micah 6:8). The humble person does not "boil up" with a great need to be first or gain acclaim. A humble person is not threatened by the success of others.

WISE WAYS In what kinds of situations do you sense pride "boiling up" within you? Why do you think those situations affect you so? [Note: If you have a copy of *Mere Christianity*, read the chapter on pride.]

Today, Lord, free me from that strong urge to promote myself, to be noticed, to receive acclaim, and to be arrogant toward others. Teach me how to humble myself so that you can exalt me at the proper time.

April 12

Item 1: Billions of dollars are spent each year on legalized gambling, even though it has been proven that one is more likely to get hit by lightning than to ever hit the jackpot.

Item 2: Exercise and diet products that promise *big* results in exchange for *minimal* effort are flying off the shelves.

Item 3: Over the last ten years, more people than ever before have poured more money than ever before into "get rich quick" schemes.

What's going on? The answer is simple: People want "something for nothing" (or, more accurately, "lots for very little"). Forget the notion of long-term discipline and slow, steady progress. Nothing less than instant, spectacular results will do.

God's Word offers an opposing view. We are urged to reject the frantic pursuit of "get rich quick" fantasies. The true secret of success (financial, physical, or spiritual) is hard work spread out over a long time. Diligent effort, not wishful thinking, is the way to prosperity.

WISE WAYS What is "instant gratification," and how much does this kind of thinking affect you?

Today, Lord, keep me from believing the lie that I can prosper without hard work. Help me to be diligent and to think long-term, not short-term.

**Read
Proverbs 12**

GET RICH QUICK?

Hard work means prosperity; only fools idle away their time.
Proverbs 12:11

April 13

**Read
Proverbs 13**

THE SECRET OF LONG LIFE

The life of the godly is full of light and joy, but the sinner's light is snuffed out.

Proverbs 13:9

At Great-Grandma's hundredth birthday celebration, someone inevitably asks, "How did you do it? What's the secret to such a long life?" The answer will no doubt surprise you. Centenarians have been known to credit their longevity to everything from strawberry ice cream to daily naps to crossword puzzles!

Today's proverb addresses this question. In the ancient Near East, "light" symbolized physical life. For example, without the light of a campfire at night, a traveler was susceptible to danger, even death.

The point is that a wise, godly person will tend to have a long life. He or she will "walk in the light" (Isaiah 2:5; John 12:35)—keeping God's rules that provide for safety. Foolish, sinful people, on the other hand, tend to die early. They dwell in a kind of moral darkness that is fraught with traps and life-threatening trouble.

WISE WAYS What are some behaviors in your life that could possibly shorten your life? How do things like worry and anger take their toll on you physically?

Today, Lord, help me remember that my life is in your hands. Help me to avoid sinful attitudes and actions that put me at risk spiritually, emotionally, and physically.

April 14

The story is told of a deathbed visit paid to Walden author Henry David Thoreau by a Christian aunt. When she inquired if he had made his peace with God, he is reported to have said, "Why, I didn't know we had ever quarreled."

This is the mind-set of the skeptic or the cynic—or what Proverbs routinely calls the "fool." The concepts of guilt and repentance are laughable. The thought of needing to make amends with God or others is a joke.

Contrast this strong-willed arrogance with the response of the godly person. He or she owns up to wrong actions and the hurt they have caused. More than that, the upright person seeks to make restitution, to set things right. Reconciliation (literally "good will" with God and people) is his or her primary goal.

This one pithy sentence explains how the humble find favor with God and people and why the proud never will.

WISE WAYS Can you think of any relationship in your life that is strained because of your refusal to admit wrong and seek forgiveness? Rehearse what you should say to make things right.

Today, Lord, I want to experience the blessing of right relationships with you and others. Show me what I need to do to make this a reality in my life.

Read
Proverbs 14

MAKING AMENDS

Fools make fun of guilt, but the godly acknowledge it and seek reconciliation.
Proverbs 14:9

April 15

**Read
Proverbs 15**

❋

THE CRITIC'S CORNER

*Stop judging others,
and you will not be
judged. For others
will treat you as you
treat them. Whatever
measure you use in
judging others, it will
be used to measure
how you are judged.*

Matthew 7:1-2

In the current "climate of tolerance," it is taboo to call into question the behavior of others. When someone dares violate this unwritten cultural rule, even irreligious people (who seldom think of Jesus and certainly have no desire to follow him) are quick to paraphrase the words of Christ: "Who are you to judge? Let him who is without sin cast the first stone!"

This kind of noble-sounding rhetoric is not only foolish, it is also a distortion of what Christ meant. Today's "New Testament proverb" is primarily a call to examine ourselves before we criticize others. Jesus recognized how easy it is to be hypocritical, to spot the flaws of our neighbors even as we are blind to our own faults.

The biblical standard is to take a hard look at ourselves first (Psalm 26:2; 1 Corinthians 11:28). Only then are we in a position to lovingly help others see where they are off track (Galatians 6:1; 1 Thessalonians 5:14).

WISE WAYS   Are you a critical person? Would those close to you say that you have a tendency to find fault? How do Jesus' words impact you?

Today, Lord, I want to honor you by not being harsh with others. I want to be treated with mercy, so help me to treat others accordingly.

April 16

Our human tendency is to assess sin superficially. We look at external behavior and rank it. For example, "white" lies are often viewed as "no big deal," stealing is regarded as a pretty major sin, and, well, if you really want to offend God, engage in some kind of sexual perversion—like pedophilia.

The Bible takes a deeper view of sin. God looks at the human heart and says that the root of all disobedience—from unkindness to mass murder—is the sin of pride. It's not surprising, then, to read in Proverbs 16 that God despises pride.

Pride is that powerful yearning inside each of us that says, "I will do things my way." Pride has no regard for God's glory. It has no interest in exalting his name. Pride rejects God's will for "what I want." But in the end it reaps punishment, not freedom.

WISE WAYS In what area(s) of your life do you tend to resist God's plan for you? Why?

Today, Lord, show me where I stubbornly refuse to bow my will to yours. Give me the grace I need to humble myself before you.

**Read
Proverbs 16**

THE ROOT
OF SIN

*The Lord despises pride;
be assured that
the proud will be
punished.*

Proverbs 16:5

April 17

SCARED STRAIGHT

A single rebuke does more for a person of understanding than a hundred lashes on the back of a fool.

Proverbs 17:10

Two teens get into trouble. One's brush with the law scares him straight. The other is in and out of court—and in and out of jail—for the rest of his life. How do we account for this difference? According to the Book of Proverbs, the first kid is wise; the second is a fool.

A wise person carefully and quickly heeds words of warning. He or she realizes that a rebuke, while sometimes embarrassing, is actually a gift. Coming from an older, wiser saint, the discerning soul receives constructive criticism, knowing it can save him or her from much trouble and regret.

Meanwhile, the fool is impervious to discipline. Not even excessive physical punishment can change the ways of one who is hardheaded and hard-hearted. He or she is stubborn and, barring a sudden change, headed for even bigger trouble.

We would do well to consider how we respond when corrected.

WISE WAYS Make a list of people in your church or community whom you respect and from whom you are willing to receive correction. Why do you think you respond well to them?

Today, Lord, I want to make progress in the area of being open to rebukes based on truth and offered in love. Make me teachable.

April 18

When it comes to food, what's your weakness? What scrumptious dish do you find almost impossible to resist? What delicious dessert causes you to salivate?

In the proverb for today, gossip is pictured as a mouthwatering morsel. It sure is a fitting image. Rumors tempt us like a sizzling entrée. Like addictive snack food, we can't seem to get enough. We crave more juicy details.

Dieters like to say, "A moment on the lips, forever on the hips." What seems so good in the short-term ends up causing long-term pain. According to our verse, a similar phenomenon takes place with gossip. Once we indulge, we find rumors hard to forget. They sink deep into our hearts.

The best course of action? Any dieter can tell you: Don't give in to the temptation! If you never take that first bite, you won't have to worry about the second or the third.

WISE WAYS   Grade yourself (A, B, C, D, F) in the area of gossip/rumormongering. What will it take for you to see deep, long-term change?

Today, Lord, I want to develop an aversion to gossip. When rumors are being spread, help me to turn a deaf ear and not participate.

**Read
Proverbs 18**

GRAPEVINE GOURMET?

*What dainty morsels rumors are—
but they sink deep
into one's heart.*

Proverbs 18:8

April 19

A GIFT FROM HEAVEN

Parents can provide their sons with an inheritance of houses and wealth, but only the LORD can give an understanding wife.

Proverbs 19:14

Some wise guy has noted that marriage is the only institution on earth where everybody on the outside wants in, and everybody on the inside wants out! It's a humorous quip with a kick. Why do so many put so much hope in marriage? Why do so many couples have such great struggle?

In Old Testament times, marriages were typically arranged by the parents. This provided for simplicity in courtship, but it did not guarantee marital happiness. According to today's proverb, while passing along the family fortune may have been a somewhat "fool-proof" transaction, good matchmaking necessitated the Lord's help and favor.

The same principle is still true. We need God's help to find the right mate. We need the grace of God to be a godly mate. If you're happily married, thank the Lord. If your marriage needs help, call on the Lord. Any and all good in your life ultimately comes from him (James 1:17).

WISE WAYS   If you are married, think of two simple, concrete things you could do today to express love to your spouse.

Today, Lord, I want to make a conscious effort to remember that every good gift in my life is from you—that goes for marriage too.

April 20

This proverb can be interpreted in a couple of ways. Taken at face value, it seems to be saying that we ought to be grateful for our physical senses of hearing and sight. These auditory and optical capabilities are, indeed, a wonderful blessing.

On the other hand, since the Hebrew verb "to hear" in this verse is sometimes translated as "to obey," and since "to see" often means "to understand" elsewhere in the Bible, this verse may mean that spiritual insight and obedience are a gift from God (Ephesians 2:8-10).

Whichever interpretation you prefer—that this verse speaks of physical perception or that it refers to spiritual awareness/understanding—don't lose sight of the deeper truth. God is the source of all that we have. Thank him for his marvelous, undeserved blessings! And use his blessings for his glory!

WISE WAYS   When is the last time you thanked God for your physical senses? for the spiritual perception and understanding you've been given?

Today, Lord, I want to give credit where credit is due. I want to praise you for blessing me with ears to hear and eyes to see. Help me use these to bring you praise.

Read
Proverbs 20

CREDIT WHERE
CREDIT'S DUE

Ears to hear and eyes to see—both are gifts from the LORD.
Proverbs 20:12

April 21

**Read
Proverbs 21**

BRIBING GOD?

*The LORD is more
pleased when we do
what is just and right
than when we give
him sacrifices.*

Proverbs 21:3

Consider the words of 17-year-old Heather: "When
my folks were splitting up, they showered me with
stuff, but what I really wanted and needed most was
them. I would gladly trade all the gifts—even my car—
to be close to them."

Giving gifts to alleviate guilt is a common practice—
and not just among divorcing parents. Often, people
who know they're not living as they should try to
"make it up" to God through various religious
gestures. In ancient times, this usually meant the
sacrifice of a few extra animals. Now, it generally
involves more time devoted to religious functions
or a little something extra in the offering plate.

The Bible is clear. God cannot be "bought off."
He isn't impressed by our "pseudo-devotion." To
ignore God Monday through Saturday and then
expect him to be satisfied with a few extra bucks or a
couple of hours of ritual on Sunday morning is the
height of hypocrisy. God doesn't want your stuff. He
wants you—doing his will.

WISE WAYS Are you aware of any areas of your
life in which you are disobeying the command of
God and attempting to "make it up" by religious
devotion?

*Today, Lord, you desire my genuine obedience, not my "slick"
attempts at appearing holy. Keep me from the insidious sin of
hypocrisy.*

April 22

SABBATH

What are people in our culture hungry for? If the infomercials we watch on TV are any indication, people crave rich food and buff bodies (how's that for a contradiction?). Our culture also seems to be thirsty for wealth, personal peace, and "escapist" entertainment. The problem is that such pursuits provide only temporary satisfaction. Then what?

In the Sermon on the Mount, Jesus urged his followers to hunger and thirst for "justice." Since this Greek verb is sometimes translated "righteousness," the point seems to be that we should long for things "to be made right." Our number one pursuit should be for a right relationship with God. Our continual prayer should be for the "rightness" of heaven to come down and fill the whole earth (Matthew 6:9).

When such eternal quests are our true longings, we can be assured that God will satisfy us—both now and in the life to come.

WISE WAYS   What do you crave . . . really? Would an objective observer who knew your thoughts and analyzed your actions conclude that you are hungry and thirsty for God and his will . . . or something else?

Today, Lord, I want to pursue you with greater passion. Stir my heart. Create within me a deeper desire for the things of heaven than for the stuff of earth.

**Read
Proverbs 22**

SPIRITUAL
CRAVINGS

"God blesses those who are hungry and thirsty for justice, for they will receive it in full."
Matthew 5:6

April 23

TRUE CHILD ABUSE

Don't fail to correct your children. They won't die if you spank them. Physical discipline may well save them from death.

Proverbs 23:13-14

Not so long ago, kids who got out of line got spanked. Parents administered this kind of physical discipline routinely, and most school principals also wielded a "board of education" to teach disobedient children important character lessons. No longer. Spank a kid today, even your own, and you may end up in court . . . or worse.

Obviously, we need to protect kids from child abuse, but is it wise to go to the opposite extreme? Not according to Proverbs. Today's verse encourages parents to exercise appropriate measures (even physical discipline) to correct defiant children. The goal is not merely outer conformity to a set a rules, but helping kids develop the kind of inner character and moral boundaries that will save them from potentially disastrous choices later in life.

By not correcting inappropriate behavior, we give our children the wrong idea that there are no consequences to wrong choices. Perhaps this is the ultimate child abuse.

WISE WAYS How can a parent spank a child in a way that honors God? How would you "defend" spanking to someone who views such a practice as "outdated and barbaric"?

Today, Lord, I am reminded that your truth is often at odds with the prevailing "wisdom" of culture. Give me the courage to do what is right, not just what is popular.

April 24

Pouting. Stomping. Yelling. Screaming. Crying. Worrying. Dissolving. Escaping. Enduring. Isn't it fascinating to watch the various ways people respond to adversity?

According to the Bible, trials are both normal and helpful. They enable us to develop godly character (Romans 5:3-4; James 1:2-4). Not only this, but the everyday pressures of stress, problems, and setbacks also reveal what we're really made of.

Proverbs 24:5 suggests that it is wisdom that gives strength. Therefore, the implication of today's proverb is that if we easily wilt when trouble comes, we must not be very wise.

What about you? Are you quick to wave the white flag when problems block your way? Do you quit at the first signs of stress? Don't run from adversity! Refuse to succumb to a lifestyle of whining and complaining. Remember that God is using tough situations to make you like Christ (Romans 8:29). Then call upon God's infinite power and wisdom (Ephesians 1:19-20).

WISE WAYS What pressures are you facing right now? What are your options? How can you honor God in the midst of adversity?

Today, Lord, grant me the wisdom to see your hand in my trials. I want to be strong. I want to persevere. Sustain me today with the confidence that you are in control.

**Read
Proverbs 24**

DON'T QUIT!

If you fail under pressure, your strength is not very great.

Proverbs 24:10

April 25

**Read
Proverbs 25**

PRICELESS!

*Valid criticism is as
treasured by the one
who heeds it as
jewelry made from
finest gold.*

Proverbs 25:12

Dinner at the best Italian restaurant in town: $75.
Tickets to an award-winning play: $80. Fifteen
minutes of constructive criticism expressed in love:
Priceless.

If we were to copy the popular ad campaign of a
major credit card, that's how we might paraphrase
Solomon's wise counsel regarding confrontation.

Human nature tends to recoil from any and all
criticism (even when it is valid). And yet as believers
in Christ, we have a new nature (2 Corinthians 5:17).
Rationalizing, justifying, and blaming are our natural
reactions. However, the indwelling Spirit of God
(Galatians 5:22-23) gives us the ability to respond in
supernatural ways. Consequently, we can, if we will,
come to see criticism as an instrument of good in
our life.

No one enjoys having his or her flaws pointed
out. But the next time you are confronted, resist the
urge to defend yourself and lash back. Listen.
Think. Pray. Through hard, tough words, God may
be offering you a priceless gift.

WISE WAYS Think back to the last time someone
criticized you. How did you react? What part of the
criticism was valid?

*Today, Lord, I want to be humble enough to hear the truth about
myself and wise enough to fix—with your help—whatever is not right
in my life.*

April 26

Most dogs will put up with a lot. (How else do you think they earned the title of "man's best friend"?) But few canines will let you yank their ears. Try that stunt, and even an unusually sweet lab or golden retriever may snap.

This is the surprising analogy used to warn us against meddling in the quarrels of others. By inviting ourselves into conflicts that don't involve us, we may end up becoming the target of both angry parties. It's noble to want to help, to want to be a peacemaker (Matthew 5:9), but when tempers are flaring and pride is out of control, little good can be accomplished.

The wiser course of action is to sit back, watch, listen, pray, and wait for the passions to subside. Then, if we are invited to help resolve the problem, or if we are in a position where it is our duty to intervene, we can gently and carefully weigh in.

WISE WAYS   Do you tend to be a "nosy" person? When has your intrusion into the conflict of others caused trouble?

Today, Lord, I want to be a peacemaker, but I do not want to be unwise. Give me the discernment to know if and when I should intervene.

**Read
Proverbs 26**

DON'T MEDDLE!

*Yanking
a dog's ears
is as foolish as
interfering in
someone else's
argument.*
Proverbs 26:17

April 27

✳

CANCER OF THE SOUL

Anger is cruel, and wrath is like a flood, but who can survive the destructiveness of jealousy?
Proverbs 27:4

An old Jewish fable tells of two men, one greedy and the other jealous. A certain king offered to give them anything they asked; but twice as much to him who asked last. The greedy man refused to ask first, because he wanted the double portion. The jealous man likewise refused to make the first request because he could not bear the thoughts of his neighbor receiving more than himself. Finally, the jealous man broke the impasse, requesting that one of his eyes should be taken out, in order that his neighbor might lose both.

Such is the nature of jealousy. It cheers for the ruin of others, and given the chance, will take an active role in bringing about their downfall. It was because of jealousy that Cain murdered Abel, that Joseph's brothers sold him into slavery, that the Jews had Christ crucified.

Unlike anger and wrath that typically erupt and then pass, jealousy lurks long-term in the shadows of the human heart, ravaging souls and wrecking lives.

WISE WAYS   Are you a jealous person? How? In what areas? When has your jealousy caused problems for you or others?

Today, Lord, I ask you to keep me free from jealousy. Help me rejoice when others experience success and prosperity.

April 28

Spiritual schizophrenia (aka religious hypocrisy) is a common malady among Christians. The symptoms are easy to see: talking like a follower of Christ one moment and living like an unbeliever the next; "pious" participation in worship, prayer, or Bible reading immediately followed by lifestyle choices that do not honor or even acknowledge the existence of a holy God. Those who embrace this kind of "Jekyll and Hyde" lifestyle are often quite successful at fooling other people, but God is never fooled.

This is the point of today's highlighted proverb. Those who have no intention of obeying God's Word might as well keep their prayers to themselves. God is not swayed by the religious endeavors of blatant hypocrites (Proverbs 15:8; Psalm 66:18; Isaiah 59:2). In fact, we are told here that God despises such a person's phony prayers! If we want God to hear us, we must first be willing to hear from (obey) him.

WISE WAYS   All of us are guilty of hypocrisy some of the time, but are you among those who are hypocritical all (or almost all) the time? Why does God hate hypocrisy?

Today, Lord, I want to live a consistent, God-honoring life. Show me blind spots in my life where I'm not practicing what I say I believe.

**Read
Proverbs 28**

FUTILE PRAYING

The prayers of a person who ignores the law are despised.
Proverbs 28:9

April 29

Read Proverbs 29

✳

IS IT BAD TO GET MAD?

My dear brothers and sisters, be quick to listen, slow to speak, and slow to get angry. Your anger can never make things right in God's sight.

James 1:19-20

When you get miffed, ticked, or steamed, are you more likely to: (a) flip your lid; (b) fly off the handle; (c) hit the ceiling; or (d) blow either a fuse, a gasket, or your top?

Truth is, lots of things can happen when we get too hot under the collar, and most of them are not good. Uncontrolled anger causes more grief and regret than just about any other emotion.

The apostle James, under the inspiration of the Holy Spirit, offered a wise checklist for those moments when we feel our blood starting to boil (James 1:19). First, make an extra effort to listen (especially to what God might be trying to say to you in the situation). Second, bite your tongue (careless words will only aggravate a tense situation). Third, don't let your emotions cause you to sin (see also Ephesians 4:26).

We should never ignore or deny angry feelings, but we should not let them control us either.

WISE WAYS   Think about a time when your anger got the best of you. What happened? Have you, with God's help, recently experienced victory over anger?

Today, Lord, I want to honor you in those frustrating, angry moments of life. Keep me from reacting sinfully. Help me respond graciously.

April 30

What does it mean to "add to God's words"? Religious cults do it when they put other writings on a par with the Bible. Churches do it when they emphasize man-made traditions as much as or more than they do the teachings of Scripture. Individuals do it when they discard the clear pronouncements of the Word in favor of popular ideas or personal desires.

Today's passage warns against any kind of "editing" of God's Word. Because God delivered his revelation to the world without error, we do not need to tamper with Scripture. In fact, it is dangerous and foolish to attempt to add human speculation to divine revelation. Attempting to alter or amend the Word of God is, in effect, to question God's wisdom, his goodness, or his judgment. And according to this passage, any such arrogance will lead to a divine rebuke and the humiliation of being exposed as one who has knowingly obscured the truth.

WISE WAYS   Can you think of any instances in which you may have elevated your own ideas or desires to the same level as Scripture?

Today, Lord, I want to treat your Word (and nothing else) as my ultimate authority and guide. Keep me from the great sin of adding to your words.

**Read
Proverbs 30**

NO EDITING
NEEDED

Do not add to [God's] words, or he may rebuke you, and you will be found a liar.
Proverbs 30:6

MAY

May 1

**Read
Proverbs 1**

NEW CLOTHING

*What you learn from
[your parents] will
crown you with grace
and clothe you with
honor.*

Proverbs 1:9

We have some wonderful opportunities to observe
the marvels of God's creation in those educational
shows about animals on television. It is interesting
to learn how some animals give birth to their babies
and then, almost immediately, the babies are off on
their own. On the other hand, many animal parents
have their young for a few years and they teach them
how to hunt and how to stay away from predators—in
essence, how to survive.

If God provided such training even in much of the
animal kingdom, how important it is for people! God
created human families so that parents could train
their children. Human parents also give their children "survival" skills—but they do much more by
giving spiritual, moral, and emotional training.
When parents are a good influence, the children who
listen will learn valuable lessons that will straighten
and smooth their own road in life. Such parents are
giving a great gift to their children—crowning them
with grace and clothing them with honor.

WISE WAYS What kind of "crown" and "clothing" are you giving your children?

*Lord, help me to be the parent you want me to be. May I give my
children the kind of instruction that will crown them with grace and
clothe them with honor.*

May 2

The Bible tells us that God is not only perfectly loving, merciful, and compassionate, but also perfectly just: "The Lord our God is just in everything he does" (Daniel 9:14). The word "justice" means "rightfulness, lawfulness, true, correct, administering of deserved punishment or reward." Because God is perfectly just, we can trust that everything he does is right and fair—whether we perceive it that way now or not. We know that whatever happens to us in this life has already passed through his hands—even perceived injustice. God promises to protect those who are faithful to him.

The world is full of injustice and corruption. While we watch injustice occur, we may wonder where God is. Yet the Bible assures us that he is guarding the paths of justice. In the end, the One who is perfectly just will punish all evil and reward his faithful children.

WISE WAYS   Even if you are facing what you perceive as injustice right now, can you trust that God is in control and that he will ultimately make it right?

Lord, help me to trust in your justice. Help me to know that ultimately you will make all things right, bring perfect justice to the world, and reward those who have remained faithful to you.

**Read
Proverbs 2**

ON GUARD

He guards the paths of justice and protects those who are faithful to him.
Proverbs 2:8

May 3

**Read
Proverbs 3**

BECAUSE
HE LOVES

*My child, don't
ignore it when the
LORD disciplines you,
and don't be
discouraged when he
corrects you. For the
LORD corrects those
he loves, just as a
father corrects a child
in whom he delights.*
Proverbs 3:11-12

An undisciplined child is not a pretty sight. We have
all seen a child who kicks and screams and behaves
rudely. Children need discipline because their
natural bent, like all humans, is toward sin and selfishness. Parents have to train their children to
behave correctly. Sometimes this involves discipline,
but that discipline is meant in love. Wise parents
delight in their children and discipline them, knowing that such training will crown their children with
grace and honor (1:9).

Like a loving Father, God also disciplines his children. Our natural bent is toward sin and selfishness.
Because God delights in us, he wants to teach us to
live rightly for him. So when we feel the sting of
God's discipline on our lives, we must not ignore it
or be discouraged. Like obedient children, we must
learn the lesson God has for us. God disciplines
those he loves; if we are being disciplined, we know
we are loved.

WISE WAYS Are you feeling the sting of God's
discipline—in the form of a pricked conscience, the
consequences for sin, or even the words of a trusted
friend? What lesson is God trying to teach you?

*Lord, let me remember that your discipline on my life happens
because you love me. Show me what you are trying to teach me.*

May 4

The picture of "running" through life seems to be an especially apt one for our culture. We run from this activity to that job to this responsibility to that commitment. Lots of that running, however, doesn't seem to be so wise. We may do way too much running, only to find ourselves limping or stumbling, unable to fulfill our commitments as well as we would like because we're over-committed, tired, or burned out.

There's no doubt that we will continue to "run" at a certain pace, for life is very busy for most people. To be able to run through life "guided by wisdom" means knowing your own best pace and allowing for only the amount of activity that can be done realistically and well. Wisdom means seeking God's guidance so we know when to say "yes" and when to say "no." Then we will do all things well, and we won't "limp or stumble" along the way.

WISE WAYS Are you limping and stumbling through your daily activities—overwhelmed, burned out, exhausted? Are you seeking God's guidance for what activities and service he wants you to do? How can you begin living your life guided by wisdom?

Lord, as I run through my activities, teach me how to be guided by wisdom. Show me when to say "yes" and when to say "no."

**Read
Proverbs 4**

OFF AND
RUNNING

If you live a life guided by wisdom, you won't limp or stumble as you run.
Proverbs 4:12

May 5

LISTEN AND LEARN

Oh, why didn't I listen to my teachers? Why didn't I pay attention to those who gave me instruction?
Proverbs 5:13

How many teachers have read this verse with great satisfaction? They knew that the knowledge they were imparting to their students was essential to their lives, but how many students simply didn't care? And how many of those same students, faced with difficult challenges that demanded those lessons or skills later in life, would then lament, "Oh, why didn't I listen to my teachers?"

The context of this verse is specifically the teaching about immorality. The student (the son) who does not listen will find himself facing utter ruin. He will then lament that he should have heeded the instruction of his teacher (his father) who had been exactly right about the perils of immorality.

In any situation, we would be wise to listen and learn from our teachers. And as teachers, especially of our own children, we would be wise to help them to understand the ultimate value of the lessons we try to impart.

WISE WAYS Are you listening carefully to your teachers? If you are a teacher in any role, how are you helping your students to see the value of the lessons you are imparting?

Lord, help me to respectfully learn from those you have sent to teach me. Also, help me to teach those you have given me as students with enthusiasm and urgency so that they will understand the value of the lessons I give.

May 6

Jesus had just finished talking about how we can know a person by his or her "fruit" (Matthew 7:20). In other words, people can say whatever they want, but inevitably their actions (their "fruit") will reveal who they really are and what they really believe. Therefore, Jesus knew that many people would attempt to "sound religious" by saying the right words and even referring to Jesus as "Lord." They may attend church and "look" right. They may even be able to fool a lot of people for a lot of the time.

Jesus made clear, however, that looking or sounding religious will not get anyone into the Kingdom of Heaven. The only thing that matters is obedience to God the Father. That obedience refers to accepting Jesus' sacrifice on our behalf and allowing him to save us. What matters is not what we say about Jesus, but what we do about him.

WISE WAYS Have you accepted Jesus as your Lord and Savior in obedience to God? If not, will you do so today?

Lord, let me strengthen my personal relationship with you. I want to obey your command to believe in the Son you sent to die for me. I want to bear fruit for you because I am your child.

Read
Proverbs 6

MORE THAN A TITLE

Not all people who sound religious are really godly. They may refer to me as "Lord," but they still don't enter the Kingdom of Heaven. The decisive issue is whether they obey my Father in heaven.

Matthew 7:21

May 7

Read Proverbs 7

"NO SOLICITORS"

She is often seen in the streets and markets, soliciting at every corner.

Proverbs 7:12

Temptation is easy to find. Most of us don't really have to try very hard to put ourselves into a situation where we are tempted to do wrong. The recovering alcoholic and the bar, the gambler and the casino, the sex addict and the newsstand—even the dieter and the nearest cookie jar!

In this passage, the temptress seduces the young, foolish man. She knows what she wants, and she stands brazenly "in the streets and markets, soliciting at every corner." Temptation is brazen as well, for Satan desires to lure us to commit sin. He wants to see us fail, be embarrassed, ruin our witness for Christ, or fall back into addiction. To do so, he will solicit in every corner of our lives.

How do we stay out of his traps? We follow wise teachings, guard them, and write them deep in our hearts (7:1-3), so we can say "No" to the brazen solicitations of temptation.

WISE WAYS In what areas are you facing temptation today? What do you need to do to stand firm against doing what you know is wrong?

Lord, help me to stand firm in the face of this temptation that is trying to lure me into sin. Give me words from your Word to help me to say no to temptation.

May 8

In this verse, Wisdom is the speaker (see 8:12), calling out for people to listen. Wisdom knows that "fear of the Lord" and "evil" are mutually exclusive. One cannot fear the Lord and enjoy any form of evil. In fact, God's people should "hate evil" in all of its forms. Some of the forms of evil are outlined here: pride, arrogance, corruption, and perverted speech. These should be hated by people who love the Lord and desire wisdom.

Pride and arrogance refer to attitudes of superiority that usually result in offensive displays of haughtiness. These have no place among God's people who are called to be humble (1 Peter 5:6). Corruption is moral depravity, dishonesty, perversion. A corrupt person is debased in character. In contrast, God's people are to live above reproach (1 Peter 2:12). Perverted speech leads people astray and is improper. Believers' words should always be good and helpful (Ephesians 4:29).

WISE WAYS   In what areas do you need to develop hatred for evil? In what ways are you seeking to be humble, to live above reproach, and to make sure that your speech is always good and helpful?

Lord, teach me how to live to fear you and to hate evil. May I develop humility, may I live above reproach, and may my words be helpful to all to whom I speak.

**Read
Proverbs 8**

FEAR THE LORD, HATE EVIL

All who fear the Lord will hate evil. That is why I hate pride, arrogance, corruption, and perverted speech.
Proverbs 8:13

May 9

**Read
Proverbs 9**

✳

COURAGEOUS, CONSTRUCTIVE CRITICISM

So don't bother rebuking mockers; they will only hate you. But the wise, when rebuked, will love you all the more.

Proverbs 9:8

Why shouldn't we rebuke a mocker? Because a mocker hears without listening. A mocker pays attention only to mimic, ridicule, and humiliate. Even a mild rebuke will be returned as mockery, while an effective rebuke will simply be met with hatred.

Wise people don't enjoy being told they're wrong, but they understand that a truthful rebuke reflects love. So, where a mocker only hears more fodder for ridicule, a wise person hears an expression of love.

When we have people in our lives who are willing to rebuke us when necessary, we should be thankful. We should also be courageous enough to rebuke someone we love if we realize that he or she needs it. A rebuke given out of love will help the other person. Hopefully, he or she will understand our motivation of love. And perhaps we will recognize that several rebukes we have received were actually expressions of love.

WISE WAYS Whom could you thank today for a past rebuke that you know was given in love?

Lord, help me rebuke lovingly. Help me also to hear the love in the rebukes of others.

May 10

Proverbs constantly seeks to help us understand the differences between wisdom and foolishness, and calls us to be people of wisdom. Wise people have certain characteristics; foolish people have certain contrasting characteristics. To know these characteristics gives us a mirror into our own lives. These also help us be discerning about the people with whom we choose to associate.

This proverb tells us that people who are wise "treasure" (or value and store up) knowledge. Wise people are constantly learning—from their own mistakes, others' mistakes, from the world around them, from God's Word—and they store up that knowledge so as to help them live wisely. They don't run around talking all the time, so when they speak, we trust that what they say is knowledgeable. In contrast, the fool is "babbling" all the time, talking without thinking. That "invites trouble," said the writer. We should seek to be people whose words can be counted on as having depth and wisdom.

WISE WAYS How much do you talk? Are your words carefully considered or do they flow out uncontrolled? What can you do to "treasure knowledge" and so become wise?

Lord, watch over every word I speak. Help me to consider my words and from where they come. Teach me how to treasure knowledge.

Read
Proverbs 10

DABBLING
WITH
BABBLING

Wise people treasure knowledge, but the babbling of a fool invites trouble.
Proverbs 10:14

May 11

Read Proverbs 11

✴

WHAT MONEY CAN'T BUY

Riches won't help on the day of judgment, but right living is a safeguard against death.

Proverbs 11:4

Make no mistake about it—both the Old and New Testaments describe a "day of judgment," a time when God will vanquish evil and make all things right. No matter how rich we are, our money will be worthless. We cannot purchase salvation—it was already purchased by the blood of Christ.

Of course, the writer did not know about Jesus Christ. All he knew was that a relationship with God was available and that God's people attempted to live by God's standards. "Right living" does not mean that good deeds can give salvation, for the New Testament clears that up for us. However, right living—a life lived through the power of the Holy Spirit because of one's belief in Christ—does indeed "safeguard against death." This does not mean, of course, that we won't ever die. Instead, it pictures that death is not the end, but merely a step into the next life—an eternal one with God.

WISE WAYS   Have you accepted the ultimate safeguard against death—a relationship with Jesus Christ? How do you think about your money? Do you act as if it is your salvation, or do you see it as God's gift to you to use wisely?

Lord, may I learn to see my money (no matter how little or much I have) as your gift to me. Teach me how to use it wisely to meet my needs and then to do your work in the world.

May 12

This verse has been taken many ways—with varying results. At face value, this could mean that a teenager who listens to the advice of his friends to try drugs is actually considered wise. Obviously, the principle here goes far deeper, concerning both attitude and discernment. Foolish people think they know it all. They "think they need no advice," and so they refuse to listen to anyone who might have experience, knowledge, or even just loving concern for them. They foolishly limit their ability to make good decisions.

"The wise listen to others" means that these people are able to discern to whom they should listen as well as the wisdom of the advice offered. God often does speak to us through other people, and so wise people should seek counsel from others whom they respect as spiritually sensitive. Wise people then can consider the advice and experience of others as they continue to seek God's guidance.

WISE WAYS   Do you ever seek advice or counsel? If not, why not? If so, do you seek advice from the right kinds of people, or only from those who will agree with you? What do you do with the counsel you receive?

Lord, I ask you to show me how I should seek advice. Reveal to me the people who can give wise advice. Teach me how to discern and use the counsel I receive. Help me to grow and learn so that I can give good counsel to others who have need.

**Read
Proverbs 12**

LISTEN UP

*Fools think
they need no advice,
but the wise
listen to others.*
Proverbs 12:15

May 13

SABBATH

**Read
Proverbs 13**

ALL OF WHAT?

*Jesus replied, "The
most important
commandment is this:
'Hear, O Israel! The
Lord our God is the
one and only Lord.
And you must love the
Lord your God with
all your heart, all your
soul, all your mind,
and all your strength.'
The second is equally
important: 'Love your
neighbor as yourself.'
No other
commandment is
greater than these."*
Mark 12:29-31

This marks our fifth look at this Greatest Command-ment. The first four have been general attemps to see the big picture of our relationship with God and our neighbor. Our remaining meditations on this passage will focus on individual aspects of the command.

For instance, when we quote or think about the first part of the verse, we tend to mentally shorten it to "Love the Lord with all your heart, soul, mind and strength." We leave out the clearly repeated "all your" that introduces each human component. This summary may help us clarify the main point of the commandment, but it doesn't help us apply it very well.

The task of meditation forces us to consider some important questions: What is the difference between loving God with "all your heart" and loving God with "all your mind"? What does it mean to love God with "all your soul"? How does "all your strength" fit with the other three? Keep these questions in mind. Meditate toward answers on your own.

WISE WAYS   Those who develop their ability to meditate on God's Word know that details are the key to understanding. What grade would you give to your current capacity for meditation?

Lord Jesus, you said this was the most important. Help me treat these words that way—seeking to understand and to put into practice your priorities.

May 14

Many people live in sin, never sensing that they are doing anything wrong. They are doing what pleases them, so it must be right, they reason.

In his letter to the Romans, Paul wrote, "When you were slaves of sin, you weren't concerned with doing what was right. And what was the result? It was not good, since now you are ashamed of the things you used to do, things that end in eternal doom" (Romans 6:20-21). Just because people "feel good" about what they are doing doesn't necessarily make it right. No matter how it "seems," it may be a pathway only to death.

So what is the right path—the one that doesn't end in death? It is the path we get on when we accept Jesus Christ as our Savior. We follow that path as we serve him in the world. On that path, we are truly set free to "do those things that lead to holiness and result in eternal life" (Romans 6:22).

WISE WAYS   Which path are you on in life—the one that "seems" right to you, or the one you have been guided toward because of your relationship with Jesus Christ?

Lord, walk with me. Help me to take steps in my life not because they "seem" right, but because I have sought your guidance and am walking closely with you.

**Read
Proverbs 14**

✳

CHECK THE MAP

There is a path before each person that seems right, but it ends in death.
Proverbs 14:12

May 15

HAPPY FACES

*A glad heart
makes a happy face;
a broken heart
crushes the spirit.*

Proverbs 15:13

It seems so obvious, why make it a proverb? When people's hearts are light and joyful, their faces reflect happiness; when people are sorrowful and brokenhearted, their spirits are crushed. While this may be true, does it have to be that way all the time?

The author may want us to consider how we react to the situations that come into our lives. It's easy to be happy when our hearts are glad; it's much more difficult to reflect deep joy even when we are hurting. Yet all of us experience hurt, sorrow, and grief in our lives at one time or another. While we are not called to be happy about our difficulties, we can still reflect an attitude of strength and faith in God, refusing to let our circumstances crush our spirits. Such an attitude understands God's love and sovereignty and trusts him to be a "rock and fortress" through times of difficulty.

WISE WAYS How do you act during times of difficulty? Are you a crushed spirit, or do you reflect your faith in your loving and all-powerful God?

Lord, may my face reflect my love for and faith in you, regardless of my circumstances.

May 16

This verse is not saying that we should make no plans. In fact, God says that wise people seek advice (12:15) and don't just follow whatever path seems right (14:12). Surely God does not want us to idly sit, waiting for him to make things happen in our lives. We must make plans, get advice, think carefully, pray, weigh the pros and cons, and use our God-given brains to take steps forward in life.

The writer is reminding us of God's complete sovereignty. As Paul made his plans to visit various countries in his ministry, at times God simply stood in the way and said "no" (Acts 16:6-10). The point is, we make our plans and hold them loosely, allowing God to intervene and make changes according to his will. What a wonderful promise! At no time do we ever need to fear that we will miss what God wants for us. As we move, he guides and directs.

WISE WAYS   How much are you aware of God's sovereignty over your plans? How sensitive are you to his guidance?

Lord, as I make my plans, help me to remember that you are sovereign. Wherever you want to take me is exactly where I should be.

**Read
Proverbs 16**

DAY PLANNER

*We can make
our plans,
but the LORD
determines
our steps.*

Proverbs 16:9

May 17

**Read
Proverbs 17**

✳

FLOOD LINE

*Beginning a quarrel
is like opening a
floodgate, so drop
the matter before a
dispute breaks out.*

Proverbs 17:14

How vivid is the picture of quarrelsome words opening the floodgate and letting loose a torrent of anger.
However, this is not a proverb for non-confronta-
tional people to always keep their hurt and anger
stopped up behind the dam. There is a place for talking through difficulties and differences of opinion—
in fact, in healthy relationships, it has to be done.

However, the writer advises us not to begin a
quarrel. In other words, when we need to talk about
some hurt or deal with some anger, there is a way to
start the conversation and there is a way not to start
it. To begin with a volley of accusations or even a
heated voice will start a quarrel and open the flood-
gates. How much better to drop the matter, at least
for the time being. Then we can calmly find the
right way to communicate how we feel and talk it
through in a healthy manner.

WISE WAYS   How do you handle hurt, anger, and
disagreements? Are you quarrelsome, or do you
know how to bring up the matter calmly?

*Lord, help me to deal in a right way with the hurts, disagreements,
and concerns I have with people close to me. If I feel quarrelsome,
help me to wait for a better time. Help me to speak calmly and to
express myself clearly. Help me to listen to what the other person
says to me.*

May 18

At times, we just need a place to hide. Life's circumstances begin to overwhelm us, problems mount, situations are out of our control. We know we have to deal with these things, but we just can't do it right now. Instead, we just want to get away and regroup.

God knows that life is like this. He knows that sometimes we feel like we can't handle anything more. So he provides himself as a fortress, a place of safety, a place to hide. With high walls, battlements, and soldiers on the lookout, our fortress is a place for us to run and find safety. The gate swings open for us and locks securely behind us. There in the fortress we can talk to God, get his guidance, and receive his strength. We will indeed have to go out and face whatever is before us, but not before God has prepared us behind the walls of his fortress.

WISE WAYS   Where do you go when life becomes overwhelming?

Lord, I need you to calm my heart, give me rest, and then prepare me for what is ahead. Please be my strong fortress today.

**Read
Proverbs 18**

READY FOR
BATTLE

*The name of the
LORD is a strong
fortress; the godly
run to him and are
safe.*
Proverbs 18:10

May 19

A HELPING HAND

If you help the poor,
you are lending to the
LORD—and he will
repay you!
Proverbs 19:17

The Bible makes no excuses for the realities of life. Some people will be wealthy; some will be poor. While we can blame all kinds of circumstances, the fact is clear that even some of the poorest people in one country are very rich by the standards of another country.

So what do we do about it? The Bible makes it very clear that God's people are to be concerned for those less fortunate. Obviously we ourselves cannot solve the entire problem of poverty; governments have tried to do that and often come up short. The most efficient and effective system involves individuals helping other individuals in whatever ways the Lord leads them. The promise is that in helping others we are helping the Lord, just the way Jesus described (Matthew 26:31-40). In addition, God promises to repay. But don't wait for a refund check in the mail. God's currency comes in many forms—not the least of which is great joy!

WISE WAYS In what ways do you seek to help those less fortunate than you?

Lord, let me be mindful of the needs of others. Show me how I can, with wisdom and sensitivity, help to meet those needs.

May 20

SABBATH

James makes the point that the tongue, while small, can cause lots of damage (James 3:5-6). We may know some people whose mouths always seem to get them into trouble, but we certainly don't expect that from people who "claim to be religious." Such people may claim to have faith in the Lord, but if their mouths are out of control—either by use of profanity, gossip, or words that wound—then they are only fooling themselves about their faith. Their "religion is worthless" because it has made no change in their hearts.

Believers have received the Holy Spirit, and one of his fruits is "self-control" (Galatians 5:23). Self-control involves tongue-control. While we may not always be able to control the thoughts that fly into our heads at any moment, we certainly ought to be able to control the words that seek to fly out of our mouths. The Holy Spirit promises to help us.

WISE WAYS Do the words that come out of your mouth reveal the fruit of the Spirit in your life, or are you "fooling yourself" about your faith?

Lord, help me to watch what I say. Give me self-control to think before I speak so that my words will reveal your Spirit in me.

Read
Proverbs 20

TONGUE-CONTROL

If you claim to be religious but don't control your tongue, you are just fooling yourself, and your religion is worthless.
James 1:26

May 21

**Read
Proverbs 21**

✳

WHEN PRIDE
GETS IN THE
WAY

*Haughty eyes,
a proud heart,
and evil actions
are all sin.*

Proverbs 21:4

God hates pride. Sure, God wants his people to realize how much he loves them; he wants his people to have strong self-esteem that comes from knowing their worth and value in his eyes. But God hates pride. Why? Because pride pushes us away from God. Pride says we don't need God watching over us. Pride says we don't want God in control. Pride says we are better than everyone else. Pride turned a glorious angel into Satan, so God knows the power of pride.

We would all agree with the second part of this verse—evil actions are sinful. But God also views "haughty eyes" and "a proud heart" as sinful. To look down on others and to separate oneself from God is to commit sin, just as surely as doing an evil act such as stealing. Pride is powerful and dangerous, so we must be ever on guard against it.

WISE WAYS   Does anyone think that you are haughty, arrogant, proud? If so, how can you change that before God and before that person?

Lord, if I am haughty or prideful in any way toward anyone, please reveal it to me. Show me how to walk humbly with you and to treat others as I should.

May 22

God hates pride (21:4). He desires that we have "true humility." Humility does not mean weakness; true humility is a proper understanding of oneself in relation to God and to others. It understands sin, but knows that God loved us enough to die for us. Humility understands that we have a place in God's plan, while we respect the place God has for others in his plan.

When we are humble and fear (respect) the Lord, God says this leads to "riches, honor, and long life." We must remember that a proverb is a "life observation," not necessarily a promise. Plenty of truly humble and reverent people have been poor, gone unnoticed, and died young. The proverb is saying that when people live this way, many times they receive these blessings simply because it is a smart way to live. We ought to strive to honor the Lord by how we live, regardless, for we will be pleasing him.

WISE WAYS Where would you fall on the scale between pride and humility? Think about how you can have a healthy self-esteem and yet be humble.

Lord, help me to begin on the path toward true humility. Give me healthy self-esteem so that I can use my gifts for you, while always being aware that you gave me the gifts to use for your glory and to build up your kingdom.

**Read
Proverbs 22**

HUMBLE PIE

*True humility and fear of the L*ORD *lead to riches, honor, and long life.*
Proverbs 22:4

May 23

**Read
Proverbs 23**

✳

WHEN THEY
HAVE IT ALL

*Don't envy sinners,
but always continue
to fear the LORD.*
Proverbs 23:17

It can be very difficult when we see "sinners" prospering—especially when they prosper well beyond us. We
see blatantly dishonest people being rewarded for
their dishonesty. People we know are anti-Christian
seem to be receiving God's blessings. Many who are
living in ways that are socially acceptable, but sinful,
are gaining fame, wealth, and power. It's difficult not
to be envious as we try to please God and yet continue
to struggle.

This proverb tells us not to envy them, but to
continue to fear the Lord. The next verse says why:
"For surely you have a future ahead of you; your
hope will not be disappointed" (23:18). No matter
what happens in this life, we must continue to fear
the Lord. He has promised to watch over and guide
us in this life so that we accomplish exactly what he
desires. And he has promised eternity in glory with
him. It doesn't get any better than that!

WISE WAYS   How much do you envy people who,
though not believers, seem to "have it all"? How do
you handle that envy? How can you strive to do as
this proverb suggests?

*Lord, show me how to continue to trust in you, even when doing so
seems to put me at a standstill while everyone else moves ahead.
Help me not to be envious of them. Show me the riches of your glory
and my blessings in you so that I have the right perspective.*

May 24

Trying to play hide-and-seek with God is what we might call a "no win" situation—for us. The context of this verse is where someone is unjustly sentenced to death and a person who could have helped remained quiet (24:11), claiming he knew nothing.

The point is that God knows everything about us. He knows our hearts, he sees us wherever we go, he keeps watch over our souls. We may be able to hide from people, fool them, and even make them think one way about us when the opposite is true. But we can never hide from God. He sees all, knows all, understands all, and—eventually—judges all.

We should seek to live honestly, truthfully, and respectably. While we don't have to wear our hearts on our sleeves for everyone to see, we should at least be transparent enough for people to know that we are sincere in how we speak and what we do.

WISE WAYS   If you were always aware of God's presence with you—wherever you went and whatever you said—how would that make a difference in your life today? Tomorrow?

Lord, may I always remember your presence with me. May I always remember that no matter what I say or do, you know the truth. Teach me to live a life of sincerity and truthfulness.

**Read
Proverbs 24**

TRANSPARENT BEFORE GOD

Don't try to avoid responsibility by saying you didn't know about it. For God knows all hearts, and he sees you. He keeps watch over your soul, and he knows you knew! And he will judge all people according to what they have done.

Proverbs 24:12

May 25

**Read
Proverbs 25**

TOO MUCH

*Do you like honey?
Don't eat too much
of it, or it will make
you sick!*
Proverbs 25:16

"You can't have too much of a good thing," or so the saying goes. Yet even the sweet taste of honey can become sickening if one eats too much of it. And a stomach full of sweet honey feels sour!

In other words, we can enjoy what God gives us to enjoy, but we are wise to always do so in moderation. It is our penchant toward overindulgence or misuse of God's gifts that leads to sin. A little wine may be fine—overindulgence leads to alcoholism. Food is for sustenance and often for enjoyment—overindulgence is gluttony. Our sexuality is a gift from God—misuse of it outside of the bonds of marriage can lead to much heartache.

We can indeed have too much of—or find ourselves misusing—things that God intended for our good. How much wiser to know from where the gifts come and how to use them in order to please God.

WISE WAYS   What gifts and pleasure has God given you to enjoy? Are you using them correctly and wisely?

Lord, thank you for all that you have given me to enjoy. Help me to use your gifts wisely.

May 26

When an insane person starts shooting, lots of people end up hurt—or dead. Senseless shootings have made us question the sanity of those who wield lethal weapons to commit such horrible acts.

Yet consider the damage our words do when we tell lies to others. Now consider the damage done when telling a lie to a friend. Now consider telling a lie, getting caught, and then trying to say we were only "joking." A little saying goes, "What a tangled web we weave, when first we practice to deceive." Telling lies to our friends may cause situations that spin out of our control. Despite the movies that try to show humorous situations that arise from this—or unhappy situations that have a happy ending—the truth is that lying and then trying to cover up is like shooting a lethal weapon. No happy ending here. Be truthful. Lies are never a joking matter—not even among friends.

WISE WAYS   Consider your own truthfulness. Are you a truthful person or do you tell little lies? Are lies sometimes seen merely as jokes? If so, how does this need to change?

Lord, teach me to see lies for what they are—as damaging as lethal weapons. Help me to value and practice truthfulness in everything I say and do.

Read
Proverbs 26

NO LAUGHING MATTER

Just as damaging as a mad man shooting a lethal weapon is someone who lies to a friend and then says, "I was only joking."
Proverbs 26:18-19

May 27

**Read
Proverbs 27**

GUARANTEED
EXCHANGE

*God blesses those
who are merciful,
for they will be
shown mercy.*
Matthew 5:7

Tucked in among the Beatitudes, we find Jesus' re-statement of what we know as the Golden Rule. Jesus gave it later in the Sermon on the Mount. "Do for others what you would like them to do for you. (Matthew 7:12).

To this profound relational principle, Jesus added the teaching that God stands ready to bless this kind of attitude, which sees others deserving nothing less than what we hope to receive. This runs exactly contrary to selfish human desires, which tend to think of benefits only at the expense or loss of others. Rather than change the desire, Jesus simply challenged us to enlarge it to include everyone. He used this same principle in the second half of the Great Commandment, "Love your neighbor as yourself" (Mark 12:31).

The application of mercy, love, and simple kindness to others ultimately benefits us. God guarantees it.

WISE WAYS Make it a practice to keep your relationship accounts up to date. If there is someone from whom you have been withholding mercy, have you considered how that affects your own expectation of mercy?

Lord, I know I pray "forgive us our debts as we forgive our debtors" without really thinking about what I'm asking. Teach me to extend mercy more readily.

May 28

Jesus made a similar statement when he told his disciples, "If anyone causes one of these little ones who trusts in me to lose faith, it would be better for that person to be thrown into the sea with a large millstone tied around the neck" (Mark 9:42). Clearly, God does not take it lightly when anyone leads others into sin. He is especially harsh on spiritual leaders because they are trusted (James 3:1). A pastor, teacher, parent, or anyone else in spiritual leadership must be worthy of trust. A spiritual leader who leads others into sin will be punished severely. Leadership is a heavy responsibility.

Honest leaders, however, will reap the fruit of their honest leadership. The results, though they may take time, will be worthwhile. They will have students who will grow and mature and so be able to teach others (2 Timothy 2:2). And they will receive a commendation from the Lord.

WISE WAYS Who is following you? Where are you leading them? How would you describe your example?

Lord, let me look at myself as those who follow me look at me. Reveal to me what kind of example I am to them. Show me where I need to improve.

**Read
Proverbs 28**

FOLLOW THE LEADER

Those who lead the upright into sin will fall into their own trap, but the honest will inherit good things.

Proverbs 28:10

May 29

LOVING DISCIPLINE

Discipline your children, and they will give you happiness and peace of mind.

Proverbs 29:17

What a very simple statement, yet how many parents fail to put it into practice. Afraid of being politically incorrect, or hurting their little child's psyche, or wanting to be best buddies with their child, too many parents are passing on the command to discipline their children. Then they wonder why their kids give them nothing but unhappiness, fear, and worry.

Of course, the word *discipline* needs to be understood. Many parents either threaten but never follow through, or they are too harsh. Wise parents need to discipline their children wisely. They must let the punishment fit the "crime." They must follow through consistently. They must also show love.

Does this guarantee happiness and peace of mind? The proverb tells us that this will be the general case. There will probably still be times of sadness and worry—for that is part of life. But parents who have wisely disciplined their children will find their efforts well rewarded.

WISE WAYS How would you rate your discipline of your children? Is it loving, consistent, appropriate?

Lord, show me how to be wise when I have to discipline my children. Show me how to help them know my love for them even as I teach them how to act appropriately.

May 30

If God were to give you any two requests, would you choose these? Agur, the writer of this passage, requested only that he never tell a lie and that he not be too poor or too rich.

We can learn from this little prayer. This need not be the pattern for all that we request in life, but it reveals a heart that trusts completely in God and yet knows its own weaknesses. Agur did not want to ever be dishonest—and so we would do well to value honesty as highly. Agur also knew that riches might lead him away from his God, and intense poverty might do the same. So he asked God to take that into account and just meet his needs. We would do well to consider the natural outcome of some of our requests, understanding that what might seem good to us may not be good in the long run.

WISE WAYS When you consider the requests that you bring to God, what might be the long-term outcome of many of them? What might happen if God really gave you everything you wanted?

Lord, may I think through the requests I bring to you. Help me to remember that you have the big picture, that you know all things, and that you may at times even say no to my requests because you know my weaknesses better than I.

**Read
Proverbs 30**

JUST TWO THINGS

O God, I beg two favors from you before I die. First, help me never to tell a lie. Second, give me neither poverty nor riches! Give me just enough to satisfy my needs.

Proverbs 30:7-8

May 31

OPEN ARMS

*She extends a helping
hand to the poor and
opens her arms to
the needy.*

Proverbs 31:20

In this portrayal of what is known as the "virtuous woman," we find, among many other qualities, a woman of compassion. While no one woman is expected to exemplify perfectly every characteristic in this description, the general portrayal is a woman of wisdom, a fitting ending to a book about wisdom. This woman has wealth that she manages carefully, and yet she is willing to help the poor and open her arms to the needy.

Compassion is a vital need in our world today. Many of us are running around trying to gain more and more, never having enough, never content, never even considering offering help to those in need. We have plenty of excuses. But this woman of wisdom stands at the end of Proverbs willingly helping those who have less. Whether she gave money, time, or resources is unknown—and not really important. The point is, she gave. And so should we.

WISE WAYS   Where would you place yourself on the scale of compassion for others—from not caring or even noticing, to active involvement in trying to help? You may not be able to save the world, but is there one person who needs your help today?

Lord, open my eyes to the needs of others. Show me how to be a compassionate person. Show me one person for whom I can do something compassionate today.

JUNE

June 1

Read
Proverbs 1

✳

GREED INDEED

*Such is the fate
of all who are greedy
for gain. It ends up
robbing them of life.*

Proverbs 1:19

It starts simply enough. We need enough stuff to get by. We want the good things of life for ourselves and our loved ones. Soon, however, "enough" just doesn't seem like enough. Greed has gotten a hook into our heart. Solomon knew firsthand what greed could do: in the quest to get more in life, true life starts to ebb away. In this passage in this first proverb, he passes on the benefit of his experience.

What happens when greed takes over? As we long for more stuff, our relationship to the Giver gradually is lost. Without this connection to the Source of life, true life in its eternal richness gets lost. But if we seek to gain more and more of the rich relationship that God offers—through prayer, reading the Word, and worship with his people—God is pleased and will bless us. Let us, in a sense, become "greedy" for the riches of a life lived in close connection with God.

WISE WAYS What kinds of earthly gains—money, fame, possessions, power—have the most attraction for you? Think about how much they pale in comparison with spiritual gain.

Lord, may I seek the riches that you offer and not those of the world. Make me greedy for a deep relationship with you.

June 2

Good teachers and trainers know that their role in their students' lives is temporary. The student pilot will eventually fly solo. The intern will someday make independent diagnoses. The trainee truck driver will be alone one day behind the wheel of a big rig. All will have to make decisions and perform tasks alone, but only after they have learned and internalized all they have been taught.

God is the ultimate teacher and wants us to so learn and internalize his lessons that we "will know how to find the right course of action every time." Just as a well-taught pilot does not panic when things go wrong but can instead call upon ingrained knowledge and skills, so we can be confident that, when the time comes, we can know what is right, just, and fair. How can we have this assurance? We can open our minds and hearts to God's wisdom, shown in his Word. With such knowledge comes a bonus: joy.

WISE WAYS   How confident are you that God's wisdom is already in your heart?

Today, Lord, teach me more of what is right, just, and fair in your sight. Thank you for the joy that comes with your wisdom and knowledge.

**Read
Proverbs 2**

FIND THE RIGHT COURSE

Then you will understand what is right, just, and fair, and you will know how to find the right course of action every time. For wisdom will enter your heart, and knowledge will fill you with joy.
Proverbs 2:9-10

June 3

SABBATH

**Read
Proverbs 3**.

LET IT SHINE

*You are the light of
the world—like a city
on a mountain,
glowing in the night
for all to see. Don't
hide your light under
a basket! Instead,
put it on a stand and
let it shine for all. In
the same way, let
your good deeds shine
out for all to see, so
that everyone will
praise your heavenly
Father.*

Matthew 5:14-16

At first glance, Jesus seems to be encouraging his followers to call attention to themselves. These are surprising words from him who at other times condemned religious leaders who tooted their own horns. What could Jesus be thinking? Does he want his followers to have big heads?

The answer, of course, is no. The glowing, standing out, and shining have a higher purpose: the praising of our heavenly Father. The light within us that deserves attention is the light of Christ, he who was and is the light of the world (John 9:5; 12:46). People must know the source of the good and light—that it comes from the Light, not from a sunny disposition or a commitment to a good cause. These words of Jesus come from the Sermon on the Mount, not long after the Beatitudes, a list of the many ways God blesses us. We are called to a bold display of the bright goodness of God at work in us and through us.

WISE WAYS In what ways might you be hiding Christ's light under a bushel? How can you "let it out" so that the praise goes to God?

Today, Lord, give me the courage and the humility to let your light shine out through my life.

June 4

Much of life is spent traveling, and a path is an apt image for the way we live. We choose a path. We cross paths. We follow a path. We stray from the path. But the author of this proverb had something much more literal in mind when he spoke of "the path of evildoers." Our feet can take us on paths that will lead us away from God.

If we have struggled with or even succumbed to a particular sin in the past, God urges us to steer clear from the places that will put us in a compromising position. A compulsive gambler would do well to pick Rapid City over Atlantic City for a vacation. One who has struggled with drinking should stay away from bars, especially when alone. As the proverb urges, pick a new destination, for life is a journey. In the Lord's Prayer, we ask God to "lead us not into temptation." Why would we then tell our feet otherwise?

WISE WAYS   What are the actual places that are off God's path for you? What people make it hard for you to stay away from these places?

Lord, help me to stay on your path. Give me fellow pilgrims on the journey so that we can encourage each other not to stray.

**Read
Proverbs 4**

THE PATH
NOT TAKEN

*Do not do as the
wicked do or follow
the path of evildoers.
Avoid their haunts.
Turn away and go
somewhere else.*

Proverbs 4:14–15

June 5

Read
Proverbs 5

THE VOW THAT REFRESHES

Drink water from your own well—share your love only with your wife.
Proverbs 5:15

The idea of comparing drinking water with marital love is most certainly an image sent from God to the author of this proverb. After all, who better than God would know that, just as water refreshes us and even sustains our life, fidelity within marriage refreshes and sustains. In addition, just as there is no true substitute for water—despite all the colas, sports drinks, and simulated fruit juices—all other sexual relationships are impostors compared to that of husband and wife.

God loves the very concept of marriage and wants us to know that any other coupling is far from his best. He wants us to experience his best for each of us. We must never settle for imitation sex or even compromise another person's marriage. Let us concentrate on and be thankful for what and whom God has provided to each of us.

WISE WAYS   Consider some couples you know who have been married for a long time. What lessons can you learn from their relationships?

God, help me to hold on to your view of marriage. Give me strength to be faithful to you and, if it is your will that I marry, to the spouse you give to me.

June 6

Honesty and good communication in relationships are elusive enough in and of themselves. God knows this well, just as he knows us well. God is therefore particularly upset by those who lie and promote disharmony within a family: hate and detest are not words to be taken lightly.

The image of a person pouring out lies as one would pour out a watering can on a garden is vivid indeed. It shows an intention—not accidentally spilling, but pouring—that betrays a heart at cross purposes with God. In much the same way, sowing discord—as if planting a garden of disharmony in a family—indicates how far the guilty party has strayed from God's best in relationships. Such actions often grow out of small things—the "little white lie" that seems harmless but leads to a habit of falsehood, or the gossip and taking of sides that pits family members against one another. Let us guard our ways, striving to be people who tell the truth and promote harmony.

WISE WAYS   Is there evidence that a false witness has been at work in your church community? In what ways might you inadvertently "sow discord" between spouses, between parent and child, or among siblings, in your own family or other families?

Today, Lord, give me your sense of truth and harmony, that I might be your force for good in my family, church, workplace, and neighborhood.

Read
Proverbs 6

DISCORD VERSUS HARMONY

There are six things the LORD hates—no, seven things he detests . . . a false witness who pours out lies, a person who sows discord among brothers.
Proverbs 6:16, 19

June 7

**Read
Proverbs 7**

CAME OUT AND CAME ON

*It's you
I was looking for!
I came out
to find you,
and here you are!*
Proverbs 7:15

Some people stumble into temptation never realizing that "one thing can lead to another," and suddenly they find themselves inappropriately involved with someone. Then, there are other people who most certainly do not stumble into sexual sin; indeed, they march purposely toward it, seeking it out, and finally say, "It's you I was looking for!" In the movies or in novels, it can look romantic, even "destined to be," but God knows it for what it is . . . and so should we.

We must not be naive about the world. In order to safeguard our own and others' marriages, we must look out for those who would seek extramarital relationships, steering clear of them and any involvement with them. Those of us who are married must do whatever it takes to continually strengthen our marriages and our willpower.

WISE WAYS Are there people in your circle of friends, workplace, community organizations, even church who do not have God's view of the sanctity of marriage? How have you prepared to counter any advances they might make?

Lord, you are such a good God for making marriage. Give me your wisdom and strength to recognize any challenge to my marriage or others' marriages.

June 8

Proverb 8 gives one of the richest, most vivid personifications in the Bible: the traditionally abstract concept of Wisdom presented as a woman. She describes her creation so long ago, before anything else was created, and her appointment to a timeless role for the benefit of all humankind. Yet what she offers in this verse is so needed today. Indeed, we might mistake these words for the promises on the dust jacket of a self-help book: good advice, success, insight, strength.

Many people read the Bible—or, if they are honest, comment on the Bible without having read it—and say that God is inscrutable. They think that he enjoys confusing his people, that no one can even begin to know his ways. Yet here is Wisdom offering the insights of the ages, making herself visible and accessible. She foreshadows the clear teaching and godly advice of Jesus, the ultimate teacher. We would do well to read, listen, and humble ourselves before the Wisdom of God.

WISE WAYS Who and what has God used to communicate his Wisdom to you?

Lord, I thank you for your willingness to teach and guide me. Give me an open mind and a devoted heart.

**Read
Proverbs 8**

ADVICE AND SUCCESS

Good advice and success belong to me. Insight and strength are mine.

Proverbs 8:14

June 9

**Read
Proverbs 9**

WISE, WISER,
WISEST

*Teach the wise, and
they will be wiser.
Teach the righteous,
and they will learn
more.*
Proverbs 9:9

In the world of words, whether it be a newspaper column, a magazine article, a 945-page novel, or anything in between, one thing is certain: Everybody needs an editor. Even the best writers, out of sheer overfamiliarity with their material or good old human imperfection, need someone to point out the inconsistencies, the missing transitions, the faulty logic, the shaky plot lines. In fact, good writers have become good because of what they have learned from critique and instruction. The good get better. Those resistant to editing never improve and grow.

In similar fashion, the wise get wiser. They listen to the words of Wisdom. They "take it personally," but in the best sense of the phrase. Rather than allowing their feelings to be hurt, they listen and change, much as a writer reads all the red-pencil markings rather than wallow in self-pity and the claim that "no one understands my work." God has so much to teach us, so much that he has entrusted to Wisdom, who in turn entrusts it to us. We simply must be willing to be edited.

WISE WAYS What lessons or criticisms have you been resistant to hear? How does it help that it is God's chosen messenger, Wisdom, who wants to help you?

Lord, I thank you for the persistent work of Wisdom. Teach me to be wise. Teach me to be righteous.

June 10

SABBATH

How many times have you loved with all your heart? We often find it surprisingly easy. The idea of loving with our whole heart appeals to us. We understand and desire the intensity of such love.

Our problems arise from the objects of our affection: We love what we shouldn't love. In fact, it is easier to be wholehearted in our love for almost anything other than God. Jesus warned that our hearts tend to be wrapped around our treasures (Matthew 6:21), and few of us treasure God as we ought. Yet obedience begins by loving God with our whole heart. Jeremiah recorded this starting point in the Lord's own words: "You will seek me and find me when you seek me with all your heart" (Jeremiah 29:13).

What we don't seek and love with our heart, we will not love with our soul or strength. Since we will love God only to the degree that we have "found" him, we must intensify our search. We must persist in asking God to reveal himself to us, noting the way the character and mind of God were revealed in Jesus. Everything we need to know about love we find in Jesus.

WISE WAYS How much of "all your heart" loves God? In what ways could you improve that amount?

Lord, show me one part of me that is not entirely committed to loving you. Give me your grace and strength to conform that part.

**Read
Proverbs 10**

WITH ALL YOUR HEART

Jesus replied, "The most important commandment is this: 'Hear, O Israel! The Lord our God is the one and only Lord. And you must love the Lord your God with all your heart, all your soul, all your mind, and all your strength.' The second is equally important: 'Love your neighbor as yourself.' No other commandment is greater than these."
Mark 12:29-31

June 11

**Read
Proverbs 11**

CAN YOU KEEP A SECRET?

*A gossip goes around
revealing secrets, but
those who are
trustworthy can keep
a confidence.*
Proverbs 11:13

Many think of it only as a tongue twister, but its meaning rings true: Loose lips sink ships. Whether the ship represents a relationship, a reputation, a career, a person's faith, or the trust within a community, gossip and rumors can lead to disaster. What can seem harmless and fun eventually can cause disaster. Gossiping becomes a habit that needs to be stopped.

Even Christians can fall into the habit of gossip, often under the pretense of "sharing" or informing others "just so you can know how to pray for the poor dear." But today's proverb labels it for what it is: breaking a trust. If keeping a secret is hard for us, we can be assured that God is more than able to help us end this habit. It is that important to him. If we consider the Golden Rule (would we want our secrets revealed?), pray for the person, and ask God for strength, he will see us through to be people of integrity who have better uses for communication than breaking a confidence.

WISE WAYS   How easy or hard is it for you to keep a confidence? What people or situations make it more difficult?

Today, Lord, help me to be a person of integrity. Show me how to avoid gossiping.

June 12

In many cultures, defending one's honor is not merely acceptable, it is mandatory. "What are you, a wimp?" others chide. "Are you going to let him talk to you that way?" Soon harsh words or even fists are flying. But the Bible prescribes a better way.

A wise person realizes that an insult says more about the insulter than the insulted. He or she takes a deep breath and takes the long view. Staying calm, in this case, becomes not a passive, wimpy reaction but an active response drawn from inner strength and assurance that what the other person thinks or says is not the final word. We take our cue from God himself; the prophets spoke often of his being "slow to anger." The apostle James, whose letter often counsels us to be patient and calm in various situations, picks up the theme of today's verse from Proverbs when he writes, "My dear brothers and sisters, be quick to listen, slow to speak, and slow to get angry. Your anger can never make things right in God's sight" (James 1:19-20).

WISE WAYS   In what situations this week have you been tempted to react in anger? How did you deal with that impulse?

Lord, help me to be "slow to get angry" and to stay calm in the face of insults, real or perceived.

**Read
Proverbs 12**

STAY CALM

*A fool is quick-
tempered,
but a wise person
stays calm
when insulted.*
Proverbs 12:16

June 13

**Read
Proverbs 13**

FAST FORTUNE?

*Wealth from
get-rich-quick
schemes quickly
disappears;
wealth from hard
work grows.*

Proverbs 13:11

If we want proof of the timelessness of the wisdom of
the Book of Proverbs, we need look no further than
this verse. Whether solicited through pyramid scams,
self-help books, infomercials on television, junk
e-mail, or a dozen other means, get-rich-quick
schemes are alive and well in our culture. Human
nature has always been attracted to the fast track to
fortune, but God has always known that the money
rarely lasts, if it comes at all.

For the Christian, however, wealth should not even
be the goal. Instead, obedience to God's call is our
objective, with monetary rewards one of the possible—
not promised—benefits. Hard work, in whatever field,
is godly work, and God will reward us in whatever way
and in whatever amount he deems best for us and for
his purposes. Even when we convince ourselves, and
try to convince God, that we could do so much more
for God's kingdom with a quick buck, we have still
taken our eyes off the real prize: the satisfaction of
plain-old hard work and obedience.

WISE WAYS   What get-rich-quick schemes have
come your way lately? Which are the hardest to resist?

*Today, Lord, may I concentrate on you and on working hard at the
tasks you have given me.*

June 14

The term "backslider" is an interesting word. It implies that the person once had faith, that they used to be committed. Somehow these believers took a step back from God and slid away from him. We know that God is just, so if they are getting "what they deserve," that first step of retreat must have been conscious. They cannot claim to be innocent victims of circumstance or moan, in the words of a television character years ago, "The devil made me do it."

What do they get? More precisely, it is what they lose that matters: their relationship with God. This is the very thing that good, faithful people receive. We who remain "good" can stand proudly on the mountaintop in judgment of the backsliders, but the footing is shaky up there. We must remember that it may only have been one small, false step away from God that started the whole downward motion. God is the judge. It is for us to remain faithful and in prayer for our fellow hikers in the mountains of faith.

WISE WAYS What are the ways that might lead you (or have led you in the past) to backslide? How can you counter them?

Lord, I want a deep relationship with you. Help me keep my eyes on you and not in judgment of others.

Read Proverbs 14

RECEIVING REWARDS

Backsliders get what they deserve; good people receive their reward.

Proverbs 14:14

June 15

TRUTH OR
TRASH?

*A wise person is
hungry for truth,
while the fool feeds
on trash.*

Proverbs 15:14

What a picture! Falsehood and dishonesty sit in the Dumpster, covered with spoiled leftovers and half-eaten sandwiches. In a quest for sustenance, some will actually choose these forms of "nourishment." But the real food lies somewhere else entirely, far from the Dumpster in the alley.

Truth is the true food that not only sustains us, but also helps us grow. Wise people recognize hunger for what it is and fill their mind and heart with truth. We can find this kind of nutrition in the Word, in solid teaching and counsel, and in humble prayer that asks God directly for it. Or we can settle for the quick and easily-found snacks of lies and deception that the world offers. The axiom from computer programming will apply, however: garbage in, garbage out. The menu choice is ours.

WISE WAYS What trash have you been fooled into "eating" in recent years? What alternatives does God offer you?

Today, Lord, I thank you for the feast of truth that you spread before me in your Word.

June 16

Today's verse may conjure images of celebrities or politicians who were riding high, did not see the precariousness of their proud position, and eventually fell from grace. We sometimes take a secret pleasure in seeing such famous folk, their chests still puffed out, take a major tumble.

We need to note, however, that this verse is not addressed solely to those in the public eye. There is no preface that reads, "Hey, all you whose faces frequent the popular magazines, this message is for you!" No, God's word of warning is for all of us. Whenever the source of our pride is something other than God, whenever we have confidence in ourselves alone, we are in danger of losing altitude quickly. We must seek the proper perspective on ourselves in relation to our Creator. It is on the basis of Jesus' life and sacrifice, not our own accomplishments, that we have our worth restored. The proper source of our pride? The one who humbled himself and then was lifted up, Jesus Christ.

WISE WAYS What and whom are your sources of pride?

Today, Lord, may I stay proud of Jesus' work and not my own. Thank you that you will keep me from falling if I remain faithful to you.

Read
Proverbs 16

PRIDE AND
PRECIPICE

Pride goes before destruction, and haughtiness before a fall.
Proverbs 16:18

June 17

Read Proverbs 17

GODLY POSSIBILITIES

He replied, "What is impossible from a human perspective is possible with God."
Luke 18:27

He had seemed so earnest and eager for the truth. The rich, religious leader had genuinely wanted to know how to get eternal life. But when Jesus gave him the truth about salvation, he could not accept it. His earthly wealth meant more to him than heavenly treasure and Jesus' call to discipleship—and the Savior knew it. It was not the wealth itself that kept the man from salvation; it was his dependence on it.

The disciples, and we who read this story, heard from Jesus that because of this dependence it would be extremely difficult for the rich to enter the Kingdom of God. They wondered aloud if anybody could therefore be saved. Jesus replied with one of the most powerful statements in the Bible—with God, the impossible becomes possible. Anybody's dependence on wealth—measured in money, fame, friends or family, possessions, intelligence, giftedness, or any other currency—must be set aside in order to receive God's gift of salvation. The offer still stands today.

WISE WAYS On what kind of wealth do people you know (including yourself) depend? What can break this dependence?

Today, Lord, I thank you for the riches of salvation that you offer. I accept the treasure in heaven that you promise.

June 18

Over the centuries, cultures and groups have devised all sorts of defensive buildings and barricades using the materials and technology of the time. Inside, the leaders and their people feel secure and protected. But time and again, history records that the city walls are scaled, the castle doors are rammed open, the wooden fort is burned to the ground, the steel beams melted. What was thought impregnable is soon found wanting.

So it is with people's dependence on wealth to defend them against all harm. Either the money does not last, or they find that no amount of it can protect them from the problems and losses of this life. Any one of us can be attacked by outside circumstances, disease, injury, broken relationships, or more. But the true defense is not found in anything but God who, if we trust him, will shield us from the crushing effects of life's problems. His promise, however, is his care in the midst of problems, not freedom from them. In the words of Martin Luther's powerful hymn, "A mighty fortress is our God, a bulwark never failing."

WISE WAYS How has God protected and cared for you in the face of the "slings and arrows" of life?

Today, Lord, may I rest secure in the fortress of your strength and love.

**Read
Proverbs 18**

OFFENSIVE DEFENSE

The rich think of their wealth as an impregnable defense; they imagine it is a high wall of safety.
Proverbs 18:11

June 19

Read
Proverbs 19

WHILE THERE IS HOPE

*Discipline
your children
while
there is hope.
If you don't,
you will ruin
their lives.*

Proverbs 19:18

When parents worry about ruining their children's lives, they often think of things such as not giving them enough material things, not providing the shelter and food they need, or making them endure their parents' separation or divorce. All these circumstances certainly can affect girls and boys, but today's proverb has a bigger culprit in mind. Lack of discipline can actually ruin their lives, not merely produce annoying adults.

Why the strong language? Isn't the word *ruin* a bit extreme? No, because the lack of discipline establishes a pattern of behavior and attitude that will follow children until the day they die. They can lose out on the hope that the first part of the verse mentions—the hope of living a life that has been disciplined to love and serve God. Undisciplined people have an attitude of entitlement and assumption that they are immune to punishment; if they got what they wanted as kids, then they will get what they want as adults. Parents can despair over this, or they can turn to God for the strength and consistency to discipline while there is still hope.

WISE WAYS Are you a parent or do you know parents who struggle to discipline their children? What new perspective do you have on what is at stake?

Today, Lord, give all parents the strength and grace to discipline their children.

June 20

According to an old saying, "It takes two to tango." In other words, responsibility for many forms of wrong-doing is shared. Today's verse expresses this truth in the context of spreading gossip, which is often a problem even among Christians. God detests gossip, as we can surmise from all the injunctions against it in the Book of Proverbs alone. His directions for dealing with it, therefore, are certain and strong.

Part of the problem is that gossip is extremely contagious. What may seem like harmless, even positive, "sharing" is actually the telling of secrets, the revealing of parts of another person's life that are not ours to reveal. Because of the communicability of this disease of rumor, we must put the chronic gossiper into a sort of isolation ward. God does not mix words: do not hang around with someone who talks too much, which we can infer is not just any kind of talk but specifically gossip. We will not "cure" a gossip; we will more than likely be infected ourselves.

WISE WAYS Are there chronic gossipers in your life? How can you avoid, or at least reduce, your contact with them?

Lord, I want to be a person whose speech is positive and uplifting. Give me strength to avoid the gossipers in my life.

Read
Proverbs 20

TOO MUCH TALK

A gossip tells secrets, so don't hang around with someone who talks too much.
Proverbs 20:19

June 21

MISTY MONEY

Wealth created by lying is a vanishing mist and a deadly trap.

Proverbs 21:6

Financial matters may seem the stuff of dry numbers, endless columns of stock quotes, boring business analysts on public television, and impersonal banks. In truth, however, money matters are highly emotional when you add to the picture siblings squabbling over inheritances, spouses arguing over debt, long-time business partners cheating each other, and a host of other scenarios. The stakes are high, God says, and he is not talking about casino odds.

The highest stakes, and therefore the entry of death into today's proverb about money, are found when wealth has been created by lying. English has a variety of terms for such wealth: ill-gotten gain, dirty money, filthy lucre. Lest we think God only has millionaires in mind, we should note that the amount of money is not specified here, only the manner in which it is gained. We must be honest in all our financial deal-ings and teach this to children from the time they are old enough to pick up a penny found on the sidewalk. If we are faithful in small things, we can learn to be faithful with more (Matthew 25:21).

WISE WAYS   In what ways can you help yourself be honest in all money matters?

Lord, I know that you are the source of true wealth. Give me your wisdom and commitment to honesty in all my handling of money.

June 22

Many parents see part of their role as making good choices for their children. Certainly this is true for very young children. Adults decide what they will wear, what they will eat, where they will go any given day, and who will be their playmates. But the true job of parenting is teaching children to make their own choices as they grow, first in small things such as wardrobe, then branching out to include friends, college, career, life partner, and more.

Some parents find it hard not to make all the choices for their growing children, whether out of genuine concern or out of a selfish desire to fulfill their own dreams through their children. God gave his children free will and the guidance to use it; this is what earthly parents must do for their children. Life is full of so many choices. Paths converge and diverge before us constantly. We truly love our children when we show them how to consider options, weigh the evidence, pray, read Scripture for guidance, seek godly advice, and then choose. Just as a child's wardrobe choices gradually improve from the "interesting" ensembles of three-year-olds, children will gradually get better at the business of making choices.

WISE WAYS   How did you learn to make choices as a child? How can you use this experience with children today?

Thank you, Lord, for the gift of choice. Help me to model and teach good decision-making to the children in my life.

Read
Proverbs 22

PATHFINDERS

Teach your children to choose the right path, and when they are older, they will remain upon it.

Proverbs 22:6

June 23

**Read
Proverbs 23**

A FUTURE AHEAD

*For surely you have a
future ahead of you;
your hope will not be
disappointed.*

Proverbs 23:18

"You've got your whole life ahead of you!" we say,
whether to the newly graduated or the newly disappointed in life or love. God wants us to maintain
this long-term perspective as well. Today's verse
must be seen in context; verse 17 says, "Don't envy
sinners, but always continue to fear the LORD." It is
easy to lose sight of our good future and reason for
hope when those who do not follow God seem to be
prospering.

Actually, God is not attaching a timetable to all
this future and hope talk. So he wants us to adopt
the long, long-term perspective. His view of the
future stretches way beyond our view, and he has
hopes for us that we cannot yet imagine. We must
look to our part: continue to fear God (in the sense
of revering and being in awe of him) and hold on to
our hope. We may have mini-disappointments, but
we have the God of the future with us.

WISE WAYS   In what are you hoping? What is
your plan for keeping your mini-disappointments
from reaching macro proportions?

*Lord, I thank you that you have a future for me. I trust and hope in
your goodness.*

June 24

SABBATH

When we picture a person whose heart is pure, we may easily picture a small child or an adult who has led a quiet, sheltered life. We smile fondly. Yet look at the reward that Jesus promises to such an individual: to see God! Does this mean that the Mighty One of the universe will make a personal appearance, rather like a celebrity making a visit to the pediatric ward of a hospital? Or is the vision of God rather the ability to see him around us?

We cannot know exactly what Jesus had in mind that day up on the mountainside, when what came to be known as the Beatitudes began what came to be called the Sermon on the Mount. We can only be certain that the presence of God abounds nearby and within a person whose heart has been made pure by the blood of the Lamb, Jesus. God indeed blesses them . . . and this blessing can be ours.

WISE WAYS Where do you see God? How does he make himself visible to you?

Today, Lord, I offer you my heart. I want it to be pure for you, for I want to see you.

**Read
Proverbs 24**

PURE IN HEART

God blesses those whose hearts are pure, for they will see God.

Matthew 5:8

June 25

✳

ONCE TOO OFTEN

Don't visit your neighbors too often, or you will wear out your welcome.
Proverbs 25:17

Moderation is the watchword of many of the proverbs, and evidently this principle applies to relationships as well. The truth of this verse has proved itself through the centuries. For example, "wearing out one's welcome" has become a well-known social faux pas and the premise for many a comedy.

The other side of the picture—going right along with not taking advantage of others' hospitality—is the need to extend one's own hospitality. We need to open our hearts and homes to others rather than to always be on the receiving end. Let ours be welcoming homes where people of all ages and situations feel welcome. Going along with this is separating the notion of hospitality from entertaining. When we attend more to our guests than to the angle of the cutlery, we will be most in the spirit of Christian hospitality.

WISE WAYS   Who has welcomed you into their home in the past few months? How have you returned the hospitality?

Lord, make my heart and my home the welcoming places they were meant to be.

June 26

Solomon must have had considerable experience with gossip, if the number of proverbs dealing with the subject is any indication. Likening gossip to fuel is a powerful image and speaks to the destructive effects of idle talk.

A quarrel suggests that communication is impaired and trust is harmed, if not broken entirely. Such is also the nature of gossip, as the one talked about can no longer trust the gossiper with information. Some who gossip are unaware of the ill effects of their words. We may be aware of arguments, but we need to examine our part in "fueling the fire." If we guard our tongues and use our speech for good, we may be surprised as the animosity level goes down and the trust level between and among people goes up. Without the fuel of gossip, even the presence of small sparks of disagreement need not lead to a conflagration of argument.

WISE WAYS   In which of your circles of friends or acquaintances is quarreling a problem? What part might gossip be playing?

Today, Lord, help me speak positively of others . . . or not at all.

**Read
Proverbs 26**

QUENCHING QUARRELS

Fire goes out for lack of fuel, and quarrels disappear when gossip stops.

Proverbs 26:20

June 27

**Read
Proverbs 27**

WELCOME WOUNDS

Wounds from a friend are better than many kisses from an enemy.

Proverbs 27:6

Try as we might, it is easy to cringe when we hear the words "Now, you know I wouldn't say this if I didn't care about you, but. . . ." It is a rare person who does not mind being criticized, but it helps to realize that there truly is such a thing as constructive criticism. True friends who offer constructive criticism are seeking to help us become better people; the wound is merely the means to that end. Motivation is the key; true friends have our best interest at heart.

Motivation is also the key when an enemy "kisses" us. He or she certainly does not have our best interests at heart; the motive is of the ulterior variety. Perhaps the goal is to trick us into thinking the person is a friend, then gaining an advantage over us. Others may hope merely to use us against another person. The question for us is the foundation of the relationship: Is it trust or distrust?

WISE WAYS When was the last time a friend said some hard yet valid words to you? How did you receive this "wound"?

Lord, help me to recognize my true friends and to accept the ways that you use them to make me a better person.

June 28

Cover your tracks. Cover your bets. Cover your rear. Solomon's own father, King David, attempted to cover over his sin of adultery with Bathsheba with hypocrisy and more sin. He certainly suffered for it, and many of his relationships and dealings were hindered as a result. But he also experienced the truth of the rest of the verse: he confessed, he turned away from his sins, and he received God's mercy—that is, he did not receive what he deserved (see 2 Samuel 11:1—12:25).

Like people in Old Testament times, we are no strangers to the art of the cover-up. From high levels of government to the office building down the street to our own bedrooms, we "modern" human beings are tempted to sin and then further tempted to cover over our sins. Eventually we are discovered or so wracked with remorse that the truth comes out. But the experience of David can be ours as well: we can confess, forsake our sins, and hold open our hands to receive God's mercy.

WISE WAYS Are there sins that you are covering up? What is preventing you from confessing them, forsaking them, and receiving God's mercy?

Lord, I praise you that you are a merciful God. Be merciful to me, a sinner.

**Read
Proverbs 28**

CONFESS AND
FORSAKE

*People who cover
over their sins will
not prosper. But if
they confess and
forsake them, they
will receive mercy.*

Proverbs 28:13

June 29

**Read
Proverbs 29**

✳

WILD THING

*When people do not
accept divine
guidance, they run
wild. But whoever
obeys the law is
happy.*

Proverbs 29:18

Running wild or happily obedient? Are those the only choices for humans? Solomon says yes, and his life is testimony to the truth. He stopped listening to and following God's will, drifting further and further away from God. People need not be dashing through the streets to be effectively running wild. If our lives are out of control, it is not always apparent to passers-by. Rejection of God's guidance can take many forms and can run at many speeds.

Making the journey God's way are the people who are obedient . . . and happy. Listening to and following God's rules, we acknowledge that the One who made us did not lose interest and move on to another project. If he guides us by communicating his laws, it is with the motivation of him who loves us and knows what's best for us. In short, he knows better than we do what makes us deep-down happy.

WISE WAYS   In what ways have you "run wild" in your life? How have you experienced the truth that obedience can make you happy?

Lord, I thank you for loving me and knowing me so well that even your laws have my best interests at heart.

June 30

Slander is a serious charge; it represents an attack on a person's character. When this attack threatens a person's livelihood, the damage increases. The accused may turn on the accuser, and the latter's judging attitude may backfire. The accuser also then is accused, and the cycle of character assassination continues.

We each must be responsible for our own behavior. Judging and accusing others is not our responsibility. Following God's will and ways is a full-time occupation; no time should be left for "tattling." If reporting infractions is a requirement of our job description, that is another matter, and procedures must be followed. But slander has a different motivation, for it desires to damage another's character. The Christian has no call to this mean-spirited behavior. We are called to faithfulness to our own responsibility and empathy for other people.

WISE WAYS Are you in a position to "tell" on your coworkers? Is this a legitimate part of your job, or are you engaging in slander?

Lord, help me to keep my eyes on my own behavior. Help me view my coworkers as fellow sojourners.

**Read
Proverbs 30**

THE COST OF SLANDER

*Never slander
a person
to his employer.
If you do,
the person
will curse you,
and you will
pay for it.*
Proverbs 30:10

JULY

July 1

**Read
Proverbs 1**

EXPECTING
TROUBLE

*I have told you all
this so that you may
have peace in me.
Here on earth, you
will have many trials
and sorrows. But
take heart, because I
have overcome the
world.*
John 16:33

Everyone experiences trials and sorrows in this life. However, Jesus reminds us that these are limited to this earth only. We can "take heart" because Jesus has overcome this world, and as a result of his death and resurrection, we too know that "overwhelming victory is ours through Christ, who loved us" (Romans 8:37).

Because we have been made right with God, we can approach him in confidence. Not only did Jesus overcome the world, but we also "may have peace" in him. This is not a random promise but a theme in Scripture as found in two powerful confirmations. The first is in John 14:27: "I am leaving you with a gift—peace of mind and heart. And the peace I give isn't like the peace the world gives. So don't be troubled or afraid." The second is found in Philippians 4:6-7: "Don't worry about anything; instead, pray about everything. Tell God what you need, and thank him for all he has done. If you do this, you will experience God's peace, which is far more wonderful than the human mind can understand. His peace will guard your hearts and minds as you live in Christ Jesus."

WISE WAYS   How do you react to the trials and tribulations you face every day in this world?

Lord, grant me peace that I may endure the trials and sorrows I face, and help me to look forward in hope to the eternal glory I will share with you in Heaven.

July 2

Read any book on success and the number one ingredient is having a plan. Major corporations do not achieve success through procrastination, households cannot run smoothly without organization, and students cannot fully apply themselves unless they make wise use of their time. To achieve our goals, we need to have a plan.

God's will for us is to reach our full potential in life, whatever that may be. Having a map is essential if we want to reach that goal. However, the second part of this verse reminds us that having a plan is not the end of the matter. God is in control of everything. Only a firm understanding of who we serve will enable us to avoid the pitfalls of success, whether in business or in ministry. All our planning is for nothing if the goal is not part of God's plan.

WISE WAYS   What plans have you made recently in your work, home, or church? What steps have you taken to ensure that these plans are leading you to a goal that is part of God's will?

Today, Lord, as I make my plans, help me to remember that you are in control and my ultimate goal in life is to glorify you. Guide my paths today and speak to me about the direction I should go.

**Read
Proverbs 2**

A LIVING STRATEGY

Wise planning will watch over you. Understanding will keep you safe.

Proverbs 2:11

July 3

**Read
Proverbs 3**

✳

WISDOM'S APPRAISAL

*Wisdom is more
precious than rubies;
nothing you desire
can compare with
her. She offers you
life in her right hand,
and riches and honor
in her left. She will
guide you down
delightful paths; all
her ways are
satisfying.*

Proverbs 3:15-17

"Wisdom" has come to mean many things in today's society, but here it refers specifically to God's wisdom. When we seek wisdom and understanding from God, we are consciously making a decision to reject the ways of the world and to desire what the world cannot appreciate.

God's ways are higher than our ways. God created this world and everything in it. He alone knows what is best for us. "Seeking wisdom" is seeking communion with God. It means to lay aside what we think is the best way of doing things and finding through the Bible how the Lord would have us live instead.

The promises in the proverb describe a satisfying life, a life without regrets. Wise living may not always be easy living, but the paths are delightful along the way. The truly wise seek to know God, who desires to be known. Nothing compares with the joy of knowing God (Philippians 3:7-8).

WISE WAYS What steps are you taking to seek God's wisdom in your life? How are you treasuring the wisdom of the Lord?

Today, Lord, please teach me about your wisdom and help me to gain a deeper appreciation for all that I can learn from you.

July 4

Righteousness is the state of being "right" with God. In the Old Testament, the path to righteousness was through obedience to the law. But in our sinfulness, we were not even able to do that. We cannot obtain righteousness by ourselves—it is a gift from God. There is nothing we can do to earn it. We are so buried in sin that only Jesus, being free from sin, has the power to pull us out and make us right with God. When we choose Jesus, when we reach for that hand he holds out to us, we are reaching out to the light.

Salvation is like the dawn of a new day—a fresh start—and the more we seek God, the brighter it gets. Whereas righteousness is a life with God, wickedness is a life apart from God. It can only be darkness because without God's light in our lives we have no way to understand this world, no meaning, no purpose. How wonderful that God, in his grace, shines the light of Jesus into our darkness. No wonder one of Christ's titles is "bright and morning star" (see Revelation 22:16).

WISE WAYS Next time you see the sunrise, think about God's saving grace in your own life and the light that is growing stronger every day as you walk closer with Jesus.

Today, Lord, help me to remember that in you I am a new creation, I have left the darkness and chosen to walk in the light. Speak to me today about the ways I can walk more closely with you and shine brightly for your kingdom.

**Read
Proverbs 4**

NEW DAY

The way of the righteous is like the first gleam of dawn, which shines ever brighter until the full light of day. But the way of the wicked is like complete darkness. Those who follow it have no idea what they are stumbling over.

Proverbs 4:18-19

July 5

**Read
Proverbs 5**

✳

SACRED RESERVOIR

*Why spill the water of
your springs in
public, having sex
with just anyone?
You should reserve it
for yourselves. Don't
share it with strangers.*

Proverbs 5:16-17

Sexual purity is not a very popular topic of conversation today. In movies, television, and books, sex is portrayed as something that is "no big deal," something we have a "right" to, whether or not we are married. Society seems blind to the rampant spread of sexually transmitted diseases and the epidemic of divorces. Immorality gets flaunted while virtue is held up for ridicule.

But God calls us to a higher standard. He created sex as something special that would happen within a marriage relationship only. God did not create it as something to be treated lightly, abused, or shared with strangers. When we have sex outside of marriage, for whatever reason, we are disobeying God, plain and simple.

To use the powerful imagery of this proverb, those who derive life from them must guard the springs. Otherwise, they will become polluted and of no good to anyone.

WISE WAYS With divorce on the rise among Christian couples, think about some of the ways that you can deepen the bond of your own marriage. If you are not married, how can you surround yourself with other people who are equally committed to remaining sexually pure before God?

Today, Lord, help me to have the strength to resist the temptations of this world and to remain pure in your sight.

July 6

Parents have a crucial role to play in contemporary society. There are more and more pressures on families today as they attempt to function within a world that rejects truth, traditional notions of marriage and family, and basic moral guidelines for living. One of the basic building blocks of society is under attack, and there is little recognition of the chaos that will follow if the family structure should collapse.

Teaching cannot be left to schools or churches; the primary people in a child's life are his or her parents. The responsibility is unavoidable. But this proverb is not just for parents; it also calls on children to listen to their parents. This proverb conveys the words of a loving heavenly Father saying to children, "More than anyone else in this world, your parents love and care for you and desire to see you fulfill your potential. As your parents are listening to what I teach them, you should also be listening to what they are teaching you."

WISE WAYS   Think about the positive ways your parents influenced you. If you are a parent, how can you remind yourself of this responsibility before God?

Lord, help me to be a great parent to my children and a great son or daughter to my own parents. Impress your commands on my heart and fill me with love for my family members.

**Read
Proverbs 6**

TWO-WAY
STREET

My son, obey your father's commands, and don't neglect your mother's teaching.
Proverbs 6:20

July 7

**Read
Proverbs 7**

FALSE ADVERTISING

*"Come, let's drink
our fill of love until
morning. Let's enjoy
each other's caresses,
for my husband is not
home. He's away on
a long trip."*

Proverbs 7:18-19

When no one is around, and seemingly no one will find out, it is very hard to resist the temptations of this world. A little lie here, a furtive glance there, a curse uttered in anger. These little transgressions seem small and insignificant at the time, but they are sin nonetheless.

In these cases Satan scores a double victory. Not only are we doing something that goes against God's will, but we are doing so because we don't think anyone is around. At that moment, we have accepted the bold-faced lie that we can get away with something because "no one is watching." And that, perhaps, is the greater problem, for it means we have forgotten that God is with us always. No one else may see you, but God does, and your sin breaks his heart. It is a lie from Satan that we can enjoy sin while no one is around, while the coast is clear. It ignores God's high standards for us and, worst of all, it ignores God's presence in our lives.

WISE WAYS What sins do you commit when you think no one is watching?

Today, Lord, remind me of your wonderful presence in my life. Help me to remember that you are with me always, and I can turn to you for strength when I feel weak.

July 8

Of these four ways to love God, loving him with "all your soul" may sound the least familiar. The soul doesn't get much attention these days, but it should. Jesus pointed out the danger of being extremely successful at the price of our soul (Matthew 16:26). He taught that our soul is the one thing about ourselves that we dare not lose. Within the great commandment, loving God with all our soul means loving him in any and every way that goes beyond our heart, mind, or strength. In other words, we are to love God when we don't feel like it.

Here are three training exercises in loving God with your soul: (1) Read, meditate, and imitate those psalms that mention the soul in action (such as Psalms 23, 31, 42, 62, 63, 103); (2) Learn several of the popular worship choruses that express love for God; and (3) Practice using these to train your soul in loving God. The next time you become aware that you're not actively loving God, use one of the resources listed above to love him anyway.

WISE WAYS   How many choruses do you know already that mention the soul?

Today, Lord, keep me thinking about my soul. Help me to appreciate how precious a gift from you it is. Help me never to exchange it for something cheap.

**Read
Proverbs 8**

SOUL-LOVE

Jesus replied, "The most important commandment is this: 'Hear, O Israel! The Lord our God is the one and only Lord. And you must love the Lord your God with all your heart, all your soul, all your mind, and all your strength.' The second is equally important: 'Love your neighbor as yourself.' No other commandment is greater than these."

Mark 12:29-31

July 9

Read
Proverbs 9

HEALTHY FEAR

Fear of the Lord is the beginning of wisdom. Knowledge of the Holy One results in understanding.
Proverbs 9:10

Most of us are familiar with John 3:16, "For God so loved the world. . . ." He loved us so much that he provided a way out of our sin through the death of Jesus Christ. So what does it mean to "fear" him? This does not mean that he is "out to get us."

However, stopping to contemplate the personhood of God should put us in complete awe. God created everything. He made this world. He put the planets in motion. He knows the universe. Shouldn't we fear someone with that much power? It's beyond the scope of our imagination to even begin to think about "who" God is. He is beyond definition. Even a label of "omnipotent" seems somehow limiting for the one who invented power. "Omniscient" is a joke for the one who made thought, language, words. Our God is a mighty God. He isn't an old man with a long beard; he isn't the best of several other gods. He is the *only* God.

God is not only the beginning of wisdom, he is the beginning of everything. God is worthy of our utmost awe and worship.

WISE WAYS   How can you retain a biblical viewpoint regarding who God is? In what ways can your fear of God lead to a deeper understanding of his will?

Today, Lord, give me a glimpse of who you are and what you can do in my life. Help me to fear you more, so that I might come into a deeper relationship with you.

July 10

It seems pretty obvious to most Christians that we should not be "squandering" our money on sinful activities. But at the same time, we sometimes try to "get around" this proverb by altering God's definition of sin to fit our current situation. For example, we may feel good about not spending money at a certain store or subscribing to a particular magazine. However, we might then go and pour more money than is perhaps wise into our house or car.

When we stop to realize that it is all God's money, there is a shift in perspective. When we turn to God for advice and guidance in what we spend and where, it can only enhance our lives. We are enriched not through the things we purchase, but through the direction we are led to use our funds for the glory of God's kingdom. When we choose to spend our earnings without consultation or guidance from God, we often squander the financial opportunities that God has presented to us.

WISE WAYS   How are you spending your earnings? In what ways can you use them to glorify God and his kingdom?

Today, Lord, help me to use your blessings to enhance my life and others in accordance with your will. Help me to avoid the pitfalls of my sinful heart and to focus on serving you in everything that I do.

**Read
Proverbs 10**

STEWARDSHIP

The earnings of the godly enhance their lives, but evil people squander their money on sin.

Proverbs 10:16

July 11

Read
Proverbs 11

✳

LEADERSHIP BACKUP

Without wise leadership, a nation falls; with many counselors, there is safety.
Proverbs 11:14

Without God's direction in our lives, we would be hopelessly lost in sin. Indeed, whenever we try to strike out on our own path and go in a direction different from God's, we invariably fail. The same is true at all levels—in the family, in a church, at a business, and in the government. It is impossible to have wise leadership without the presence of God, for true wisdom comes from God alone.

Furthermore, every leader needs good counselors. From the president of the country down to the family unit, we all rely on a close-knit circle of friends and advisors for advice and guidance. Sometimes, when we are far from God, it is only the wise counsel of a spouse or close friend that can bring us back. Thank God for the good counselors in your life.

WISE WAYS   How do you incorporate God into your leadership roles at home or at work? Take a close look at your "counselors"—are they men and women who truly desire to follow the Lord?

Today, Lord, remind me that true leadership is based on you and you alone, that your wisdom is the source of life. Please use the people in my life to guide and mold me and keep me on the path that you have set forth for me.

July 12

Just about every courtroom drama revolves around someone not telling the truth. The judge and jury have to figure out who is being honest and who is not. As Christians living in the world no one should ever have to call our truthfulness into question. With the Holy Spirit dwelling within us there is no reason why we cannot tell the truth. Yet we continually slip up, and little untruths can quickly become big lies.

Part of the problem lies in our perspective. In any given situation in our day-to-day routine, it can be very easy to come up with a good reason for not telling the whole truth. But this proverb calls our attention to a larger purpose, a bigger calling. We are all witnesses for Christ and his love. We are living, breathing examples of the work he did for us on the Cross. And our witness to the world should be honest and true. For if our truthfulness is called into question on small things, how can we expect people to believe us about the massively important truths of salvation and forgiveness?

WISE WAYS In a world that denies almost all types of truth, what are some ways that you can stand firm as an honest witness for truth?

Today, Lord, give me the courage to stand firm for you. Help me to be an honest witness, proclaiming your truth to the world in all that I do.

**Read
Proverbs 12**

WITNESS STAND

*An honest witness
tells the truth;
a false witness
tells lies.*

Proverbs 12:17

July 13

**Read
Proverbs 13**

LONG-TERM HOPE

*Hope deferred
makes the heart sick,
but when dreams
come true,
there is life
and joy.*

Proverbs 13:12

Read the front page of any newspaper and it's hard not to get depressed at the state of the world. Wars, unrest, fighting, terrorism, natural disasters, diseases, failing economies—the list goes on and on. How can we have any hope in such a fallen world? Some Eastern religions gloss over these troubles and suggest that through meditation we can remove ourselves from caring about the suffering around us. Others try to accept it all as just being the way the world works. For them, there is no meaning or purpose, just a hard life followed by death. But neither of these approaches is true, and neither of them is God's will for us.

This proverb says that when hope is deferred, it makes the heart sick. But God wants us to have enduring hope—hope for a future, hope for the return of Jesus Christ, hope for a time when all suffering and persecution will end. Some might call this "hope" nothing more than the foolish wishes of a child who doesn't yet understand the harsh realities of life. But the proof is in Jesus Christ. His life, death, and resurrection are the reasons for our hope. We may not get what we hope for, but the One in whom we hope will never fail us.

WISE WAYS   In what ways have you been struggling with deferred hope?

Today, Lord, grant me a deeper sense of hope for the future. Fill me with an abundance of your love, and help me to look forward with a longing heart for your return.

July 14

As Christians, we have nothing to fear anymore. Satan has lost the war once and for all, and we can move forward in full confidence. However, there is a difference between confidence in Christ and overconfidence, or pride in ourselves. There is no trial, tribulation, or struggle that is too great for Christ to bear, but there are many things that we cannot bear. We should be confident because of Christ and through Christ, but not outside of Christ. The foolish can only blunder forward out of too much self-confidence.

Furthermore, it is foolish to rush forward and, out of pride, think that everything will be OK. Christians are not immune to stupidity. God will often allow gracious lessons in humility and endurance to occur because we have confused confidence in ourselves with confidence in him. Instead, we want to live with a wise caution that makes decisions neither out of fear and anxiety nor out of prideful overconfidence.

WISE WAYS What wisdom have you taken from the Bible today? How can you use that to help you be confident in Christ, but cautious in dealing with the world?

Today, Lord, I want to be your servant. You have shared your wisdom with me through your Word and through your church, but I pray for extra guidance as I go out today. I pray that you would help me to be cautious and prudent, and not rush into anything prematurely.

**Read
Proverbs 14**

INFORMED RISK

The wise are cautious and avoid danger; fools plunge ahead with great confidence.

Proverbs 14:16

July 15

SABBATH

Read Proverbs 15

TIGHT SQUEEZE

How hard it is for rich people to get into the Kingdom of God! It is easier for a camel to go through the eye of a needle than for a rich person to enter the Kingdom of God!
Luke 18:24-25

There are two things here that we know Jesus was not trying to say. First of all, it is not impossible for rich people to be born again. God has blessed each one of us differently, and while one person may have been born in poverty, another may have been born into wealth. God can use people in all walks of life, no matter how much money they have. Surrendering our will to him first is imperative, because unless we are born again, there is nothing we can do for God. Second, we do not need to be poor in order to be good Christians. The Bible does not say that we must sell everything we own in order to be holy.

That said, it is often much harder for wealthy people to be exposed to God's Word and for it to sink in and take root. The problem lies most often with the distractions of the world. Cars, houses, schools, jobs, 401k plans—the amount of time spent each day worrying or thinking about money tends to outweigh devotional time. This is why money makes it so hard to worship God—and why Jesus offered stern warnings to those with wealth.

WISE WAYS   How can you make more room in your schedule for God this week?

Today, Lord, help me to clear away the distractions and the lies of this world and focus on you and your eternal wisdom.

July 16

Do you remember the first time that you read the words of Jesus? Do you remember the thrill of reading something that you knew deep down in your heart was absolutely, eternally true? Throughout the Bible, it is experiences with this absolute Truth, the Creator of the world, that drives the changes in people's lives, makes leaders out of the most unlikely people, and shapes the fate of nations.

True wisdom can only come from God—through prayer, quiet times, reading his Word, and earnestly seeking his will. But most of all, wisdom will come from an attitude of service and obedience. No amount of Bible study or church activity can cover up our hearts before God. He can only bless us when we are genuinely seeking to follow him.

God also uses some of his followers as teachers and leaders who must pass on their understanding to others. "Presenting" instruction well means that leaders, pastors, and teachers have a responsibility to seek God's wisdom first and foremost because they are teaching not what they know, but what they have been taught by God. When the source is truth, instruction is not just appreciated, but actively sought.

WISE WAYS How can you seek God's wisdom and share with other people what God has taught you?

Today, Lord, help me to find wisdom in your Word and share it openly and confidently with others.

**Read
Proverbs 16**

WISDOM
SENSITIVITY

The wise are known for their understanding, and instruction is appreciated if it's well presented.
Proverbs 16:21

July 17

Read
Proverbs 17

THE HIGHEST COURT

The LORD despises those who acquit the guilty and condemn the innocent.
Proverbs 17:15

We've all heard stories about prisoners being set free after spending years in prison for a crime they did not commit. Whatever the reason, the results are always devastating. It fills our hearts with joy to hear of an innocent man being set free after a false imprisonment.

Regardless of what we see on the news or read in the papers, God keeps tabs on everything. This proverb tells us about God's response when he sees lies take precedence and the innocent condemned. The story of Jesus is the ultimate wrongfully accused story—a man who came to save us, who had done nothing wrong at all, was imprisoned, tried, and convicted without a fair trial.

This is the depth of God's love for us. Although he despised the situation, he used it to defeat Satan and his lies once and for all, and to grant us all eternal life. Although as sinners we were part of that crowd that called for Jesus to be crucified, now that we are born again we can have right standing with God and have the ability to live a life that is pleasing to him.

WISE WAYS What are some of the difficult decisions that you have to make every day, at work or at home, that involve holding people responsible? How are you seeking God's help?

Today, Lord, I choose you. I choose honesty and truth, and I pray that you would help me to live out these ideals today as I face so many different challenges from Satan. Protect me and give me the strength that I need to stand firm for you.

July 18

Frustrating as it may be, at some point in our lives we've all rushed to give advice without listening to the complete story. On the other end of the spectrum, almost everyone has had the misfortune of receiving advice before being allowed to finish explaining first. This proverb encourages us to rein in our tongues and listen more than we usually do. It makes it easier to then give accurate and helpful advice and avoid the pitfalls of pride.

Why is this true? Often, if we speak too quickly, the advice we give turns out to be the first thing the person already tried. Listening can help us realize how little help we have to offer and remind us to ask for wisdom and help from God on behalf of our friend. Waiting to hear the whole story is itself the action our friend needs the most from us. Our attention conveys care and concern in ways we can't measure.

WISE WAYS What are some practical steps you can take to ensure that you are hearing people fully before dispensing advice, both at work and in the home?

Today, Lord, I want to hear all the facts before passing judgment. Help me to rein in my tongue and focus on listening to other people.

**Read
Proverbs 18**

TONGUE BITING

*What a shame,
what folly,
to give advice
before listening
to the facts!*

Proverbs 18:13

July 19

**Read
Proverbs 19**

✳

REPEAT OFFENDERS

*Short-tempered
people must pay their
own penalty. If you
rescue them once,
you will have to do
it again.*

Proverbs 19:19

Tough love gets rave reviews from those who have learned its lessons. Those in the middle of undergoing the tough love experience, however, rarely like it! Short-temperedness is simply one of numerous character traits that cannot be corrected or eliminated by cooperation. If a person's short temper proves effective to move or cower people, that person will continue to use it.

Trying to help a short-tempered person requires calm and the use of effective negative consequences. One such consequence, described as a "penalty" by this proverb, is the cost created by short temper: fines, repair charges, restrictions, restitution, and others. If a short-tempered person is shown in any way that others are willing to "cover the costs" of his or her behavior, the behavior is simply reinforced.

Tough love is hard on the one being loved as well as the one loving. We want to help. But we aren't helping when we deflect the consequences that can teach a valuable lesson.

WISE WAYS Reflect on the valuable lessons you have learned in life from the consequences that have followed your actions. When appropriate, share those lessons.

Today, Lord, I pray for the short-tempered people in my life. If I'm one of them, I include myself in my request for your help. Teach me to pay attention to the penalties.

July 20

Almost all of us have, at some point, cursed a parent in some way (just think about when we were teenagers) and yet we are still here, alive. So obviously, this proverb is not saying that a word uttered in anger, frustration, or ignorance against a parent will result in a bolt of lightning from on high.

However, that said, curses result from anger. Anger expressed outwardly comes from anger in the heart, which is the same emotion that can lead to many more dreadful and hurtful acts. Jesus said that although the law condemns murderers, those who are merely angry with another will be judged also (Matthew 5:21-22). And it is this relationship that the proverb is drawing us toward—anger is not part of God's plan for us or for the world. It is a sinful emotion that tends to lead to more sin and more hurt. We need to repent and seek forgiveness for any time that our anger takes control in our lives, and turn to God for the patience and strength that only he can provide.

WISE WAYS   Try to catch yourself today when you get angry about something—anything—and instead of letting it boil up inside, talk with God about the aggravation. Think about some ways that you can let God have more control over your emotions.

Today, Lord, as yesterday, I need you to help me with anger. Help me to put your Holy Spirit back in control instead, so that you are in complete control of my life.

Read
Proverbs 20

VERBAL HONOR

If you curse your father or mother, the lamp of your life will be snuffed out.

Proverbs 20:20

July 21

**Read
Proverbs 21**

HEARING AID

*Those who shut their
ears to the cries of the
poor will be ignored
in their own
time of need.*
Proverb 21:13

Anyone who lives in a big city hears cries from the poor every day. Even in the suburbs, homeless people are out on the streets. This is aside from the working poor, who may not be living on the street, but barely make it from day to day. The situation in developing countries is even worse—the quality of life is often terrible, running water may not be available, children are homeless, and wars destroy entire towns. Sometimes we are tempted to deal with all this suffering and heartache by steeling our hearts against it all, blocking it out. There is, after all, only so much we can do.

But nowhere in the Bible does God call on one individual to fix all the problems of the world. That is his job, not ours. Jesus told us, "Those who are last now will be first then" (Matthew 20:16). In the meantime, we are called to respond to the leading of the Holy Spirit in our lives. What can a dollar do for a homeless person? Maybe not much at all, but that's not for us to decide ahead of time. If you feel a tug on your heart, don't let Satan rationalize it away, but respond freely and openly. Let God worry about what happens to it.

WISE WAYS What are some practical ways that you can help a poor person today? Will you commit to sponsoring a child or donating to a homeless shelter this week?

Today, Lord, give me a heart for the poor. It is hard to see so much suffering and not shut it out. It's a greater burden than I can bear. But you can bear it, Lord. And so, while I know I can't help everyone, I pray that you would give me an opportunity today to help one person.

July 22

"I want to work for world peace." It's a cliché we hear all the time—on TV, in newspapers, from world leaders and local leaders, politicians and beauty queens. Rarely is any real action taken, however. On the one hand, this is understandable; world peace is a mammoth task that no one person could ever hope to achieve.

However, while we may not be able to stop all fighting and wars across the globe, we can do much to heal wounds and bring peace to our local communities and personal relationships. We can stop yelling at our children and our spouses. We can stop fighting with extended family members whom we don't like or can't get along with. We can stop honking furiously at the person in front who stopped us from cruising through a yellow light. These simple acts are completely within our ability and absolutely under our control. At every difficult and stressful moment we have a choice—to escalate the problem or to defuse it. With the Holy Spirit in our lives, we should always be working for peace and glorifying God in the process.

WISE WAYS How can you work for peace in your home, in your neighborhood, in your office?

Today, Lord, help me to work for peace in my community. Help me to make the right choice when a stressful situation arises. Fill me with your love and patience and the ability to defuse such situations rather than escalating them.

Read
Proverbs 22

PEACEMAKERS

God blesses those who work for peace, for they will be called the children of God.
Matthew 5:9

July 23

Read
Proverbs 23

✳

STAYING ON THE WAGON

Do not carouse with drunkards and gluttons, for they are on their way to poverty. Too much sleep clothes a person with rags.

Proverbs 23:20-21

Lust, greed, power, money, laziness, self-righteousness, anger, and avarice—these are all things on which we can gorge ourselves. They may not be as obvious to others as the overconsumption of alcohol or food, but they are equally bad because they take control away from the Holy Spirit. And when we grab the steering wheel away from the Holy Spirit, it's going to result in a car wreck—guaranteed.

Yes, drinking too much liquor will eventually lead to bankruptcy, but too much greed, anger, lust, or laziness will also bankrupt us spiritually, taking us out of the presence of God. Although it's easy to point our fingers at those we know who are struggling deeply with such sins, we are fooling ourselves if we ignore the times we indulge ourselves as well. But while there may be pleasure in sin for a time, it always ends. Furthermore, when we get out of the presence of God, we can't be moving forward at the same time. We come to a dead halt spiritually. No more building up treasures in heaven, no more being used by God here on earth, no more anything. And unless we turn back, we will face spiritual poverty.

WISE WAYS What are some actions you can take today to avoid spiritual poverty?

Today, Lord, help me to identify the places in my life where I am most in danger of overindulging my sinful heart. Keep me from temptation, and help me to keep the Holy Spirit firmly in control of my life.

July 24

We may hate to admit it, but it's a great feeling when things start to go wrong for someone we don't like. Maybe it's an adversary at work who suddenly gets fired, or a neighbor we don't like who has to move away. *Finally,* we think to ourselves, *they are getting what they deserve.*

God calls us to a higher standard, however. Sure, we can rejoice when our enemies start to experience persecution in the way they persecuted us, but that misses the most fundamental truth of Christianity—forgiveness. It should pain us when anyone experiences trouble and difficulty. It should be a sad moment when others stumble and fall. Such occurrences should cause us to pray and show love and kindness. When our "enemies" are outside the church, it is a powerful testimony to the true life-changing power of Jesus Christ when we shed a tear for their troubles instead of laughing in glee.

Within the body of believers, it is even more imperative to step forward and help those who stumble, however much we dislike or disagree with them. We are brothers and sisters in Christ.

WISE WAYS   Who in your community could benefit from your prayers and support this week? Who has stumbled that you can help up?

Today, Lord, fill me with love for my enemies. It is hard sometimes to love them or treat them kindly when they have abused me so much. Lord, I know that you have the power to help me. Soften my heart, and help me to love more freely.

Read
Proverbs 24

WASTED CHEERS

Do not rejoice when your enemies fall into trouble. Don't be happy when they stumble.
Proverbs 24:17

July 25

HARD WORDS

*Telling lies about
others is as harmful
as hitting them with
an ax, wounding
them with a sword,
or shooting them
with a sharp arrow.*

Proverbs 25:18

When you were a child, you may have heard the phrase "Sticks and stones may break my bones, but words will never hurt me." It's a popular saying, but the Bible tells us otherwise. Whereas a stone might cause a bruise on the surface, it heals quickly and there are rarely any long-term negative consequences. Words, on the other hand, pierce to the soul and can cause long-lasting damage.

Of all the words that sting, lies are the worst. They slander our name, they spread dissension, and they destroy relationships, families, businesses, and churches. They lead to more lies and more lies again to cover up the first lies. Satan deceived Eve with a lie in the Garden of Eden. The bottom line is that lies cause far more damage than any other weapon invented by man. Thankfully, the solution is simple—don't tell lies. The command is not just for kids who stole a cookie or didn't do their homework—it's for everyone, of every age, of every station in life.

WISE WAYS What are some actions you can take today to avoid stretching the truth in your home or office?

Today, Lord, help me to stand up for truth. I know it in my head, and I can say it with my lips, but help me to feel it in my heart and live it with my life.

July 26

Touch a lit match to a piece of paper soaked in gas and you'll have a fire on your hands before you know it. Likewise, if you make friends with a quarrelsome person, don't be surprised when quarrels start to break out! But there is more to this proverb than this simple correlation.

The application of proverbs always starts best at home. This proverb provokes a good question: "Am I a quarrelsome person?" Or perhaps, "When am I a quarrelsome person?" Almost every heated discussion or confrontation has one or more important forks in the road. If any of the participants is in a quarrelsome mood, the fork taken will likely lead to a fight.

Think of the last fight you had with a spouse or friend. Can you remember the fork? Did the argument become a fight because you took the quarrelsome fork in the road? Would it have been better to call a time-out?

WISE WAYS Weak points or tendencies can be avoided. Admit to a quarrelsome mood before getting into a discussion you will probably escalate into a fight.

Today, Lord, help me think about admitting my weaknesses. Help me not to avoid truthful discussions, but to avoid ruining them with a quarrelsome attitude.

**Read
Proverbs 26**

SPARKS!

A quarrelsome person starts fights as easily as hot embers light charcoal or fire lights wood.
Proverbs 26:21

July 27

Read
Proverbs 27

GENERATIONS

*Never abandon a
friend—either yours
or your father's.
Then in your time of
need, you won't have
to ask your relatives
for assistance. It is
better to go to a
neighbor than to a
relative who lives
far away.*
Proverbs 27:10

A good friend is hard to come by. We make many acquaintances throughout life, but a friend who sticks with us through thick and thin is a special gift from God. As such, we should treasure the friends that we have.

As counselors in times of need, prayer partners, advisors, and friends can be used by God to teach and guide us. But although friends play a special role in our lives, we sometimes let the relationships slip through the cracks, and those friends become mere acquaintances again.

The Bible urges us to put the extra effort into these relationships to keep them going. We need a body of believers around us, a close group of friends who are also believers to support and pray for us. A tight-knit community is much harder for the enemy to break into.

Although the proverb seems to imply that we should favor friends over family, it really just emphasizes the special nature of a close friend. Family will always be there. But close friends are the first level of defense and support in our lives, and should be treasured as such.

WISE WAYS   Think of some ways you can thank your close friends for their support and prayers and friendship.

Today, Lord, I thank you for the friends that you have blessed me with; they are truly assets that I treasure very much. I pray for their protection, and I hope that you will continue to bless these relationships over the course of this year and the years to come.

July 28

A stubborn heart has stood in the way of many people becoming Christians. Such a heart refuses to change or listen to reason. And the sad result is that they will never know the redeeming love of Jesus Christ. But don't give up on the stubborn! They need as much prayer, and sometimes more, than those who seem more receptive to hearing about the cross of Jesus.

People with a tender conscience, on the other hand, are a joy to meet. They are often receptive and responsive to the gospel. They often have a high awareness of their sins and find the news of forgiveness in Jesus Christ truly good news! Those who are stubborn may take longer and be a harder audience, but "serious trouble" often has a way of tenderizing people's lives. That's more than enough reason to persist in praying and caring for the stubborn people in our lives.

WISE WAYS The best way to treat stubborn people is to out-stubborn them with genuine love.

Today, Lord, make me aware of someone with a tender conscience. Give me the wisdom and words to encourage and speak to them about you.

Read
Proverbs 28

TENDERIZER

Blessed are those who have a tender conscience, but the stubborn are headed for serious trouble.
Proverbs 28:14

July 29

SABBATH

Read
Proverbs 29

HORN-FREE ZONE

When you give a gift to someone in need, don't shout about it as the hypocrites do—blowing trumpets in the synagogues and streets to call attention to their acts of charity! I assure you, they have received all the reward they will ever get.

Matthew 6:2

This proverb seems so easy. We can make a gift or otherwise help someone in need, but we don't go out of our way to tell everyone how great we are for doing it. What's so difficult about that? But then we see a homeless person outside a grocery store and everyone is ignoring him, so we offer to buy him some groceries. The desire to tell everyone about our "good deed" is a strong one!

Jesus makes a serious point. The hypocrite gives to charity or helps a poor person but thinks in his heart: "It's my gift that is helping that person," or "If it weren't for me, this charity would be lost." Such an attitude takes God out of the picture and marks hypocrites—those who confess God with their lips but in their hearts feel that they are the ones making things better on this earth.

All good things come from God, and he uses us all in different ways. But our gifts and deeds are worthless outside of him. He is the one doing the work; he is the one changing lives and hearts, not us. It is a blessing and a privilege to be a part of any work for God, and we should always consider it as such.

WISE WAYS   What are some acts of charity that you can do this week? In what ways has this "proverb" of Jesus affected your attitude toward giving?

Today, Lord, help me to give freely of my time and money for the glory of your kingdom. Help me to remember throughout all that I do that you are the one in control, not me.

July 30

Respect. Honor. Talk to any teacher or parent today and you'll hear how much they struggle with kids who don't have any respect for their elders. Note how children dishonor their parents. It's a growing problem, and one that we can't ignore.

Lack of respect is at the heart of mockery; you don't mock someone whom you respect. People who have become Christians should have a deep understanding of respect. Outside of Christ, we mocked God with our rebellious hearts and lives. We disrespected and dishonored God. We were convinced that our way was better than his, but the end result of such a life is death, with no hope for eternal life. Repentance and salvation changed that.

Our relationship with our parents should reflect our relationship with God. We are bound by respect for God to honor them.

WISE WAYS   How can you show your parents how much you respect them and all that they have done for you over the years?

Today, Lord, I thank you for my parents and all that they have taught me. I pray that you would bless them and keep them safe.

**Read
Proverbs 30**

R-E-S-P-E-C-T

The eye that mocks a father and despises a mother will be plucked out by ravens of the valley and eaten by vultures.
Proverbs 30:17

July 31

Read
Proverbs 31

✳

CONFIDENT LAUGHTER

She is clothed with strength and dignity, and she laughs with no fear of the future.

Proverbs 31:25

Many women today find it hard to understand their roles and identity. On the one hand, they are expected to be 100 percent female and fulfill all the typical female "norms" and responsibilities. On the other hand, they are also expected to be just like men, competing, working, and living like men. The result is doubt and fear and confusion. It's hard enough to live up to one set of expectations, but to live up to two sometimes opposing expectations is impossible.

A woman whose life is planted firmly in the Lord's hand is able to live free from these societal constraints, and instead live according to the way God made her. A life built on Christ's redeeming power and the wisdom of the Lord opens the heart to a source of strength that comes only from a relationship with God. True dignity comes from a firm belief in God's love for each one of us. And such a woman can indeed laugh at the future—not in mockery, but with confidence, for there is nothing to fear when she is walking with the Lord.

WISE WAYS If you are a woman, what are some ways you can "clothe" yourself with strength and dignity? Otherwise, based on this proverb, how can you better encourage the women in your life?

Today, Lord, I give you all my fears and doubts. You created me. You love me. You alone know what is best for me. I put my life in your hands and seek your will.

AUGUST

August 1

**Read
Proverbs 1**

HEARING TEST

*Come here and
listen to me!
I'll pour out
the spirit of wisdom
upon you and
make you wise.*
Proverbs 1:23

A memorable distinction we learn from watching children is the difference between hearing and listening. Sure, children hear what adults say. "Stop that." "Come here." But do they listen? The answer to that question is, "selectively," at best. Many parents are mystified by a child's uncanny ability to heed the tinkling of the neighborhood ice cream truck still blocks away, while feigning acute deafness when being summoned for dinner from the next room.

In the same way, we may halfheartedly hear what God says through a pastor or our own personal Bible study. But are we really listening to God? Listening implies open hearts as well as open ears. As with children, obedience is the sign that listening has taken place. When we listen to God in this way, he promises to pour out his wisdom on the soil of our hearts. We grow wise as a result.

WISE WAYS   Need wisdom to deal with a particular situation you are facing? How can you set aside time today to listen to God's counsel?

Today, Lord, make my ears quick to listen to your voice. Make my heart ready to respond with obedience.

August 2

The story is told of an unfortunate woman whose accelerator became stuck as she was leaving the parking lot of a local bank. The self-propelled station wagon bolted across four lanes of traffic, sideswiped two telephone poles, and steamrolled a postal box before finally boomeranging back through the evacuated lobby of the bank. Her teary testimony about her foiled attempts to wrangle the wild beast into reverse, neutral, or even park was silenced when the officer at the scene merely asked, "Did it occur to you to turn off the ignition?"

Sometimes common sense eludes us when we need it the most. What disastrous chain reactions common sense can avoid! Often the precursor to wisdom, common sense is an insider's tip. It's the voice inside that alerts us to others' mischievous motives and questionable quandaries. Common sense makes us take note that something's not quite right. Wisdom follows in the form of a choice—a decision not to partner with impiety. Fools, too, hear the same voice—they merely decide to ignore it.

WISE WAYS   How often do you waiver when trying to discern the right thing to do? In what scenarios can you ask God for the ability to choose wisely today?

Today, Lord, may I use common sense in dealing with others in order to choose wisely. Save me from foolish mistakes before it's too late.

Read
Proverbs 2

TURN IT OFF

Wisdom will save you from evil people, from those whose speech is corrupt.
Proverbs 2:12

August 3

**Read
Proverbs 3**

✳

WORTHY COMPANIONS

*My child, don't lose
sight of good
planning and insight.
Hang on to them, for
they fill you with life
and bring you honor
and respect.*
Proverbs 3:21-22

Sometimes in our rush to "do" the next thing on the horizon, we don't take time to thoughtfully create a plan of action. As a result, we stumble into the future, fueled only by the ravenous desire for a dream. When our eyes are focused on a future goal, we can steady our gaze with a firm grasp on a good plan.

Before treading on new ground, it is a good idea to take a look over our shoulder. Enthusiasm is a poor substitute for evaluation. Pinpointing prior mistakes in previous ventures decreases our chances of repeating them. Also, incorporating the insights of those who have already achieved similar life-goals (buying a home, adopting a child, etc.) ensures that our own choices will be laced with an honorable legacy. Most importantly, we must diligently seek God's counsel along the way. Goals change, and so do our plans for reaching them. Fortunately, we can rely on God's relevant advice whenever a change of course might arise.

WISE WAYS Who or what is your best earthly resource for planning personal future goals? How are you taking advantage of this resource?

Today, Lord, help me to pattern my plan for the future after your godly ways.

August 4

Ever wonder why a single, well-placed paper cut can create such relentless agony? Even the smallest task like folding letters or jotting a note becomes an impossible feat—comparable to water torture. How can such a small thing command such focus from the entire body?

The Bible refers to the human heart as facing a similar experience. The condition of our heart affects each undertaking without exception. Sure, our lips may let a lie slip past them, but our heart feels the pain. Our fingers may deal a dirty hand to a neighbor or business partner, but our heart is soiled. Guarding our hearts from leading the rest of our members to sin is a full-time job.

Thankfully, God is willing to take our shift. He alone can safely monitor an irregular heartbeat—one that can be arrested by sin at any moment. Through Christ's death on the cross, we can surrender our hearts to his keeping.

WISE WAYS Where is your heart leading you today? Toward ever-increasing godliness? Roads unknown? Perilous pathways? Surrender your heart to God in this moment.

Today, Lord, I surrender the leanings of my heart to your keeping.

**Read
Proverbs 4**

HEART WOUNDS

*Above all else,
guard your heart,
for it affects
everything
you do.*

Proverbs 4:23

August 5

Read
Proverbs 5

SOLID SAVINGS

*If you try to keep
your life for yourself,
you will lose it.
But if you give up
your life for me,
you will find
true life.*
Matthew 16:25

At times life seems like an unsolved mystery. We park in the driveway and drive on the parkway. We say feet "smell," and our noses "run." Likewise, Jesus' method for finding true life may sound like a riddle. Yet, it is no mystery because his truth has been tried and proven. A significant few have discovered the secret to mortal happiness goes something like this: Go last to be first. Lose to win. Die to live. Jesus' words are an ill fit with our natural instincts, yet they are a salve to our spiritual nature. Surrendering selfish pursuits allows us to experience the joy of fulfilling others' needs. Giving up personal gain is the gateway to outrageous satisfaction from God's hand alone.

We must, however, understand that it is impossible to grasp Jesus' intent unless we take him at his word. Experience is the best way to unravel the riddle.

WISE WAYS What selfish pursuits keep you from experiencing the true life Christ offers?

Today, Lord, I will give up finding my own route to satisfaction so I can find favor with you instead.

August 6

A popular female humorist, Erma Bombeck, titled one of her books, *Family: The Ties that Bind . . . and Gag.* How often the words our parents spoke to us in our childhood find their way into our lives, applying just enough pressure to remind us of their timelessness. Regardless of our family experience, the wisdom of the more experienced has girded us throughout our lives. Whether it was a trusted teacher growing up, a godly grandparent in our young adulthood, or a colleague in our first job, most of us have gleaned guidance from others.

Proverbs is just such a collection. It serves as a permanent document of godly wisdom. Were these words written in today's culture, the author might suggest entering words of wisdom in our PDAs or planners—whatever paints a picture of a constant companion. God is able to remind us of the wisdom garnered from others in our moment of need. The words we have stored in our minds and memories can serve to lead, protect, and advise us day to day.

WISE WAYS What is the most helpful advice you've ever received and why? How have you applied that piece of wisdom?

Today, Lord, I am grateful for those who have influenced my life. Remind me of their wisdom and ways when I need it.

**Read
Proverbs 6**

WISDOM STORAGE

Keep their words always in your heart. Tie them around your neck. Wherever you walk, their counsel can lead you. When you sleep, they will protect you. When you wake up in the morning, they will advise you.
Proverbs 6:21-22

August 7

Read Proverbs 7

JUMP!

So she seduced him with her pretty speech. With her flattery she enticed him.

Proverbs 7:21

A scientific experiment once proved that a frog would strangely allow itself to boil to death if placed in lukewarm water that was gradually warmed to a boil. When placed in boiling water first, it naturally leaped to safety. However, the gradual increase in temperature lulled the frog into a false sense of security, for it hardly noticed its weakening muscles until it was too late to jump to safety.

Sound familiar? Perhaps we can't remember the last time we viewed life from the inside of a kettle. But how about being flattered to death within the walls of our own workplace? It starts out slow—a subtle need for people's approval. The extra attention we may receive for a job well done feels nice, soothing. However, we can find our resolve gradually weakened by the warm feelings we get from having our ego stroked. Our craving for affirmation from others can lead to a number of questionable ethics on the job. We may join the office gossip loop to feel included. We may fudge figures to appear successful to our boss. When it boils down to pride, there's a lot to be learned from the frog in the kettle.

WISE WAYS In what ways are you potentially weakened by flattery? Do you consider yourself easily enticed by your ego? Why or why not?

Today, Lord, I praise you for the ways you have protected me from myself. Help me be alert and prepared for temptation of all forms.

August 8

Fifty-one weeks, three days. That's the average amount of time an individual spends in a lifetime looking for lost keys. Wouldn't it be nice to know that once we began searching for a needed item, its location would be instantly revealed? No more wracking our brains to remember the last time we saw it, used it, or heard it. What time we would save from looking between sofa cushions or underneath beds. Instant gratification, guaranteed.

The Bible says that what the natural world cannot offer, the spiritual realm does. Those who seek for wisdom will surely find it. If we treasure wisdom, wisdom will prove invaluable in return. God will not withhold his counsel from us when we earnestly desire to have it. He promises to richly reward our efforts. Satisfaction, guaranteed. With a guarantee like that, what are we waiting for? Let the search begin!

WISE WAYS   If you're reading this, your search for God's wisdom has already begun. What major insights do you feel you've discovered about God's truths so far?

Today, Lord, I pray you will lead me down new paths in my hunt for wisdom. May I search your ways with all my heart.

**Read
Proverbs 8**

SURE OUTCOME

*[Wisdom says,]
"I love all
who love me.
Those who search
for me will surely
find me."*
Proverbs 8:17

August 9

*Wisdom
will multiply
your days and
add years
to your life.*
Proverbs 9:11

It's not a pill, a diet, or a complicated daily regime; however, it is the top-producing technique for increasing our longevity. It has nothing to do with guava juice, gravity weights, or wrinkle analysis, yet it does wonders for our health and vitality. Don't look for it on the Home Shopping Network anytime soon. It can't be sold, bartered for, or bought, yet its value is priceless. Men and women have turned to it with guaranteed results throughout the centuries. It boasts the longest running ad history of any product—its formula has been unchanged since its inception.

Known as Wisdom, it is both prescribed and described within the pages of the Bible. Whoever takes wisdom to heart will experience the quality of life we were meant to share. It relieves stress under pressure. It cures our heartaches and changes our attitudes. It offers perspective on persecution. Wisdom can lance our emotional ailments and thereby increase our physical health as well. Indeed, is it any wonder that it is the greatest health secret of the ages?

WISE WAYS   How can you apply the practice of wisdom to decrease the sources of stress in your life?

Today, Lord, I need help applying wisdom to my life's ailments. Deliver me from my insistence on fixing my own pain. Instead, may I lean on your counsel.

August 10

Correction is a blessing; constructive criticism is a gift. However, no one looks forward to receiving either one! The Bible concedes that discipline is not enjoyable, but it is necessary for our growth.

We can consider it this way. Suppose a fellow driver points out that we have a flat tire. How ridiculous it would be for us to get mad at the person who pointed out the flat. If we continued driving with our flat tire, we would then become a hazard for others on the road, as well as causing damage to our car.

Those who refuse to be corrected allow pride and insecurity to take the wheel. They are a road hazard on the pathway to peace. It's best that we stay out of their way. In contrast, the person who responds to correction is able to enter the roadway again—better equipped for the future.

WISE WAYS   What is your first reaction to correction when you are wrong? Why is that?

Today, Lord, open the parts of me that I have closed off to correction. May your discipline bring me up to speed on the pathway of life.

Read
Proverbs 10

OVERLOOKING THE OBVIOUS

People who accept correction are on the pathway to life, but those who ignore it will lead others astray.

Proverbs 10:17

August 11

Read Proverbs 11

LEFT BEHIND

Evil people get rich for the moment, but the reward of the godly will last.

Proverbs 11:18

Hearses do not have hitches—a reminder that when our time comes to take a ride in a hearse, whatever we have amassed on earth is staying right here. Believers and unbelievers alike have the same return on material investments—they will all lie in the dust at the end of our earthly life. While a corporate culprit may take in hoards of ill-gotten gain (holed away in Swiss accounts), a righteous person's portfolio is more diversified. As any financial advisor will reveal, it is the length of the term, not the amount of the investment, that matters.

Earthly gain for the moment cannot compare to an eternal reward. A virtuous person maintains a heavenly account of spiritual rewards that has thousands upon thousands of years to accrue unlimited interest. Understandably, Wall Street has nothing on heaven. One measures wealth in a teacup over time; the other doles it out in perpetual waves across eternity. The godly can amass untold heavenly wealth from a lifetime of Christlike living.

WISE WAYS   In what ways are you investing for eternity? How does your focus on momentary wealth compare?

Lord, help me keep my sights set on the long-term benefits of loving and serving you.

August 12

SABBATH

When Jesus quoted Deuteronomy 6:5, he purposely included the mind as one of the personal channels of our love for God. By doing so, he clarified the scope of our relationship with God. We are expected to love the Lord completely. In this case, our love must be conscious and thoughtful.

In a world where faith is often described as a characteristic of people who don't think, Jesus' words point to the importance of engaging our minds as a central aspect of what we believe. Jesus spoke of himself as the truth (John 14:6). The Bible repeatedly claims to be true and reliable (Psalm 19:7-11; 119:151; 2 Timothy 3:16).

Truth keeps the mind healthy. Every day, our minds have to digest large quantities of mental junk food. If we do not include truth in our thought diet, we will have malnourished minds. The daily discipline of thinking about God's Word will result in spiritual health.

WISE WAYS   The mental effort of these daily thought-exercises in Proverbs will be good for your mental and spiritual health.

Lord Jesus, teach me to apply my mind to think about you and your Word as part of loving you.

Read
Proverbs 12

MINDFUL LOVE

Jesus replied, "The most important commandment is this: 'Hear, O Israel! The Lord our God is the one and only Lord. And you must love the Lord your God with all your heart, all your soul, all your mind, and all your strength.' The second is equally important: 'Love your neighbor as yourself.' No other commandment is greater than these."
Mark 12:29-31

August 13

**Read
Proverbs 13**

LIVING WATER

*The advice of the
wise is like a life-
giving fountain;
those who accept it
avoid the snares
of death.*

Proverbs 13:14

It's like the full-body rush we feel when we dive into a swimming pool on an August afternoon. Getting the right advice in the time of need can't be beat. But not just any kind of advice will bring us relief.

Unfortunately, soliciting advice from the wrong source is like diving into the deep end of failure. This proverb encourages us to seek the counsel of the well advised. Think of it as creating an advisory board for our lives. Imagine eight empty chairs around a large conference table, with Christ seated at the head. These chairs represent where our most trusted advisors reside in our minds. One chair represents someone we would turn to in financial areas; another chair is for our spiritual advisor; another seats the one called upon for family concerns, and so on. In times of need, the benefit of their resources and experience may only be a phone call away.

WISE WAYS What names come to mind on the advisory board of your life?

Today, Lord, I am thankful for the times I have received godly advice from good people. Bless them today for their faithful work.

August 14

If this proverb referenced only our literal neighbors, some of us would be hard-pressed to find a financially challenged one in the bunch. We can broaden the principle revealed in the proverb by considering anyone in a poor, pitiful situation to be "one's neighbor." Ironically, the poorest "neighbors" of all can include those who may be substantially wealthy, yet without a friend in the world. They find themselves in the unenviable position of loneliness at the top. Our "neighbors" are those who have gone through a messy divorce, bankruptcy, or other public humiliation and suddenly find their social circle has shrunk significantly. Those whom the world finds easiest to despise—perhaps in fear of becoming like them and sharing their fate—are our neighbors.

The Bible reminds us that it is wrong to ride with the tide of public opinion when it despises those in need. Instead, we are called to help our neighbor by offering friendship and the reassurance of support. We are commanded to welcome those "survivors" whom society has voted off the island. In fact, we are to consider them as close as . . . neighbors.

WISE WAYS Who comes to mind when you think of "neighbors" in this way? What can you do to help them and so receive God's blessing?

Today, Lord, keep my eyes fixed on those from whom I'd rather turn away. Move me to help them however I can.

**Read
Proverbs 14**

GOOD NEIGHBORS

It is sin to despise one's neighbors; blessed are those who help the poor.
Proverbs 14:21

August 15

**Read
Proverbs 15**

REAL TREASURE

*It is better to have
little with fear for the
LORD than to have
great treasure with
turmoil.*
Proverbs 15:16

Imagine being offered a luxurious town home filled
with all the comforts and conveniences money can
buy. It is the ultimate offer in terms of finery and
decorum. There is only one stipulation. The quarters
must be shared with one, modest-sized elephant.
That's all. The zenith of luxury living offered in
exchange for enduring a gigantic problem.

The reality of this ridiculous illustration is no
exaggeration for some folks. Some people have the
freedom to buy anything their hearts desire, yet they
are confined by mammoth-sized grief, divorced
families, spoiled children who haven't spoken to
them in years, so-called friends who use them for
position, or impatient lawyers bringing bad news.
For them, that fleeting but terrifying feeling just
before retiring at night is that the weight of their
growing grief may one day trample them. Meanwhile, the God-fearing family with comparably little
material wealth sleeps soundly in their beds. The
Bible teaches that God's awesome presence is a
believer's true treasure.

WISE WAYS   In what ways have you personally
experienced or observed the truth of this Proverb?
What lessons have you learned?

*Today, Lord, I praise you for being my true treasure. Help me value
my relationship with you above all else.*

August 16

Gossip is to a friendship what weeds are to a garden. As weeds choke a garden, so gossip saps the strength and chokes the growth of relationships. The Bible highlights dozens of friendships and relationships built on qualities like trust, affection, mutual purpose, and mission. Such words characterize the intense bond between biblical characters like David and Jonathan, Priscilla and Aquila, and Paul and Silas.

When we gossip with close friends, a subtle change affects our friendship. Our dearest friends may become haunted by the persistent thought that maybe they would find their own name as our hot topic in another social circle. Who's to say we wouldn't slice and dice them, too, if the opportunity arose? We may never betray a best friend by gossip, but human nature allows the suspicion to remain. By publicly dismantling another person's dignity, even within the intimacy of a close circle of friends, we have demonstrated the destruction we are capable of doing.

WISE WAYS How do you deal with the temptation to gossip? When are you most tempted to gossip?

Today, Lord, help me deal with gossip in a godly way. Help me spread only good news instead.

**Read
Proverbs 16**

GOSSIP CROP

A troublemaker plants seeds of strife; gossip separates the best of friends.
Proverbs 16:28

August 17

Read
Proverbs 17

✳

LESSON ON
LOYALTY

*A friend is always
loyal, and a brother
is born to help in
time of need.*
Proverbs 17:17

We can choose our friends, but not our families. A less touted observation is the Bible's reminder against cafeteria-style loyalties with friends or family members. We don't have the option to pick and choose which friends or family members we will be loyal to at which times. When families run into hard times, Proverbs boasts that the idea of the family unit was birthed for just such a purpose. Similarly, true friends are not only loyal; they are always loyal in their intent. Going the second mile is second nature to the believer. If a friend or family member is in need, a believer does whatever is possible to meet that need.

Why such an emphasis on loyalty? Christian relationships—friendships or marriages or families—are to model Christ's own relationship with believers as a witness to the world. In fact, the Bible emphasizes that the world will take note of our loyalty or lack thereof. How well we demonstrate our willingness to honor a commitment to family or friends is a strong testimony for or against the legitimacy of the Christian faith.

WISE WAYS Which relationships are easiest for maintaining loyalty? Which are most taxing? How can you strengthen your resolve today?

Today, Lord, I am aware of friends and family members with whom I have struggled. Motivate me to work on my commitments as a testimony to your grace.

August 18

Although believers are privy to a supernatural experience, we are not superhuman. While we dwell on this earth, we will get mud on our shoes and rain on our heads. We may become well acquainted with illness, disease, calamity, and catastrophe. Through all this, God can infuse the human spirit with courage to bear up through whatever earthly trials come our way. Though we may reach the depths of depression, we can endure because of the hope of Christ.

However, the Bible teaches that the ultimate sadness is the devastation of a crushed spirit apart from Christ. God infuses the spirit with life; sin bears down on the spirit with ever-increasing pressure, crushing it with hopelessness. These broken lives pass us in the aisles of grocery stores and stand in line beside us at the theater. They are a reminder that we are unable to save ourselves from the hopelessness of life without Christ. Whatever believers may experience, we can endure because of Christ. However, no one can bear up alone under a life with no hope.

WISE WAYS   How often do you consider your situations or trials hopeless? How does the hope of Christ's presence help change your perspective?

Today, Lord, I know I can endure my trials because I am relying on you. Encourage my spirit and make me strong.

**Read
Proverbs 18**

RUN DOWN

The human spirit can endure a sick body, but who can bear it if the spirit is crushed?

Proverbs 18:14

August 19

**Read
Proverbs 19**

PRICELESS SOUL

*And how do you
benefit if you gain
the whole world but
lose your own soul
in the process?
Is anything worth
more than your
soul?*

Matthew 16:26

How many people gain a promotion only to lose
their principles along the way? How many business
tycoons focus their mental energies on gaining
material fortune only to lose their families due to
neglect? As pitiful as these stories are, Jesus points
to a more frightening proposition. It is possible to
gain everything this life has to offer and yet lose our
souls. We risk losing the only thing we take with us
from this life into the next: our soul. Jesus proves
the point of his proverb in the form of a question—
not a mandate. No one can answer for us—we must
answer his inquiry for ourselves.

What will we benefit from our earthly gains?
When we are caught up in a materialistic moment,
we can lose sight of what really matters in light of
eternity. Jesus reminds us that preparedness is
essential when it pertains to eternal life.

WISE WAYS In what ways are you tempted to lose
sight of what really matters in life? How can you
tighten your grip on eternal matters?

*Today, Lord, many things will attempt to draw away my focus from
what really matters. Steady my gaze and tighten my grip.*

August 20

There are a few select phrases that delight the ears of almost anyone: "Let me do the dishes" or "Who wants this last piece of cake?" for example. Moreover, there are particular words that just feel good on the tongue: "I have the day off" and "I think I'll take a nap" are near the top of the list. However, there is a unique phrase (with many variations) that we may love to say, but dread hearing from anyone else: "I will get even."

Vengeance—it's the variation on a theme repeated throughout literature, prose, history, film, and fantasy. Whenever we are harmed, we rush to our idea of justice. Taking matters into our shaky hands, we often handle the situation poorly. Instead, the Bible offers a panacea to personal injury: wait. Wait on God to handle the matter. Like a mother arranging for the father to deal the goods to an undisciplined child, so we can bequeath our right to repay. We can summon our heavenly Father to right the wrong according to his ways.

WISE WAYS How can you keep from seeking vengeance on those who hurt you? What is the most difficult thing about waiting on God to repay?

Today, Lord, grant me the wisdom to wait. When I am hurt, angry, or frustrated, help me to set vengeful thoughts aside.

**Read
Proverbs 20**

DIVINE BACKUP

*Don't say,
"I will get even
for this wrong."
Wait for the LORD to
handle the matter.*

Proverbs 20:22

August 21

**Read
Proverbs 21**

JUSTICE
ASSURED

*Justice is a joy
to the godly,
but it causes
dismay among
evildoers.*
Proverbs 21:15

Justice is a two-sided proposition. One side represents the joy we experience when we see a wrong righted. An abuser is arrested. A criminal is caught. If we are on the proper side of justice, fear is unnecessary. We can relax and rejoice when justice is administered in a situation. In contrast, those who receive its penalty experience another side of justice altogether. Guilty participants ponder life in the penitentiary as punishment for their crime. The penalty that accompanies justice disheartens an unrepentant delinquent. Such indignant offenders don't want justice to be rendered in their case.

Ultimately, justice is a joyous experience for believers because of the certainty of heaven's reward. Likewise, evildoers find nothing to celebrate. Final justice will rest upon them. The Bible warns us to be on the proper side of justice—both in an earthly and eternal sense. We can then live without fear and with great joy, celebrating God's justice on earth and in heaven.

WISE WAYS In what ways can you actively promote justice in your home, work, school, or community?

Today, Lord, may I stand for what is right in all situations and rejoice.

August 22

Analogy is a favorite tool of Proverbs. Comparing two items demonstrates the relationship between them. In this case, the rich rule the poor because of the balance of power. Their relationship is dependent upon the concept of supply and demand. The rich have what the poor need. In the same way, this proverb exposes the balance of power between a lender and a borrower. A servant is dependent upon another in the same way borrowers become dependent upon a bank or other lender. Whether or not we should borrow money is not at issue.

This truth simply emphasizes the seriousness of such a move. The comparison is a vivid picture of our commitment to repaying our debt. Though we may enjoy the benefit of a loan, the balance of power remains in the lender's hands. We ought to fully understand the dependent relationship that is created whenever we borrow money. Understanding is the first step to applying what the Bible teaches about integrity and money.

WISE WAYS Why do you think a servant is a good picture for understanding the relationship between a lender and borrower?

Today, Lord, help me realize that I am indebted to you for all of my resources. May I be a good manager of what you give to me.

**Read
Proverbs 22**

DEBT SERVICE

*Just as the rich
rule the poor,
so the borrower
is servant to
the lender.*
Proverbs 22:7

August 23

**Read
Proberbs 23**

✳

WISDOM
SHOPPING

*Get the truth and
don't ever sell it;
also get wisdom,
discipline, and
discernment.*

Proverbs 23:23

When spiritual hunger strikes, we have options. We can starve, we can bargain-hunt in earthly resources, or we can turn to God for the goods. Too often, we are tempted to go to the convenience store of earthly resources instead of God's Word. We pick up a bargain brand of humanism in place of God's truth. Instead of scriptural self-discipline, we take home the latest self-help CD. We would rather skim a horoscope than whisper a prayer for wisdom.

In contrast, Proverbs is a shopper's paradise—a wealth of resources at our fingertips. We can pick up exactly what we need: a handy answer to that nagging problem, a bit of advice concerning a family member. This particular proverb contains a shopping list of the essentials for Christlike living. They are a saint's staples—a farmer's market of fundamentals. As if they were called out by a hungry soul to a hastening shopper: "While you're out, get Truth. Also get Wisdom if you see it. Discipline. And one more thing: Discernment." We can make a meal out of these goods that will truly satisfy our soul.

WISE WAYS Where do you most often "shop" to find the answer to a problem? Why is bargain-hunting for truth so tempting yet so disappointing?

Today, Lord, thank you for the resources you have given me in Scripture. Help me to turn to your Word for my daily needs.

August 24

When the ruthless beat out the righteous for the next promotion at work, we may begin to envy them. When the malicious go unpunished, the disparity between what seems fair and what is reality causes great frustration. We become convinced that if we are "nice," we are destined to "finish last." However, that's just it: we're not finished yet. Like a hiker cresting the top of a mountain peak, only to see the horizon littered with higher and higher peaks, we must remember that the journey has just begun.

Life on earth—for the godly and the ungodly—is but one peak from God's perspective. Many people may cheat to climb higher, stepping on the heads of the righteous for a foothold. However, while they may enjoy the pinnacle experience of life on earth, sadly, it will be their only summit. The Bible teaches that there is no future for evildoers. While the righteous will continue to ascend the light of eternity, evildoers are "snuffed out" and doomed to descend into darkness.

WISE WAYS   Why might you envy the wicked? How does God's perspective help you deal with this temptation?

Today, Lord, may I not waiver between worry and envy when it comes to the wicked. Help me to trust that righteousness will win out in the end.

**Read
Proverbs 24**

WISE JOURNEY

Do not fret because of evildoers; don't envy the wicked. For the evil have no future; their light will be snuffed out.
Proverbs 24:19-20

August 25

**Read
Proverbs 25**

✳

SENSITIVE REPERTOIRE

*Singing cheerful
songs to a person
whose heart is heavy
is as bad as stealing
someone's jacket in
cold weather or
rubbing salt in a
wound.*
Proverbs 25:20

Early radar systems functioned with such dulled sensitivity that they often picked up a flock of birds as a formation of planes. Imagine the resulting mishaps, wrong landings, and missed calculations! In the same way, our sluggish sensitivity to others' needs causes us to misfire when it matters most. We are often too preoccupied with ourselves to even pick up on others' feelings or emotions. Instead, we carry on with our own cheery selves—indifferent to those with heavy hearts.

This proverb vividly illustrates coming upon someone in need, only to leave that person in worse condition! Proverbs sharpens our radar images, teaching us to notice. Instead of overlooking and further saddening a person who already feels ignored, we can stop and take note. Practicing the proverbs makes us helpful in that moment. Instead of unrealistic platitudes or other efforts likened to salt in a wound, we can learn heartfelt ways that offer salve to someone who is hurting.

WISE WAYS Who may need your encouragement today? How can you notice and help today?

Today, Lord, I want to be tuned in to the needs of others. Show me how to be helpful with my words and actions.

August 26

SABBATH

Like wearing rival colors at our alma mater's home football game, the Bible teaches that godliness is countercultural, often resulting in persecution. We can be thankful that the typical Western experience of persecution is not life threatening, but it remains uncomfortable, aggravating, and, at times, lonely. We may be ostracized from social events because of our faith. We may undergo criticism for upholding standards for our children—sometimes even within our own ranks. Persecution in the workplace may mean being passed over for promotions. Amid all our persecution, God's promise is his presence and power.

Like a medal of honor, the kingdom of Heaven is a reward for such endurance. However, just as veterans alone know the true value of a medal of honor, we will only realize the truth of this verse if we experience it. The goal is not a higher rating on the persecution meter. Rather, we should only be concerned with how overtly we live out our faith.

WISE WAYS   In what areas do you feel you are persecuted because of your faith? Why do you think God chooses to bless those who are persecuted?

Today, Lord, there are those who don't understand what I am about. Encourage me with a spirit of rejoicing whenever I am misunderstood.

Read
Proverbs 26

POSTHUMOUS AWARDS

God blesses those who are persecuted because they live for God, for the Kingdom of Heaven is theirs.

Matthew 5:10

August 27

SUNRISE EXUBERANCE

*If you shout a
pleasant greeting to
your neighbor too
early in the morning,
it will be counted as
a curse!*
Proverbs 27:14

Like a linguist, Proverbs explores the power of the tongue in a number of different ways. It weaves together the words we say and the motives behind them to create revelations about human nature. At first glance, the emphasis in this proverb appears no deeper than a chuckle—clearly, this neighbor is not a morning person. However, consider the motive of the zealous greeter. Why was the greeter up at such an hour? Why go out of the way to call for the neighbor's attention? Perhaps the pleasant greeting was a form of flattery with a person of influence— one with high standing in the community. Maybe that person had something the eager greeter desperately wanted. Whenever we trip over ourselves to get another person's attention, we present a questionable motive. Are we trying too hard to impress? Are we attempting to elevate ourselves in society or the workplace instead of waiting on God's direction?

Proverbs reminds us that such a venture often meets with disappointment. We can actually lose ground with such a "greeting." Better to wait on God's timing than force our own.

WISE WAYS How are you tempted to impress people of influence for personal gain? What is the better way to make a good impression?

Today, Lord, I know that I have tried too hard sometimes to impress someone. Help me to maintain pure motives in all my interaction with others.

August 28

Late-night TV's sleep-inducing, snowy rendition of "The Star-Spangled Banner" (signaling the television was going to bed before we were) has new competition in town: the dawn of the infomercial. Now, we can enjoy back-to-back testimonials from fellow insomniacs who ordered the latest moneymaking ploy package and retired in an Italian villa six months later.

The Bible warns us of the get-rich-quick scheme, but not because making money is inherently evil. Money is not the issue. The pursuit of money is more the point. Those who want money above all else are destined for troubling temptations. Tax evasion. Fraud. Debt. Chapter 13.

When we want to be faithful more than we want to be rich, a funny thing happens. Money finally finds its proper place in our lives. We begin to see the fruit of faithfulness, such as ripened relationships nourished by integrity, as a more valuable commodity. Though our bank statements may never be summoned as a television testimonial, the quality of our lives will testify to our rich reward.

WISE WAYS How do you know you hold money in the right perspective? In what ways is faithfulness richly rewarded?

Today, Lord, help me to want to be faithful above any other earthly desire. Lead me to taste and enjoy the fruit of being trustworthy.

Read Proverbs 28

DANGEROUS SPEED

The trustworthy will get a rich reward. But the person who wants to get rich quick will only get into trouble.
Proverbs 28:20

August 29

Read
Proverbs 29

✳

GRACEFUL
LIVING

*There is more hope
for a fool than for
someone who speaks
without thinking.*

Proverbs 29:20

Miss Manners, Peggy Post, and Martha Stewart make a robust living off the premise that some things are just not done. The published pontiffs of politeness agree: opening our mouths with our foot nearby is one of them. This proverb reminds us how someone who speaks without thinking is worse off than the fool who doesn't know any better. There is hope for fools to recover gracefully—no one expects anything from them. However, when it comes to being able to inflict pain with our words, friends, not fools, have the edge.

Proverbs reminds us that our tongues contain the power to ravage a friendship when our speech is not in sync with our minds. Until we have prayed through a piece of advice for a friend, we have no right to share it. Unless we have thought through our own responsibility in the matter, we can't adequately bring up a grievance against another person. Thinking it through before speaking our minds can save many people a lot of wasted and hurtful words.

WISE WAYS   How can you avoid saying something you might regret? When are you most tempted to speak without thinking?

Today, Lord, may my words be few. Give me wisdom to speak only what is important and encouraging today.

August 30

The bully of the big screen is a familiar stereotype. The bully walks into the school cafeteria and snatches a meatball sandwich out of the scrawny kid's fumbling fingers. After gorging on the poor kid's meal in plain view, the remorseless bully eyeballs the cowering crowd and says incredulously, "What are you lookin' at?" End of scene.

The star of this proverb acts out a similar screenplay—only with much higher stakes. It is a frightening picture of how we can be so driven by our sinful appetites that it becomes impossible for us to be remorseful. The imagery is of a woman shrugging off her indulgence. It warns us of times when, instead of repenting of our actions, we justify them. Not only are we steeped in sin; we cease to see our sin as sinful. Many people call such action a choice, a mere lifestyle like any other. Scripture calls it "amazing."

WISE WAYS When do you find yourself rationalizing questionable behavior? How do you deal with the temptation to justify sin?

Today, Lord, may I remember what it is like to be truly sorry for my sins. Teach me how to repent.

Read Proverbs 30

DENIAL IS NO RIVER

Equally amazing is how an adulterous woman can satisfy her sexual appetite, shrug her shoulders, and then say, "What's wrong with that?"
Proverbs 30:20

August 31

**Read
Proverbs 31**

WISDOM APPLIED

*When she speaks,
her words are wise,
and kindness
is the rule
when she gives
instructions.*
Proverbs 31:26

Which is easier: giving instructions or following them? While it is often easier to make up the rules than follow someone else's, life requires us to be adept at both. In the same way, leadership is both leading and following.

This proverb gives us insight into a person's reputation for leading. How often do we run across an authority figure whose words are wise each time he or she speaks? How many in positions of power follow the rule of kindness in exercising their role? If others can express similar affirmations about our style of leadership, then we are in sync with scriptural command. However, too often, leaders are memorable for less than godly reasons.

Leadership may be a heady experience, though it should never be a head-trip. When we use kindness as our governing rule, we will honor, not abuse, those who are under our authority—from coworkers to family members. Our reputation for leading others should emerge from a commitment to wisdom and kindness.

WISE WAYS   How do you want others to view your style of leadership? Why is that?

Today, Lord, I want to strive for a reputation that honors you. May my words be wise and my actions result in kindness.

SEPTEMBER

September 1

AN AWESOME GOD

*I will not answer
when they cry for
help. Even though
they anxiously search
for me, they will not
find me. For they
hated knowledge
and chose not to
fear the LORD.*
Proverbs 1:28-29

In 1988 Rich Mullins wrote a worship song titled
"Awesome God." Its familiar lyrics highlight biblical
events that display the awe-inspiring character of
God. The chorus begins and ends giving honor to
God's greatness. Indeed, our God is awesome—in
the fullest sense of the word. Although we often hear
of God's great love for us and his mercy toward us,
we must never forget his incomprehensible gran-
deur. Hebrews 10:31 says that it is "a terrible thing
to fall into the hands of the living God." And
Galatians 6:7 warns us: "Don't be misled. Remember that you can't ignore God and get away with it.
You will always reap what you sow!"

Our wise, powerful, and loving God earnestly
desires to fellowship with us. But when we "hate
knowledge and choose not to fear him," we will find
the heavens as hard as iron, and our God as illusive
as vapor. Let us always approach our God with a
healthy respect for his majesty and holiness.

WISE WAYS In what areas of your life have you
hated knowledge and not feared God? Remember,
God will look upon us as we humble ourselves before
him (Isaiah 66:2).

*Today, Lord, take my hardened heart and make it fear you. Show
me the glory of your righteousness and the beauty of your ways.*

September 2

SABBATH

When God created us in his image and for his glory, he gave us gifts. He made us unique by giving us each certain abilities, talents, and character traits in a combination no one else possesses. Later, when we became believers, certain spiritual gifts were added to the original package (see 1 Corinthians 12).

Each of us has different gifts and in differing measures, but God would have us all use them for his purposes. Sometimes we doubt that we're gifted, or we're not sure how to use our gifts in the situations in which God has placed us. As we remember that the very air we breathe is a gift from our Creator, we can trust that he has total creative rights over all his creation, and that he will guide us in the use of our giftedness.

Accordingly, as we remember his goodness and kindness towards us, we can come before him and say, "Father, all that I have is yours, and I lay it at your feet." Then, we can go out into the world, determined to use the gifts that he has given us to glorify his awesome name.

WISE WAYS Are you seeking to use your gifts for God's glory? In what ways can you make use of the gifts God has given you?

Today, Lord, help me to recognize my gifts and to use them in ways that glorify you.

Read
Proverbs 2

A USEFUL GIFT

To those who use well what they are given, even more will be given, and they will have an abundance. But from those who are unfaithful, even what little they have will be taken away.

Matthew 25:29

September 3

**Read
Proverbs 3**

✳

AN INCLINATION TO SERVE

*Do not withhold good
from those who
deserve it when it's in
your power to help
them. If you can help
your neighbor now,
don't say, "Come back
tomorrow, and then
I'll help you."*

Proverbs 3:27-28

Have you ever met someone whose good intentions
were just on the other side of a winning lottery
ticket? You know, the kind of person who says, "If I
just win this money or that sweepstakes, I'll do all
these wonderful things."

We may all fantasize about what we would do with
a million dollars, but God wants to use us to do
wonderful things right now. We must remember that
our Father's heart overflows with love and compassion for the poor and hurting. As we walk more fully
in his will, we should reach out to help those in need
with whatever resources we already possess.

This proverb points out how easy it is to withhold
help from others under the excuse that we need what
we have in order to have even more to give in the
future. Such an attitude actually betrays a tendency
to never give at all. Remember, Jesus promised a
reward to those who did good to others, for he
likened it to doing good to him (Matthew 25:40).

WISE WAYS How can you start giving practically
toward those around you who are in need?

*Today, Lord, show me someone who needs to be shown your love in
a practical way, and use me to meet that person's need.*

September 4

We all know that our tongues are powerful weapons. Through them, we have the power to build up a hurting friend or to mercilessly tear down those who have offended us. But do we realize that the words we speak reveal the true character of the innermost depths of our hearts? There is a direct connection between what we say and who we actually are.

Jesus said, "For whatever is in your heart determines what you will say" (Matthew 12:34). So, when we engage in "perverse talk" and "corrupt speech," we show the very sinfulness of our own hearts. In order to "avoid," we may also have to consider the company we keep. Our prayers should echo the psalmist's: "May the words of my mouth and the thoughts of my heart be pleasing to you, O Lord, my rock and my redeemer" (Psalm 19:14).

WISE WAYS Would "perverse talk" or "corrupt speech" describe any of your words today? In what ways? What do you need to do to avoid such talk?

Today, Lord, change my heart so that the overflow of my lips is pleasing to you.

Read
Proverbs 4

THE POTENT TONGUE

Avoid all perverse talk; stay far from corrupt speech.
Proverbs 4:24

September 5

Read
Proverbs 5

MARITAL BLISS

*Let your wife be a
fountain of blessing
for you.
Rejoice in the wife
of your youth.*

Proverbs 5:18

When God created people in the Garden of Eden, he created us male and female. In his wisdom, our Father created two distinct sexes that would each represent his glory throughout his creation. But he didn't stop there. God ordained that the two would become one flesh, and so present a picture of Jesus and his church (Ephesians 5:22-32), united by love. We need only look briefly at the world around us to see how that image has been attacked and distorted.

The proverb, meant for a son, highlights the effects and blessings of a healthy marriage. The "let" indicates how important it is for marriage partners to allow or expect each other to be a benefit in their lives. When we "rejoice" in our spouse, we allow him or her to know the significant and wonderful difference he or she is making in our lives.

May we recommit ourselves to loving and serving each other, and to showing forth the love of God through our families.

WISE WAYS   Are you letting your spouse be a blessing, and are you rejoicing in him or her? Are you a blessing to your spouse, someone in whom he or she can rejoice?

Today, Lord, teach me to better love and serve my family, and to rejoice in the blessings that you have given me.

September 6

We don't like to be told that we are wrong. It is an affront to our pride. And so, in our self-assuredness, we often push ahead with our own plans, presuming that we know better than God. It's the same lie that Adam and Eve bought into in the garden. Satan said, "You won't die!" (Genesis 3:4), and they believed him above God, and turned their backs on the Father.

The Proverbs reiterate over and over again that it is the fool who spurns correction. An honest look at our own lives and hearts will show us that God is infinitely better equipped to be Lord of our lives. Therefore, let us humble ourselves and seek his direction. Then, when we fail and need correction, we will have another opportunity to demonstrate that we do trust him to straighten us out.

WISE WAYS How have you ignored the commands and correction of your heavenly Father? What do you need to do to listen to him better?

Today, Lord, teach me the way of life. Soften my heart to yield to your truth and to rejoice in the beauty of your commands.

**Read
Proverbs 6**

REPROOF
FOR LIFE

For these commands and this teaching are a lamp to light the way ahead of you. The correction of discipline is the way to life.

Proverbs 6:23

September 7

Read Proverbs 7

✳

SIN'S ATTRACTION

He followed her at once, like an ox going to the slaughter or like a trapped stag, awaiting the arrow that would pierce its heart. He was like a bird flying into a snare, little knowing it would cost him his life.

Proverbs 7:22-23

Oh, the compelling attractiveness of sin! Even though we know that what we're pursuing will destroy us, our hearts lust after that which can only give us passing pleasure at best. This proverb pictures that all-too-familiar moment when we consciously decide to go our own way. The sinful temptation may not be as obvious, but our sudden fall shares similarities with the young man's choice.

The Apostle Paul wrote candidly about his struggle: "I don't understand myself at all, for I really want to do what is right, but I don't do it. Instead, I do the very thing I hate" (Romans 7:15). We love our sins so much that we follow them blindly to our destruction. May God revitalize our hearts and open our eyes to the reality that "everything else is worthless when compared with the priceless gain of knowing Christ Jesus" (Philippians 3:8).

WISE WAYS   In what areas of your life are you valuing the world's offerings more than God's righteousness?

Today, Lord, show me the folly of my sinful ways. Help me to desire your righteousness more than anything that this world has to offer.

September 8

Why would it matter that the first thing formed in all Creation was wisdom? Before God began to create the physical items—earth, stars, moon, animals, fish, plants, and planets—God decided on a way, an approach, he would use in Creation. That way was wisdom. Creation didn't result from a random, miscellaneous approach to building an intricate system. God may have created instantly, but he didn't create haphazardly!

We've discovered that even what appears to be in chaos in the universe exhibits order at some level. Wisdom shouts from the organization, intricacy, balance, and wonder of Creation. God decided, by using wisdom, that every molecule of Creation would give evidence of its Creator. This is why the psalmist was stating a profound truth when he wrote, "The heavens tell of the glory of God. The skies display his marvelous craftsmanship" (Psalm 19:1).

WISE WAYS You can reflect God's wisdom when you express wonder and gratitude for his Creation. In what ways can you express that thankfulness today?

Today, Lord, teach me to see myself and those around me as incredibly precious, made for your glory, and created through wisdom.

Read
Proverbs 8

PRIORITY IN
CREATION

The LORD formed me from the beginning, before he created anything else.
Proverbs 8:22

September 9

Read
Proverbs 9

STRONG LOVE

Jesus replied, "The
most important
commandment is this:
'Hear, O Israel! The
Lord our God is the
one and only Lord.
And you must love the
Lord your God with
all your heart, all your
soul, all your mind,
and all your strength.'
The second is equally
important: 'Love your
neighbor as yourself.'
No other
commandment is
greater than these."

Mark 12:29-31

The phrase "all your strength" must not lead us to the conclusion that a robust and energetic love for God would be something impressive. We sometimes read this verse as if Jesus said, "Love the Lord your God with . . . all your great strength." Instead, we ought to quietly consider that what he meant was, "Love the Lord your God with all of what little strength you actually possess."

Jesus measured qualities like strength and faith by comparing them to mustard seeds (Matthew 17:20). In the context of the great commandment, if heart-love is characterized by spontaneity, then strength-love involves a conscious effort. For instance, attentive worship takes energy. If we stay out late Saturday night, we may fall asleep during our worship. What are we communicating to the Lord when we say "I love you" while yawning? The "little strength" we have should come as a result of effort expended for the Lord, not because we are too tired to give even our leftover strength to God.

WISE WAYS   Consider where you are expending most of your "strength." Is God getting your best? What one new thing can you do today to show your love for God?

Today, Lord, help me to love you with everything I am, in everything I do.

September 10

Sometimes, we just like the sound of our own voices. We may be tired, excited, or angry; but we need to tell someone what's on our mind. Yet how often in the midst of those talkative times do we say something that we later regret? Whether it's a juicy bit of gossip or a rash comeback, our intemperate tongues can bring upon us a multitude of troubles.

That's why God counsels us to guard our words. The flow, says this proverb, "fosters sin." The wise observation has to do with percentages; the more we talk the greater the chance we will say something we regret. Silence not only allows us to avoid error; it provides added time to consider what we are saying before we eventually speak!

WISE WAYS   What can you do to remind yourself to control your tongue in difficult situations?

Today, Lord, help me to speak in ways that honor you. Help me to be silent when that honors you as well.

Read
Proverbs 10

A VERBAL FAUCET

Don't talk too much, for it fosters sin. Be sensible and turn off the flow!
Proverbs 10:19

September 11

Read
Proverbs 11

✳

GOD'S VALUE
SYSTEM

*The LORD hates
people with twisted
hearts, but he
delights in those who
have integrity.*
Proverbs 11:20

Our value system and God's value system are often at odds. Whereas we may admire someone for his or her intelligence, beauty, athletic ability, or charisma, God may remain unimpressed. The Old Testament tells the story of Samuel going to anoint a new king of Israel after Saul had disobeyed God. Samuel came to the sons of Jesse, and he saw David's older brother, Eliab, a tall, handsome man. But God spoke to Samuel, saying in part, "I have rejected him. The LORD doesn't make decisions the way you do! People judge by outward appearance, but the LORD looks at a person's thoughts and intentions" (2 Samuel 16:7).

God is not interested in anything else as much as he is interested in our hearts. It's the place where his presence is rooted or absent in our lives. When God looks in our hearts, he wants to find integrity. May we summon the courage to give him our everything, no matter what the cost, and to be people of integrity.

WISE WAYS   Do you think that your level of integrity causes God to delight in you? Why or why not?

Today, Lord, guard my heart from the twisted path and show me how to walk in the integrity of your ways.

September 12

When a carpenter begins to build a house, his primary concern is a proper foundation. He knows that no matter how beautiful or well built the rest of the structure is, if the foundation isn't solid, the whole building will go awry. It may take time, but gravity will eventually prove whether or not a foundation is plumb and true.

So it is in our lives. If we build our values and priorities on the foundational truth of the one who claimed to be truth—Jesus (John 14:6)—then time will bear witness to the righteousness of our choice. However, if our foundations aren't true, then all of our flimsy facades will be exposed for the shams that they are. We must pursue God's truth as if our lives depended on it. They do!

WISE WAYS What values have been foundational in your life? In what ways do these foundations honor God?

Today, Lord, lead me into your eternal truth. Show me where I have built on wrong foundations, and help me to build on the truth.

Read Proverbs 12

A WORTHY FOUNDATION

Truth stands the test of time; lies are soon exposed.

Proverbs 12:19

September 13

**Read
Proverbs 13**

A HEALTHY INDECISION

*Wise people think
before they act;
fools don't and
even brag about it!*
Proverbs 13:16

Oh, those pitiful fools! First, they don't fear God, saying that he doesn't even exist. Then, they make rash decisions and brag about their foolishness. How we must pity them—that is, until we realize that sometimes those characteristics strike a little too close to home.

We all have moments of foolishness. We can be thankful that God hasn't given up on us. He may discipline or reprove us, yet, as the Apostle Paul said, "I am sure that God, who began the good work within you, will continue his work until it is finally finished on that day when Christ Jesus comes back again" (Philippians 1:6). Let us be prudent in our decision making, choosing to rely on God and his wisdom, rather than bragging about our foolishness.

WISE WAYS   What action have you done without thinking—and then regretted? How do you think God would have had you respond in that situation?

Today, Lord, help me to lean on you. Keep me from rash decisions. Teach my heart to be patient.

September 14

There are a great many causes of concern in our lives, covering a broad range of importance. Will our income cover our expenses? Will there be a nuclear war? Are my children safe? Will I get cancer? Is there anything I'm missing that I should be worried about?

In the midst of these concerns, there exists a God who has always been and always will be. He created us, he loves us, and he knows our past, present, and future. How great our confidence can be when we bask in the glow of his sovereignty and goodness. We can turn to God—not only in the midst of our hardship, but also in the midst of our prosperity. We can find our identity and value in him. He will always be a refuge—to us and to our children.

WISE WAYS   How has God demonstrated his faithful protection toward you in the past? Recall his goodness, and walk in the confidence your remembrances bring.

Today, Lord, teach me to place my whole trust in you. I want you to be my eternal, unshakable refuge.

**Read
Proverbs 14**

A LASTING PEACE

*Those who fear the
LORD are secure;
he will be a place
of refuge
for their children.*
Proverbs 14:26

September 15

Read
Proverbs 15

✳

THE ULTIMATE FEAST

A bowl of soup with someone you love is better than steak with someone you hate.
Proverbs 15:17

We all long for intimate fellowship with people who care about us enough to speak the truth and love us enough to endure our weaknesses. The Proverbs are full of definitions of true friends. A favorite of many is Proverbs 17:17: "A friend is always loyal, and a brother is born to help in time of need."

When we are with true friends, we don't worry about every little thing we say, we don't try to make awkward conversation during times of silence, and we don't bother composing an appealing facade. We are free to be who we are. It is in that atmosphere of love and acceptance that true fellowship is found. What's on the menu isn't nearly as important as who is sharing the meal with us. We should always strive to be "bowl of soup" friends to those around us.

WISE WAYS   What "bowl of soup" friends do you have in your life? Thank God for his goodness in blessing you with faithful companions.

Today, Lord, help me to be a friend to those around me. Teach me to value them above earthly pleasures.

September 16

Whether we are working our way through Proverbs or turning to the New Testament, the Bible doesn't compromise its position regarding our tongues. We are repeatedly warned to guard our mouths, to think first, and to be slow to speak. While we may reason that our speech isn't so bad, we would do well to consider that God probably knows more than we do. Our tongues have an incredible potential to destroy people. Careless words can cripple friendships, jeopardize relationships, and bring great amounts of hurt into people's lives.

James offers us a proverb with a particularly devastating judgment: "No one can tame the tongue." We may be helpless but we're not hopeless. What is impossible for people is not all that difficult for God. We need God to sanctify our tongues and to make our speech edifying and holy.

WISE WAYS What can you do to remind yourself to guard your tongue? When do you find it better to keep it locked up?

Today, Lord, help me to tame my tongue. Keep me from speaking evil.

**Read
Proverbs 16**

TAMING THE BEAST

People can tame all kinds of animals and birds and reptiles and fish, but no one can tame the tongue. It is an uncontrollable evil, full of deadly poison.
James 3:7-8

September 17

**Read
Proverbs 17**

WITH OPEN EYES

*It is poor judgment to
co-sign a friend's
note, to become
responsible for a
neighbor's debts.*
Proverbs 17:18

When we fell into sin in the Garden of Eden, we fell
hard. Our very natures became corrupted, and one
of the main areas where that sin is manifest is in our
financial decisions. We love money. We love the
power and fun that buying and owning things brings.
One of the danger signs that we may be spending
beyond our stewardship responsibility occurs when
we have to ask someone to co-sign with us for a loan.
What kind of friends are we if we ask others to take
responsibility for our debts?

Jesus cautioned us about loving money, saying,
"You cannot serve God and money" (Matthew 6:24).
Paul warned that "the love of money is at the root of
all kinds of evil" (I Timothy 6:10). In this atmosphere
of corruption, the above proverb provides us with a
welcome caution.

WISE WAYS   What place does money have in your
heart and life?

*Today, Lord, help me to understand how you would have me handle
my finances. Help me to have my financial decisions reflect your
priorities.*

September 18

There's a classic story of a powerful king who was building a mighty new capital for his empire. At the culmination of the construction, he summoned all the wise men of his kingdom and asked them to inscribe a sign that would hang over his castle as an eternal testament to his accomplishment. So, the wise men collaborated and debated for days. When all their work was done, they unveiled their bit of eternal wisdom. Its message: "This Too Shall Pass."

Change is a constant in our lives. Every day brings new challenges and new blessings, and we are fools if we try to live in the past. Churches stagnate under lifeless traditions. People stagnate under empty rules. God created us to be creative, just as he is. The truth of God's Word often comes to us as a new idea; until a certain moment, we were not ready to hear it. If we remain open to the Scriptures, we will discover that they always have a new lesson to teach us.

WISE WAYS Which areas of your life need a flow of new ideas? Ask God to grant you creativity.

Today, Lord, help me to be open to new things. Challenge the parts of my life that have lain dormant for too long, and bring new life to me.

Read
Proverbs 18

SEEKING
WISDOM

Intelligent people are always open to new ideas. In fact, they look for them.
Proverbs 18:15

September 19

**Read
Proverbs 19**

LIFELONG LEARNING

*Get all the advice
and instruction you
can, and be wise the
rest of your life.*
Proverbs 19:20

The Bible teaches that we are wise to honor our elders. This verse tells us that those who are wise have probably reached that level after years of hard work and experience. Some of the greatest storehouses of godly wisdom are found in the elder members of our families and churches. Are you an older saint? Share your hard-earned wisdom with those who follow you. Are you younger? Pursue those who have so much to share.

So how do we become wise? By seeking advice and instruction, acknowledging that we don't know it all and that we have much to learn. One of the great motives for gratitude in our lives comes when we realize how many people have given to us the gifts of wisdom along the way. We can benefit greatly from the counsel of others, for they can help us to avoid their mistakes along the way.

WISE WAYS   In what areas would you like to be more knowledgeable? Who can you ask for godly advice and instruction?

Today, Lord, keep me humble and teachable. Grant me wisdom to walk in your truth.

September 20

When we go to a foreign country for the first time, the changes can be overwhelming. Besides the differences in language and currency, cultural differences may catch us unawares. At those times, knowledgeable and reliable guides are worth their weight in gold.

This principle can be seen in all of life. If we are honest, we can all admit to experiencing moments when we are simply overwhelmed. The weights and concerns of this life can crush us beneath their mercilessly relentless load. But Jesus told us that he would always be with us (Matthew 28:20), that he would send the Spirit to guide us into all truth (John 16:13), and that we have no need to fear, for our Father cares for us (Luke 12:6-7). We should always turn to him as our guide, for then we can walk in confidence that he is directing our steps.

WISE WAYS   In what ways has Jesus been a knowledgeable and reliable guide to you?

Today, Lord, help me to look to you as my guide. Incite in me a passion to pursue your path as the way of ultimate satisfaction and joy.

Read
Proverbs 20

A RELIABLE GUIDE

How can we understand the road we travel? It is the LORD who directs our steps.
Proverbs 20:24

September 21

HONORABLE PURSUITS

Whoever pursues godliness and unfailing love will find life, godliness, and honor.

Proverbs 21:21

The world is full of pursuits that seem worthy. However, we can easily spend too much time seeking out those pursuits that are the most elusive, such as financial security, fame, or power. At times, we even "catch" what we are pursuing, only to find that it cannot satisfy our desires. To adapt one of Jesus' warnings, we may catch the whole world, but if we've left our soul behind in the process, we've actually lost everything (see Matthew 16:24-28).

According to this proverb, there are some goals worth pursuing in life—godliness and unfailing love. The first points to the quality of our relationship with God. To pursue godliness is to desire to reflect God's character, to pursue God himself. The second points to the quality of our human relationships. To pursue unfailing love is to strive to love our neighbor as ourselves.

God promises us that if we pursue these goals, we will find the true worth of life and gain what we will never lose.

WISE WAYS   In what ways are you pursuing godliness and unfailing love? How has pursuing God's values brought about worthwhile character in your life?

Today, Lord, teach me to follow hard after you. Excite my heart to desire your godliness and unfailing love.

September 22

When God called Abraham to leave his home and family and to set off as a wanderer, he made a great promise to Abraham: "I will cause you to become the father of a great nation, and I will bless you. . . . All the families of the earth will be blessed through you" (Genesis 12:1-3). Abraham was blessed to be a blessing to all the families of the earth. In the same way, God continues to bless his people so that they can be blessings to others. God shows us his goodness and blessing—not for our own selfish fulfillment, but so that we can be channels of blessing to those in need.

The wonder is that God chooses to use us, imperfect and sinful as we are, to bless those around us. "Remember this—a farmer who plants only a few seeds will get a small crop. But the one who plants generously will get a generous crop" (2 Corinthians 9:6). The measure of our generosity is the degree to which we give to those who cannot give in return.

WISE WAYS What one thing can you do today to bless those who are in need?

Today, Lord, thank you for your great blessings in my life. Teach me to be generous, to be a blessing to others. Give me an opportunity to give to those who need. Grant me the love and compassion to reflect your love as I do so.

**Read
Proverbs 22**

SOWING TO
RIGHTEOUSNESS

*Blessed are those who
are generous, because
they feed the poor.*
Proverbs 22:9

September 23

**Read
Proverbs 23**

SUFFERING
BLESSINGS

*God blesses you when
you are mocked and
persecuted and lied
about because you
are my followers. Be
happy about it! Be
very glad! For great
reward awaits you
in heaven. And
remember, the
ancient prophets
were persecuted, too.*

Matthew 5:11-12

Jesus promised us that we would be persecuted.
"Since they persecuted me, naturally they will perse-
cute you" (John 15:20). So did the Apostle Paul.
"Yes, and everyone who wants to live a godly life in
Christ Jesus will suffer persecution" (2 Timothy
3:12). So what are we to expect? Trouble.

God's value system and the world's value system are
in direct opposition. In the above verses, however,
Jesus gives us a wonderful promise. A great reward
awaits us in heaven. Not only that, but we can also
expect that our suffering will produce a more intimate, authentic relationship with our Lord, as was the
case with Job. After suffering the loss of his family, his
livestock, and his health, Job said to God, "I had
heard about you before, but now I have seen you with
my own eyes" (Job 42:5). In his sufferings, Job met
God. The principle remains true for us as well (I
Peter 4:14).

WISE WAYS   In what areas of your life have you
suffered for the sake of Christ?

*Today, Lord, grant me the courage to stand for your righteousness.
Help me to treasure you above the approval and flattery of people.*

September 24

In the famous statue that adorns the entrances of many courts, the woman called "Justice" wears a blindfold. The implication is clear: she is blind to the criteria that we normally use to distinguish amongst ourselves, whether physical appearance, riches, or rank. So too this proverb points to justice on earth, and the justice to come with the last day.

We know that "God has no favorites" (Galatians 2:6). As Jesus told the apostle John, "Let the one who is doing wrong continue to do wrong; the one who is vile, continue to be vile; the one who is good, continue to do good; and the one who is holy, continue in holiness. See, I am coming soon, and my reward is with me, to repay all according to their deeds" (Revelation 22:11-12).

An awareness of God's promise of eventual and absolute justice ought to lie behind every judgment we make. Otherwise, we place ourselves in the position of being liable for God's judgment.

WISE WAYS   Consider how you make judgments. Do you show favoritism, or are you fair? How do you live in light of the justice of God?

Today, Lord, help me to walk in righteousness. Help me to not attempt to excuse my offenses against you.

Read
Proverbs 24
✳

UPHOLDING RIGHTEOUSNESS

It is wrong to show favoritism when passing judgment.
Proverbs 24:23

September 25

Read
Proverbs 25

✳

GODLY
OPPOSITION

*If your enemies are
hungry, give them
food to eat. If they
are thirsty, give them
water to drink. You
will heap burning
coals on their heads,
and the LORD will
reward you.*
Proverbs 25:21-22

What is our natural reaction toward our enemies?
Don't we generally seek their ruin, rather than their
well-being? But Jesus reversed the order: "You have
heard that the law of Moses says, 'Love your neighbor'
and hate your enemy. But I say, love your enemies!
Pray for those who persecute you!" (Matthew 5:43-
44). The apostle Paul reminded us to leave room for
God's vengeance, rather than seeking our own, and
ended by saying, "Don't let evil get the best of you,
but conquer evil by doing good" (Romans 12:17-21).
Perhaps our kindness in the face of adversity will help
to change our enemies' hearts and draw them to the
Savior.

There is probably no greater training ground for
the soul than the endurance course of treating
enemies with kindness. If our vision of the LORD'S
pleasure and reward are not clear or large enough, we
may not even try. Perhaps the image of Jesus, forgiving his enemies while hanging on the cross, will help
us endure—that, and the help he will give if we ask.

WISE WAYS   What enemies do you have in your
life? How can you show them God's love?

*Today, Lord, help me to love my enemies. Show me your heart
toward those around me, that I may walk in the love that only comes
from you.*

September 26

Some childhood lessons make a lasting impression. Proverbs can be illustrated by life experiences.

A young man tells the story of his father, who is a carpenter. When he was a boy, his father and he were building a deck for a model home. The plans called for a hot tub enclosure on the deck, but the builder didn't want to actually pay for a hot tub to just sit in a display home. So, they built an enclosure in the shape of a hot tub, and fashioned a wooden lid to cover the opening. It looked like a hot tub, but there wasn't actually one there. The redwood they used was beautiful, but ultimately it was of little worth. It was just a shell covering an empty space.

In the same way, we can pursue beautiful veneers in our lives that cover the coarseness of our cores. True godliness must penetrate every fiber of our being. It searches the recesses of our hearts and lays us bare before the Almighty.

WISE WAYS   How have you used smooth words as a cover-up for what you were really feeling or thinking?

Today, Lord, show me my sin. Grant me a repentance that leads to refreshing (Acts 3:19-20). Take your truth to the core of my being.

Read
Proverbs 26

DECEPTIVE FACADES

Smooth words may hide a wicked heart, just as a pretty glaze covers a common clay pot.
Proverbs 26:23

September 27

Read Proverbs 27

✳

A PROPER TOOL

As iron sharpens iron, a friend sharpens a friend.

Proverbs 27:17

Imagine a carpenter who has a dull saw blade and takes it to his workshop for sharpening. What does he use to regain its usefulness? He knows that a piece of wood, a bar of soap, or some other "soft" item is not going to do the job. If he wants to sharpen his saw, he needs a real sharpener that is made of steel—strong and tough.

Like that craftsman, we can improve our usefulness to God by having friends who sharpen us. "Don't be fooled . . . for 'bad company corrupts good character'" (1 Corinthians 15:33). We may choose to hang around those who flatter us, those who deceive us, or those who manipulate us, but in the end, they cannot "sharpen" us. They are soft, and so will we be. However, if our friends are pursuing godliness and desiring God's highest, then they will sharpen us, as surely as iron sharpens iron. Let's pursue relationships that bring us closer to God and challenge us to live for him alone.

WISE WAYS   How do your friends sharpen you?

Today, Lord, help me to learn godliness from those around me. Teach me how to be a friend that would sharpen others.

September 28

In Genesis 25:21-34, we are told the story of Jacob and Esau. Jacob, though younger, was the child of promise. God had decided to use him to continue the lineage begun by Abraham and Isaac. But Jacob wasn't content to wait for God's plans. He schemed to take what by law belonged to his brother. So when Esau came to Jacob starving with hunger, Jacob sold him a bowl of lentil stew and a piece of bread. The price? Esau's birthright, which came with being the first-born. Esau exchanged his birthright for table scraps.

We can look at this story from the distance of several thousand years and see Esau's folly. But what trifles do we settle for in our lives? Our Father offers us incredible blessings if we would love him, but how often do we despise his offerings and seek out our own provision (Jeremiah 2:12-13)? The wrong, the cheap, and the momentary are never worth enough to exchange for what God can give us.

WISE WAYS In what ways have you settled for a piece of bread? Look instead to God's banquet of righteousness.

Today, Lord, teach me to value most what is infinitely valuable, namely yourself.

Read
Proverbs 28

A GREATER COST

Showing partiality is never good, yet some will do wrong for something as small as a piece of bread.
Proverbs 28:21

September 29

Read Proverbs 29

ETHICAL WORK

A servant who is pampered from childhood will later become a rebel.

Proverbs 29:21

You discover during a downpour that your home has a leaky roof. You call the roofers and ask them to come and replace the shingles. But when they show up, you tell them to sit down, have some lemonade, eat some cookies, and chat awhile. You ask about their families, their business, and what you can do to help them. If the roofers were your sons, you would be acting like any normal parent. But if they were only your hired help, you would be considered a fool to pay them for sitting around. In fact, you would discover that the longer they sit around "on the clock," the less motivated they will be to fix your roof!

God has called us to work in a way that reflects his character. Our work is important because it is the fulfillment of God's mandate to Adam and Eve to "fill the earth and subdue it. Be masters over the fish and birds and all the animals" (Genesis 1:28). Remember, "Whatever you eat or drink or whatever you do, you must do all for the glory of God" (I Corinthians 10:31). Our relationship with God is often evaluated by others on the basis of the way we work.

WISE WAYS   How does your work reflect the glory of God?

Today, Lord, help me to work for your glory. Show me how to honor you through my occupation.

September 30

The book of James gives us a very thorough picture of faith. He writes about its true nature, "So you see, it isn't enough just to have faith. Faith that doesn't show itself by good deeds is no faith at all—it is dead and useless" (James 2:17). And again, three verses later, "Fool! When will you ever learn that faith that does not result in good deeds is useless?" God would have us live out our Christianity in a manner that impacts every area of our being: our values, our financial decisions, how we spend our time, how we talk, and more.

Sometimes, we may ponder, "What does God want me to do with my life?" Yet if we read the Bible, we find that God gives us many plain, unchanging commands. Love justice, seek truth, love God and our neighbor, minister to the orphan and widow in their distress, bring healing to the sick and freedom to the prisoner, give our cloak to the one who has need of it, honor God, fear God, delight in God, and many, many more. We need to pursue God in faith, and do what he commands.

WISE WAYS   What has God been calling you to do? What can you do today towards accomplishing that calling in faith?

Today, Lord, teach me to hear your voice and to be obedient to your call. I yield myself to you. I ask that your will would be done in my life.

**Read
Proverbs 30**

AN EFFECTIVE
FAITH

*Remember, it is sin to
know what you ought
to do and then not
do it.*

James 4:17

✴ OCTOBER

October 1

**Read
Proverbs 1**

GOD'S FLASHLIGHT

They rejected my advice and paid no attention when I corrected them. That is why they must eat the bitter fruit of living their own way. They must experience the full terror of the path they have chosen.

Proverbs 1:30-31

God does not leave us to fumble our way through the dark. Instead of watching us stumble through life, he offers us his flashlight to direct our steps. It is ironic that while we desire to make confident strides, we often choose to go down an uncertain path, forgetting to take his light with us.

It seems ridiculous that a mere human would disregard God's all-knowing, loving guidance. Our arrogance only leaves us confused and lost. The dangerous outcome is separation from God as we wander farther from him on our own dark paths.

God, however, offers his light even when we trip over sin during our journey. His light floods the spot where we've fallen, and we know to not step there again. He promises us the benefits of his light if we choose to follow it. While we don't deserve his guidance, he nonetheless offers it to us if we choose to accept it.

WISE WAYS   In what area of your life are you disregarding God's direction? How can you get back on the track God desires for you?

Today, Lord, help me to listen to your guidance. When I struggle to heed your Word, help me to trust in your light so that I will not stumble in the darkness.

October 2

There's no time for pit stops when we're on the road of obedience to God. On this road, each step aligns with God's commands and respects his wishes. Proverbs 2:16 and 19 warn us about straying off the road, even if we try to justify it as a brief "detour." Many tangents turn out to be dead ends, especially if they lead to the women mentioned in these verses. Straying from obedience to meet with either woman is unfortunate. The immoral woman represents the temptation to sin. The adulterous woman symbolizes sexual immorality and the lies that lead up to her door. Both women are dangerous because their deceit lures us from our commitment to follow God's commands.

Maybe a mere visit doesn't seem like a big deal. Once we are in their company, however, returning to the right track is a struggle. The last two sentences of verse 19 do not leave room for second chances. Once you shut the doors behind you, the path you've followed is lost. But there is grace to keep us on the right track. Meditating on Scripture will save us from any traps along the way. This is the wisdom the book of Proverbs encourages.

WISE WAYS By reading and meditating on God's Word, you build a defense against future traps. Can you commit to reading the Bible and applying it to your daily life?

Please remind me throughout this day, Lord, to seek your wisdom instead of sin.

**Read
Proverbs 2**

DOOMED DETOURS

Wisdom will save you from the immoral woman, from the flattery of the adulterous woman. . . . The man who visits her is doomed. He will never reach the paths of life.

Proverbs 2:16, 19

October 3

**Read
Proverbs 3**

✳

COPY CAT

*Do not envy
violent people;
don't copy
their ways.*
Proverbs 3:31

At first glance, this proverb appears to be of little help. It's unethical to be violent. Society condemns it. If we pause for a deeper look at Proverbs 3:31, however, we will see that it is actually a significant warning to Christians to not get sucked into sin.

The wisdom lying beneath the surface of this proverb warns us not to be jealous of power, fame, and possessions. Unfortunately, violent people can be rich, not only with money, but with influence and reputation. While being violent is not a socially acceptable quality, having power, taking control, and demanding attention are very attractive ones. We may disapprove of the violence, but admire the perks that come with it.

Violence is a conspicuous sin, but envy brews quietly inside. Jealousy eventually wells up and spills out as action. The power you may desire convinces you to copy a "bad guy's" tactics. This is how sin starts. God understands that, so he warns us clearly with this proverb. Sometimes we don't know what we need to hear. Thankfully, God tells us anyway.

WISE WAYS   How can you prevent yourself from being dragged down by negative influences?

Today, Lord, help me to recognize the times when I am envious of people. Teach me how to model myself after you.

October 4

Obedience is not an accident—it is a choice. Just like little children, Christians decide whether or not they will follow their Father's commands. Keeping in line is not easy, however. As our divine Parent, God encourages us by offering a plan for success, and then adds a promise of safety to spur us onward.

God does not assume our passivity. Each line of Proverbs 4:25-26 contains action that propels a believer along a path of obedience. These spiritual principles closely parallel the rules for keeping a compass heading in the wilderness. We take a sighting on a distant, immovable object in the direction we must go, and then walk directly to it. When we reach that object, we take another sighting and repeat the process until we arrive at our destination.

God knows that in order for us to make it in the wilderness of this life, we have to continually keep our sights on his commands. Sharpening our focus to remove any distractions, we map out our route and then discipline ourselves to follow it. God's Word provides an immovable object that can keep us traveling in the right direction.

WISE WAYS How are you struggling to stay on the right track? God will lead you if you ask him.

Today, Lord, guide me as a little child toward obedience, and continue to bless me with your promises.

Read
Proverbs 4

AN ACTIVE TRACK

Look straight ahead, and fix your eyes on what lies before you. Mark out a straight path for your feet; then stick to the path and stay safe.
Proverbs 4:25-26

October 5

**Read
Proverbs 5**

FRONT PAGE NEWS

*For the LORD sees
clearly what a man
does, examining
every path he takes.*
Proverbs 5:21

If every sin we commit were printed on the front page of the New York Times, we might live life in a slightly different fashion. While we think most of our sins are hidden from the public eye, they are always exposed to God. He sees what we do and where we go, and he knows our thoughts and motives.

Our attitude determines how we will live in the presence of God's omniscience. We will either be joyful or resentful. A joyous perspective rests secure under God's watch. We are never out of God's protective reach. A resentful perspective considers God's presence to be threatening and controlling. One can never get a moment of privacy.

God's watch over us convinces us of something else, however: he loves us. He knows us better than anyone. Only a caring father would keep such a steady eye on us.

WISE WAYS How are you taking advantage of God's closeness? He is willing to enhance his relationship with you if you let him.

Today, Lord, I thank you for your ever-present watch on my life, that you care about me enough to take an active interest in my life.

October 6

Exchanging an old, rusty car for a new, shining one is hardly a risk—it's a fantastic swap. But almost nobody would trade a classic Porsche for a teenager's clunker. It is easy to risk something that you do not value. As Solomon warns his son in Proverbs 6:26, it is not worth risking a valuable possession to indulge a sin. The possession at risk in this proverb is sexual purity.

The truth is, exchanging purity for sin is not a fair trade. There are far more consequences than we can predict. The consequences may or may not be immediate. A sin like adultery may not automatically lead to the loss of house and family. Sometimes, terrible sins remain a secret. But they create a wall between ourselves and God. Eventually, we will be poorer than if we were in poverty. Without repentance and forgiveness, such sins may, as this proverb clearly warns, cost us our very lives.

WISE WAYS What specific steps are you taking to prevent falling into sexual immorality?

Today, Lord, give me the strength to make the right choices.

**Read
Proverbs 6**

AN UNFAIR TRADE

For a prostitute will bring you to poverty, and sleeping with another man's wife may cost you your very life.
Proverbs 6:26

October 7

Read
Proverbs 7

FROM HEAVEN'S EYE

Don't store up treasures here on earth, where they can be eaten by moths and get rusty, and where thieves break in and steal. Store your treasures in heaven, where they will never become moth-eaten or rusty and where they will be safe from thieves. Wherever your treasure is, there your heart and thoughts will be also.

Matthew 6:19-21

From your perch in heaven someday, the life you spent on earth will look very different. All of the materialistic details of your life will remain here. The world will forget you in a moment or two, but the Lord will continue to love you for eternity.

In this passage, Jesus is instructing where Christians should set their priorities. Jesus is not saying, "Live with the bare minimum. Sell your clothes, cars, home, and quit your job." Instead, he is saying, "Don't love your things, love your God." Where you set your eyes and direct your feet, there your heart will follow.

The moment you stand before God, you won't care how many cars you owned or that your house was the biggest on the block. Standing before Jesus, you won't be grieving over that stock market slump or that deal you lost. If you have treasured Jesus Christ during your life, then your heart will be fulfilled in that moment.

WISE WAYS   What dreams are you chasing that won't reach farther than earth? How are your treasures prioritized?

Today, Lord, help me to keep in mind the eternal ramifications of what I accomplish.

October 8

Imagine the top CEO of the nation leaving his job to become a janitor. Who would intentionally throw away status, power, and money to pick up a job at the bottom of the ranks? Proverbs 8:27 is a reminder that Jesus did precisely that.

It is easy to forget that Jesus demoted himself to become a mere man. How do we reconcile the image of the all-powerful God with the face of the man, Jesus? All existence was at his design as he directed and molded each detail of the earth. Why did Jesus fit so well in the world? He created it his size.

Even before the world's creation, the fullness of God dwelled in Jesus. God answers our question for us, however, pointing out that his ways and thoughts are beyond our understanding. How can we not be amazed, honored, and humbled by his choice to sacrifice his life for ours?

WISE WAYS   How can you regularly express your reverence to Jesus?

Today, Lord, I call you mighty and powerful, and thank you that you loved me enough to leave your throne in heaven to save my soul.

**Read
Proverbs 8**

WHAT JESUS LEFT BEHIND

I was there when he established the heavens, when he drew the horizon on the oceans.

Proverbs 8:27

October 9

**Read
Proverbs 9**

A WISE CHOICE

*If you become wise,
you will be the one to
benefit. If you scorn
wisdom, you will be
the one to suffer.*
Proverbs 9:12

The essence of Proverbs is a choice: will you pursue wisdom or not? The kind of person we decide to be touches every aspect of our lives. Proverbs 9:12 is a reminder that there are consequences to the choices we make. No one can make this decision for us.

Ideally, we would all scoop up wisdom as our prize and live happily ever after—but we don't. In fact, we often choose to grumble over God's commands. We don't want to hear advice from anyone. Even though God is clear that wisdom leads to a fulfilling life, we sometimes choose the opposite.

A tendency to make good or bad decisions soon becomes a habit. Despite our poor decisions, however, God is persistent to warn us of the consequences. He lets you be responsible for your decisions. He is always hoping that, in the end, Christians will choose what's right.

WISE WAYS   Have you decided to pursue wisdom? If so, how do you know it and show it?

Today, Lord, I want to do what is wise in your eyes. Thank you for your guidance.

October 10

Sometimes doing the "right" thing seems boring—
even irritating. For example, stopping for the red
light is a chore, while speeding through the intersec-
tion is tempting. What keeps many drivers braking
for the light?

From a practical point of view, most drivers realize that red lights are sensible tools. For the foolish
driver, however, running the red light may seem like
fun, only the thrill doesn't last. That type of irre-
sponsible behavior doesn't lead to genuine happiness. It only leads to a wrecked car—and perhaps a
wrecked life.

While we may not enjoy putting on the brakes, we
appreciate traffic rules for protecting us from
danger on the road. This proverb reminds us that
wise conduct is the first step toward happiness. If we
make a habit of acting wise, we grow accustomed to
its benefits. Soon, wise conduct becomes a pleasure.

WISE WAYS In what areas of your life do you
need to work on conducting yourself with wisdom?

*Today, Lord, pinpoint what I may be doing foolishly, so that with
your help I can correct the situation.*

**Read
Proverbs 10**

DRIVING
TOWARD
HAPPINESS

*Doing wrong is fun
for a fool, while wise
conduct is a pleasure
to the wise.*

Proverbs 10:23

October 11

Read Proverbs 11

CHARACTER OVER BEAUTY

A woman who is beautiful but lacks discretion is like a gold ring in a pig's snout.

Proverbs 11:22

A pig wearing luxurious jewelry? That's absurd. To compare an immoral woman with a pig's repugnance is harsh—but accurate.

Two applications of this proverb would be: (1) men should not desire the beautiful but indiscreet woman, and (2) women should not aspire to be like her. The pig prompts images of laziness and ignorance. Pigs eat trash and live in filth. A pig's stench follows it where it goes, leaving traces everywhere. A pig has no idea of the value of the golden ring on its snout.

Beauty is wasted if the person reeks of immorality. Loveliness is marred by thoughtless behavior. If we emphasize appearance over character, we soon find ourselves laughing stocks as our beauty fades. God prefers a genuine faith and wisdom—that is true beauty.

WISE WAYS   In our society, what ways do you see beauty being emphasized over character? How can you focus on developing the inner beauty that God desires?

Today, Lord, bless my efforts to condition my character rather than my appearance. Thank you for a gift that will not fade.

October 12

You may not notice a genius standing in a crowded room, but it won't take long to zero in on a fool. According to this proverb, a fool announces his poor judgment simply by the nature of his words. This proverb implies the arrogance of a fool who throws words in people's faces. The wise are not being smug by holding their tongues; they are refusing to parade their knowledge before other people. Wise people choose their words carefully. Unlike the wise, however, the foolish run out of words to say, but continue to babble.

The difference between a wise person and a fool is the ability to have quiet confidence. For example, Jesus did not need to advertise his knowledge. He simply spoke and acted wisely, and people noticed.

The tongue controls the entire body, and therefore can be a dangerous weapon or a helpful tool. We direct our speech not so much by deciding when to speak, but when to be quiet. Only then will people notice our wisdom—and it won't take a word from us to tell them so.

WISE WAYS What do your words say about you? How can you keep a humble spirit when you communicate?

Today, Lord, I will refrain from broadcasting my knowledge. Show me when to speak and when to keep my mouth shut.

Read
Proverbs 12

SPOTLIGHTING FOOLS

Wise people don't make a show of their knowledge, but fools broadcast their folly.
Proverbs 12:23

October 13

**Read
Proverbs 13**

FRIENDS
IN FAITH

*Whoever walks
with the wise
will become wise;
whoever walks
with fools
will suffer harm.*
Proverbs 13:20

The quality of our friends reflects our quality. Jesus understood the importance of choosing who would surround him during his ministry. The twelve disciples didn't just happen to become his inner circle; he deliberately picked each man. In the same way, we should choose our friends thoughtfully and carefully.

Friends influence which movies we see, which games we play, and which books we read. They have an impact on our lifestyle. This proverb uses the verb "walks," hinting at the mutual journey between friends. Just as Jesus went into the mountains to pray over his decision, we too should seek God for guidance in initiating relationships. We can expect to be affected by our friends. Socializing with people who do not honor God in their words or actions soon nudges us to do the same. At first, it may not be intentional to dishonor God because it happens subtly. But gradual compromise leads to full rebellion, which in time causes pain and suffering apart from God. A good friend will lead you closer, not farther, from God.

WISE WAYS   Do you have friends who influence you to disobey the Lord? How can you change these friendships so that you can honor God?

Today, Lord, I will consider how my relationships glorify you. Please show me how I can improve the quality of my company.

October 14

In answer to an honest question, Jesus provided a pair of central priorities for life. These two (love for God and love for neighbor) form an unbreakable bond. John recorded the following crucial test: "If someone says, 'I love God,' but hates a Christian brother or sister, that person is a liar; for if we don't love people we can see, how can we love God, whom we have not seen?" (1 John 4:20).

Jesus taught in these "love-orders" that God expects as much a public as a private relationship with us. People think too often that they can love God without anyone else finding out. But secret love for God seldom lasts. Real love for God leads to love for those whom God loves. The order is important. The Son of God himself gave us permission to express love for him by loving others (see John 13:34-35). Think of your neighbor as the last person you failed to treat with love. That's a good starting point to put this command into practice.

WISE WAYS Who is a neighbor to whom you can express the love of God? How can you deepen your love for God by treating your neighbor with love?

Lord, please let me actually see my neighbors today. Help me move toward loving by the simple act of ceasing to ignore them. I want to learn to love you through them.

Read Proverbs 14

GOD AND NEIGHBOR

Jesus replied, "The most important commandment is this: 'Hear, O Israel! The Lord our God is the one and only Lord. And you must love the Lord your God with all your heart, all your soul, all your mind, and all your strength.' The second is equally important: 'Love your neighbor as yourself.' No other commandment is greater than these."
Mark 12:29-31

October 15

**Read
Proverbs 15**

✳

A WORD OF ADVICE

*Plans go wrong
for lack of advice;
many counselors
bring success.*

Proverbs 15:22

Columnist Ann Landers feeds advice to an estimated 90 million readers. Several advice-giving radio hosts have large audiences. Their success has been based on this fact: we all have plans and problems that we can't handle on our own. Sometimes outside perspective is just what we need to see our situation clearly.

While such "anonymous" advice may be helpful, we can access wise counseling through an alternate venue: the Christian community. This advice comes with accountability and perspective. A radio host doesn't know his or her callers except from what they say. Those in the Christian community know us.

Proverbs 15:22 directs us to seek advice from a number of wise friends. This proverb doesn't tell us to follow every piece of advice we hear. We accept advice in light of the Bible. Advice should never contradict what God says in the Scriptures. Pursuing advice while studying the Bible helps us to avoid disasters we would otherwise suffer on our own.

WISE WAYS Considering a problem you have right now, who could you ask for some Christian advice?

Today, Lord, I ask you to point me toward wise friends. Use these people to send me your wisdom.

October 16

Imagine how well you could get to know God in a lifetime. Throughout life, the moments of crisis, joy, faith, and perseverance all provide opportunities to deepen our relationship with God. Gray hair, hopefully, is evidence of wisdom gained over the years. A long life is the reward for rejecting sinful instincts for godly wisdom.

A godly life involves making wise choices, which are usually the smarter, safer ones. This kind of life leads a person to naturally live longer than someone who isn't making wise choices. The godly person may suffer the same temporal consequences for sin that the ungodly suffer, but a godly person has the hope of forgiveness and eternal life. The ungodly live with the weight of unforgiveness and the dread of eternal hopelessness.

Gray hair (a crown of glory) can be worn joyfully by those who are reflecting on a life's walk with the Lord. Not only have these people spent their lives with God, they also anticipate uninterrupted fellowship with him in heaven.

WISE WAYS   Consider how you will look back on your life when you are older. What can you predict your attitude will be?

Today, Lord, I thank you for my life. Let me use it to serve you and get to know you better.

**Read
Proverbs 16**

JOY FOR THE GOLDEN YEARS

*Gray hair
is a crown of glory;
it is gained by
living a godly life.*
Proverbs 16:31

October 17

**Read
Proverbs 17**

✳

A SPOONFUL
OF JOY

*A cheerful heart is
good medicine,
but a broken spirit
saps a person's
strength.*

Proverbs 17:22

Though sorrow is burdensome, it is still possible to choose joy. Proverbs 17:22 implies that there is a choice between remaining mired in misery or taking the antidote—a joyful attitude.

Poor circumstances are plentiful, but joyful attitudes are a little harder to come by. It's tough for the little league player sitting in the dugout with a broken arm to smile. It's a struggle for the young widow to get accustomed to an empty home. Harsh circumstances drain our bodies and minds of strength, leaving us weak and overwhelmed with pain. A cheerful heart may seem out of reach. But if we decide that trusting in God will get us back to a cheerful outlook, we will have taken the first step of joy.

This proverb is a gentle warning that when sorrow strikes, we must not get bogged down for too long. We need for the clouds to part and a sunny attitude to come through. Jesus is standing ready to help you rise above the pain.

WISE WAYS Which direction does your attitude lean on a daily basis? Do you have a tendency toward a delightful attitude or a sad spirit?

Today, Lord, I will choose to have a cheerful heart. Let my joy be contagious to the people around me.

October 18

Judges can't get by with swift, impulsive decisions in court. They don't make a final ruling until they have heard both sides of their cases. Making a well-informed judgment requires questioning, listening, and patience. Analyzing numerous stories leads the judge to a knowledgeable decision.

We should listen to the stories people feed us with exactly the same caution. This proverb is a useful tip for wise listening: judge a speaker's words by putting them beside someone else's. We should be objective and fair, not putting too much weight in our initial assumptions. We must not be gullible or hasty. Instead, we should be swift to test what people claim. To "set the record straight" is to be discerning and to pursue the truth.

WISE WAYS Do you tend to be too quick about accepting people's stories as true? While it is good to trust people, Proverbs insists on wisdom and discernment.

Today, Lord, help me to consider carefully the stories I hear. I want to learn how to listen, to question, and to trust people.

**Read
Proverbs 18**

THE WHOLE STORY

*Any story
sounds true until
someone sets
the record straight.*
Proverbs 18:17

October 19

**Read
Proverbs 19**

ON TRACK

*You can make
many plans,
but the Lord's
purpose
will prevail.*

Proverbs 19:21

People tend to like what they can plan, maneuver, and control—hence the popularity of PDAs, reservations, and retirement packages. This proverb can be viewed as a way of God pulling the rug out from under us. We can plan as much into the future as we would like, but nonetheless, God is going to have his own way. All our planning seems to be pointless.

It takes the right attitude to understand that this verse is consoling, not annoying. To be annoyed at God's ultimate authority over the future is to assume that he is not looking out for our best interest. Rather, God hopes to bless his people to a higher measure than we can imagine. A better attitude regarding Proverbs 19:21 is one of relief, that no matter how we chart our own courses, God is poised to keep us on track. If as Christians we are sincere in our desire to see God glorified, than we will not argue when God's purpose overrules our own.

WISE WAYS Are you counting on a specific plan for the future? Have you considered what God may say about your plans?

Today, Lord, I admit that your purpose overrides my own. I am flexible; don't let my own desires get in the way of yours.

October 20

God loves a cheerful giver—not a nervous, anxious giver. He delights in a promise or gift presented wholeheartedly to him. And who can blame him? God doesn't need anything. It's the love and commitment behind the gesture that God enjoys.

The ominous tone of this proverb is the warning to not disappoint God. "Dangerous" is a dramatic word choice, but it is appropriate. The proverb makes its point: don't rush into a vow that you haven't thoroughly considered. Going back on your word isn't wise. Instead, contemplate your promises before offering them to God. He takes you seriously. He doesn't misplace your promise amongst the countless prayers he receives at any given moment.

If we pause to assess the motives and reasoning behind our gifts and promises to God, we will not have to fear the consequences. Then God will be at leisure to enjoy the love behind each one.

WISE WAYS What has been the state of your heart behind each promise and gift you have lifted to God?

Today, Lord, I will hold my tongue and contemplate what I have promised you. I don't want you to ever question my integrity or my dedication to you.

Read
Proverbs 20

DO YOU PROMISE?

It is dangerous to make a rash promise to God before counting the cost.
Proverbs 20:25

October 21

**Read
Proverbs 21**

WITHIN
ARM'S LENGTH

*Draw close to God,
and God will draw
close to you.*
James 4:8

God isn't pushy. He waits for us to make the next move. He is always accessible to us, eager and willing to talk. He has already moved as close as his will and plan will allow him to come. Now, it's our turn. This proverb is an open invitation to get together with God. You need not RSVP. Simply show up and God will be right there.

How close is "close"? Is it within an arm's length? Ten feet? Twelve inches? There is an implied intimacy in the word "close" that we can share with God. The closeness is not a literal distance, but a special presence of the Lord. It's within his presence that we put aside our self-focus and train our thoughts to be on him.

If we are drawing near to God, we are naturally leaving something else behind—our pride. Along with our pride, we leave behind our worldly thoughts. God replaces all this with himself. It is within this intimacy that there is freedom to grow in our relationship with him. This is where we get to know the Almighty God.

WISE WAYS   How can you make the effort to draw near to God?

Today, Lord, I want to draw near to you so that I can get to know you better. Please draw close to me.

October 22

After reading this verse, it's obvious what side God favors. He is not afraid to be partial; he shields those who act wisely and frustrates those who act deceitfully.

What spills over from this proverb is a reminder that God is omniscient, able to read the mind of every person. He knows what people will do before they do it. He can intervene where necessary and allow what he chooses. Knowing this, Christians would be smart to stick to a clean course. If we act in a deceitful, dishonest manner, we should expect God to thwart our plans. It is as if the proverb is warning us, "Don't bother with your evil ways. He is sure to catch you."

But while the proverb warns what will happen if we err, it also promises what will happen if we obey. What a wonderful promise! If we strive for wisdom, God will shield and protect us. Coming from the almighty God, this promise should make our choice obvious as well.

WISE WAYS   When has God shielded you from hardship and suffering? Thank him for the times he has spared you.

Today, Lord, I praise you that you are omniscient. You know all of my thoughts and longings. Thank you for caring enough to listen.

**Read
Proverbs 22**

ON YOUR SIDE

The LORD preserves knowledge, but he ruins the plans of the deceitful.
Proverbs 22:12

October 23

Read
Proverbs 23

✳

A JOYFUL SMILE

*So give
your parents joy!
May she who
gave you birth
be happy.*
Proverbs 23:25

A drawing on the refrigerator door, a picture inside a wallet, a graduation announcement—these are symbols of precious memories. Children bring joy to their parents throughout childhood. This proverb reinforces that natural affection parents feel for their children. It also encourages children, regardless of their ages, to act in ways that make their parents happy.

Children also bring joy to their parents when they do the right thing. They bring a smile to God's face, too. God is pleased when Christians nurture positive family relationships. That means putting other people before ourselves. It means holding on to God's Word during tough times.

So, how do we please our parents? By finding out what God's Word says and following it. Out of respect to our parents and reverence to God, we accept the commandments and open ourselves up to receive the rewards. Obeying God is not only in our own best interest. It benefits our parents, too.

WISE WAYS Have you considered how your actions affect your parents?

Today, Lord, I will take the extra precaution to live the way you want me to. I want to please you, my heavenly Father.

October 24

Sometimes it seems to not be in our best interests to tell a friend the truth. He might get mad at us. Yell at us. Even end our friendship. But friends who tell the truth, despite possible repercussions, are rare.

Regardless of whether we want to share the truth, or whether the other person wants to hear the truth, honesty ought to reign over all. The truth, though it may conjure up hurt and bitterness, always stands on its own in the end.

Jesus didn't do people any favors by candy-coating the consequences of sin. He taught people about the agony of it and the need for repentance. Jesus could have danced around the issue. He loves people. Yet he would rather tell the hard truth than relax and keep them content with their sin.

As Proverbs 24:26 states, it is an honor to be told the truth. Telling the hard truth is an act of courage, risking hurt feelings so that a friend can hear what's important. A friend who is willing to take that risk is a true friend indeed.

WISE WAYS When your friends ask for the truth, do you give it to them?

Today, Lord, I will tell the truth in love. Help me to hear and to accept the truth from my friends.

**Read
Proverbs 24**

TRUE WORD,
TRUE FRIEND

*It is an honor
to receive
an honest reply.*
Proverbs 24:26

October 25

Read
Proverbs 25

A TASTE FOR AMBITION

*Just as it is not good
to eat too much
honey, it is not good
for people to think
about all the honors
they deserve.*
Proverbs 25:27

Eating too much honey is not sweet. This simile in Proverbs 25:27 compares honey with pride. This comparison is notable because it highlights the tendency for people to overindulge themselves on pleasurable things. In this case, it is specifically self-glorification. The proverb teaches the usage of appropriate boundaries, marking anything past that as "too much."

Dwelling on things that glorify us is like craving delicious food. We crave it, so we indulge. The craving is satisfied, but we continue to hoard the food, consuming more than we can contain. Soon the tastiness of the indulgence diminishes. It is no longer as good as the first bite, becoming exactly the opposite: disgusting.

The purpose of this proverb is to spare us the disgust. Most people who get sick from overeating come to detest the food and avoid it all together. Understandably, it is desirable to take credit for our work. Too much of a good thing, however, swiftly becomes idolatry.

WISE WAYS How much do you focus on yourself and your ambitions?

Today, Lord, help me to crave your Word.

October 26

People with hateful hearts will do you no good. Though they may try to persuade you of their good intentions, Proverbs 26:24-25 says to remain wary of them. Sooner or later, their true motives and intentions will come out.

So how do Christians recognize people who are evil? Just as people can't contain the joy in their hearts, so they would be unable to keep evil from overflowing. The last line of this proverb stresses that these people's hearts are full of evil. That leaves no room for anything else.

Christians can determine the evil in a person's heart by watching his or her actions. Words may disguise them for a time, but evil people will eventually act on the content of their hearts. This is a crucial proverb for our times, when a lot of interaction takes place between faceless persons talking over modems. People who can manipulate words have a distinct advantage. This kind of communication must be carried out with extreme caution, lest we find ourselves tricked by someone's words whose actions reveal "all kinds of evil."

WISE WAYS   Are you aware of the ways Christians reflect their faith on a regular basis? What do you notice?

Today, Lord, I will keep an eye open for an evil that wants to harm me. Help me to be discerning.

**Read
Proverbs 26**

A FALSE FRONT

People with hate in their hearts may sound pleasant enough, but don't believe them. Though they pretend to be kind, their hearts are full of all kinds of evil.
Proverbs 26:24-25

October 27

**Read
Proverbs 27**

SHARING A PIECE OF HIS FRUIT

Workers who tend a fig tree are allowed to eat its fruit. In the same way, workers who protect their employer's interests will be rewarded.

Proverbs 27:18

God has chosen us to take care of the world and to tell people about Christ. God's promise in Proverbs 27:18 applies to us when we are faithful with the jobs we are given. God is the employer; we are the workers.

In the broad sense, Christians are called to be stewards of the world. We are allowed to "eat its fruit," to enjoy many good things. We must never forget, however, that the world is not our eternal home, nor does it ultimately belong to us. Part of our duty is to "protect our employer's interests." God also grants to us individual jobs that are unique to our capabilities and talents.

There is a sense of justice in this proverb. God knows how well we are performing and how much we will be rewarded. The proverb is an invitation to work with him and share in his goodness. It is extraordinary that God offers to reward us. As master of Creation, humans should be ready to serve him for nothing. But he chooses to let us enjoy his benefits, to eat his fruit though we could never work enough to truly deserve it.

WISE WAYS   How are you being faithful with the jobs God has given you?

Today, Lord, I will be aware of my responsibilities. I will serve you and realign my focus to your purposes.

October 28

SABBATH

The word *offensive* is a label for any trend, belief, person, or idea that is discomforting or insulting. It is possible to be offended by what we don't understand. Most people don't enjoy being called offensive, yet some considered that an appropriate label for Jesus.

Trouble is, most people need to feel uncomfortable before they see a need to change their perspectives or behaviors. People don't like discomfort, and they don't like change. Matthew 11:6 emphasizes the need for discernment regarding these feelings. Why do we feel a burden when we hear Jesus speak? Is it because we are offended by his words, or are we actually being convicted to hear him out?

It takes humility to see that his words are meant to correct us, not to antagonize us. They are spoken to guide us, not alienate us. His motive is to love us, not to offend us. Recognizing God's intentions allows us to enjoy the gifts he has for those who don't stand offended. Jesus risked offending us in order to save us.

WISE WAYS   Have you disregarded any of Jesus' instruction because you were offended by his words? If so, how can you return to those words and look at them with a humble heart?

Today, Lord, I will remember that you had my best interest in mind when you inspired the Bible. I will remember that when I study your Word.

Read
Proverbs 28

YOUR REACTION TO JESUS

God blesses those who are not offended by me.
Matthew 11:6

October 29

**Read
Proverbs 29**

KEEPING COOL

*A hot-tempered
person starts fights
and gets into
all kinds of sin.*

Proverbs 29:22

"Hot-tempered" describes a person who reacts quickly and badly. A hot temper leaves no time for questions, reconsideration, different perspectives, or changes of heart. This kind of character assumes the worst before the best. How many ways can an angry person mess up? Today's proverb tells us that such people get into "all kinds of sin."

Compare the ill-tempered person with Jesus. What were the occasions for his anger? His anger did not add to the evil in a circumstance. He used his angry emotions as a red flag signaling that something was not right.

If we hesitate before acting on our angry feelings, fights and quarrels can be avoided. By modeling ourselves after Jesus, anger can be handled in a way that does not cause us to sin.

WISE WAYS How do you experience anger? What are some other ways that Jesus addressed his anger?

Today, Lord, I will hesitate before losing my cool. I don't want to fight or sin against you.

October 30

Our attitude after we have sinned determines if we will commit the sin again. Do we easily laugh off the guilt, talk ourselves into apathy, or deny the consequences? Or are we embarrassed about the way we faltered, storing a memory of what the guilt feels like deep in our minds? If we do the latter, the memory of the guilt we felt over our sin will come to the front of our minds when we ponder committing the sin again.

This proverb is discipline for our disobedience, but it is also a declaration of love. God foresees us acting foolishly. He plans on us messing up. In fact, he granted us salvation knowing that we were going to sin even after we received it. He loves us enough to keep getting us back on track. He hates pride and he hates sin. God wants us to avoid committing the same sin twice. It's our responsibility to see that we don't.

We are not forbidden from speaking about past sins and mistakes. They can often be helpful illustrations when we are teaching others. But there must be no hint of pride for those things that have been our downfall in the past.

WISE WAYS   Has apathy trapped you in a specific sin? Thank God for continuing to love and pursue you.

Today, Lord, I won't be cocky about my sin. I will keep my attitude humble.

**Read
Proverbs 30**

EMBARRASSED BY SIN

If you have been a fool by being proud or plotting evil, don't brag about it—cover your mouth with your hand in shame.

Proverbs 30:32

October 31

**Read
Proverbs 31**

THE PERFECT
WOMAN

*Her children stand
and bless her. Her
husband praises her:
"There are many
virtuous and capable
women in the world,
but you surpass
them all!"*

Proverbs 31:28-29

The woman who receives the praises of Proverbs 31:28-29 has obviously been doing something right. She's an extraordinary wife and mother who touched the lives of her children and husband in an extra special way. Reading the entire chapter, we understand the reasons why her family rises to praise her.

The husband's praise says that his wife is doing something noteworthy among other moral, skillful women. The question is, what makes her so different? It is most likely her spirit and attitude that are leaving marks on her family. Proverbs 31 runs through a list of duties she handles. The text conveys that it is her heart that makes her stand out from the rest. Her family is delighted that she brings such richness into their home!

Not only is this a woman whom we can aspire to be like, but she is also an example of the type of person we should aspire to find as a life-mate. When a marriage is formed between a woman and man with these qualities, the result is a healthy, loving home.

WISE WAYS   Do any of the woman's traits ring true in you? How can you emulate her?

Today, Lord, I recognize my need for your help if I am to emulate any of the qualities of the virtuous woman described in Proverbs 31. Build these character traits into my life.

✷

NOVEMBER

November 1

**Read
Proverbs 1**

✳

FRUITLESS
EFFORT

*For they are
simpletons who turn
away from me—to
death. They are
fools, and their own
complacency will
destroy them.*

Proverbs 1:32

Many nonbelievers accuse the spiritually inclined of being mindless. They simply cannot accept the leap of faith as anything other than abandoning one's intelligence. However, God warns that those who abandon his ways in deference to their own are the real fools.

For example, consider a nonbelieving executive who climbs eighty-hour weeks to the top. This person would hardly be described as unintelligent. The word *lazy* is likely absent from his or her vocabulary. Yet, the Bible refers to such a spiritually independent soul as a complacent simpleton. The issue is not effort itself, for many people work hard at unbelief. Rather, the baseline for a fool is misguided effort. The thesaurus describes a fool this way: ill-advised. They determine their life's priorities by working hard at earthly things to the neglect of spiritual things. A fool can be a corporate dynamo and a spiritual loafer wrapped up in one. He or she can achieve temporary earthly success and yet be destined for eternal destruction all at the same time.

WISE WAYS What are the consequences of spiritual loafing in your life? When are you most tempted to be complacent in your relationship with God?

Today, Lord, I can't afford to play the fool, relying on my own ways. Help me to look to you for guidance today.

November 2

"Follow the leader" is perhaps one of the more popular playground pastimes in childhood. The phrase has the power to spontaneously motivate children to line up in succession behind their lead adventurer, anxious to follow one child's whims across the playground. Up the slide. Down the slide. Across the monkey bars. And around the basketball goal. The display of trust is enormous. The crowd unquestionably follows the path's surprising twists and turns, finding joy in the journey. Fortunately, good leaders can be trusted to avoid pitfalls and lead the group in safe passage.

In the same way, we must follow the example of godly men and women—our lead adventurers in life. The mere mention of this proverb should call to mind the image of trusting children who are committed to following the one in front. If we stay on the path of the righteous, we will experience the adventure of faith walking. We may not know for ourselves what lies ahead, but we simply trust in the footsteps of the godly one who goes before us.

WISE WAYS   Whom do you consider a godly "leader"—an example you can follow? In what specific areas of your life is it helpful to have a godly example to follow?

Today, Lord, I thank you for those who live a godly life for me to follow. Help me see the path of righteousness and stay on it.

**Read
Proverbs 2**

THE RIGHT LEADER

Follow the steps of good men instead, and stay on the paths of the righteous. For only the upright will live in the land, and those who have integrity will remain in it.

Proverbs 2:20-21

November 3

Read Proverbs 3

✳

HOME INTERIORS

The curse of the LORD is on the house of the wicked, but his blessing is on the home of the upright.

Proverbs 3:33

A well-manicured lawn is not necessarily the sign of a blessed home. Nor does a godly residence imply faultless inhabitants. Both Christian and godless homes can be prone to problems. In truth, the home of the upright is not perfect—only perfectly blessed.

This blessing referred to by this proverb comes in the form of God's presence and power. A godly home can experience tragedy and yet endure in spite of it. A godly home can have a rebellious child. The home of the upright can be cramped, yet still be full of love. All this is due to God's presence and power within that imperfect home. However, what hope is there for a family apart from God's blessing? That family can only experience God's curse—the very opposite of his blessing. The house of the wicked is simply that—a house. God's blessing transforms a house into a home.

WISE WAYS   What does it mean to you to be blessed by God? What makes a godly home?

Today, Lord, I am thankful for your blessings, your presence, and your power in my life.

November 4

SABBATH

The last thing a person in today's society wants is to be responsible for someone else. Those in the public eye, from sports figures to movie stars, shrug off the idea of being role models for young people. After all, "kids will be kids."

Many people—the famous as well as the not so famous—have enough trouble handling responsibility for their own lives, much less the lives of others. The invention of the no-fault divorce represents just how far we've come with this idea. We don't want to take responsibility for our own actions—and, by default, we can't bring ourselves to assign blame to others either. We cower as a culture behind the motto "To each his or her own." However, Jesus peers over our shabbily constructed defenses to deliver the news: we are responsible. We are responsible for our influence on others. What a terrible and terrifying proposition for a culture that would rather look the other way.

WISE WAYS   In what ways might you unconsciously contribute to others' wrongdoing? How do you consider yourself a role model for others?

Today, Lord, I know others are watching me as I try to live for you. Help me be conscious of my character and not tempt others to sin.

**Read
Proverbs 4**

ACCOUNTABLE
EXAMPLES

How terrible it will be for anyone who causes others to sin. Temptation to do wrong is inevitable, but how terrible it will be for the person who does the tempting.
Matthew 18:7

November 5

**Read
Proverbs 5**

TRAPPED!

*An evil man is held
captive by his own
sins; they are ropes
that catch and hold
him.*

Proverbs 5:22

This proverb pictures a person who, spiritually speaking, trips over his or her own feet. Although we rarely enjoy accepting responsibility for our mistakes, we have to admit they are our mistakes. Though we live in an adversarial culture, we cannot blame our sinfulness on it. Though we may be bombarded with temptation in everyday circumstances, we are not so easily let off the hook.

We are like a deep-sea tuna following its instincts toward bait, only to be ensnared by a fisherman's net. Likewise, in our natural habitat—the world—we follow our natural instincts toward the things we want. Money. Power. Sex. Yet we soon find ourselves ensnared by such vices. We are soon roped in, caught, and tightly held in sin's grip. Ironically, we find ourselves in such a predicament because of personal choice. We are our own captors. This proverb reminds us that everyone sins by nature and by choice.

WISE WAYS   How are you tempted to blame your mistakes on others? What does it mean to you to sin "by nature and by choice"?

Today, Lord, free me from my sin and the temptations that ensnare me.

November 6

One of the distinctive features of a proverb is its ability to put a new spin on an old truth. Common sense appears uncommonly wise when phrased in the form of a proverb. So it is with this particular truth concerning the inevitability of punishment for sin. Certainly, the context of sexual promiscuity is particularly relevant, although the principle can apply to any wrongdoing. Sin brings consequences—plain and simple.

The proverb details a "what goes up, must come down" common sense philosophy. Yet, consider the lengths many people will go to to defy common sense. We rationalize wrongdoing. We believe we are the exception to the rule. Like a driver racing across a lowered railroad crossing guard, we interpret the odds in our favor. We routinely practice the fool's philosophy of "just this once." Why else would we continue to stoop to sin unless we somehow believed we wouldn't be punished? This proverb reminds us of the certainty of consequences, despite our best arguments against it.

WISE WAYS   Why do you think people rationalize sin? Why are consequences good deterrents to sin?

Today, Lord, I need to be reminded of the seriousness of sin and not rationalize wrongdoing.

**Read
Proverbs 6**

CAUSE AND EFFECT

So it is with the man who sleeps with another man's wife. He who embraces her will not go unpunished.
Proverbs 6:29

November 7

**Read
Proverbs 7**

MORAL DRIFT

*Don't let your hearts
stray away toward
her. Don't wander
down her wayward
path. For she has
been the ruin of
many; numerous
men have been her
victims.*
Proverbs 7:25-26

Subtlety is one of nature's more powerful forces.
For example, single drops of water, steadily spread
over millions of years, combine to form wondrous
limestone creations, housed like sculptures within
cavernous museums. These creations provide
convincing evidence of the power of subtlety.

Likewise, perhaps one of the greater forces at
work in a person's life is subtle moral drift. It is
defined by straying choices and wayward reckonings
(which, like water droplets, don't seem to amount
to much). Yet, multiplied together over a lifetime,
these little compromises result in proportionate
consequences. Proverbs accurately pinpoints a straying heart and a wandering mind as the most likely
beginning point of a ruined character. Most people
who come to ruin do so at a gradual pace. They
don't intend to race down sin's streets; they simply
wander off the righteous path. Take a lesson from
nature—little missteps have the potential to create
gargantuan compromises in our character.

WISE WAYS What is your definition of compromise? How do you see the power of subtlety at work
when it comes to sin?

*Today, Lord, I need your help to stay on the right path. Guard my
character against little compromises.*

November 8

This proverb presents wisdom come to life—a personality filled with emotion and self-will. Scholars believe personifying wisdom in this way provides a unique background for understanding Christ himself as the very wisdom of God.

Though not necessarily a direct description of Christ, the point of this proverb is to show wisdom rejoicing in our favored status with God as his creation. Wisdom is on our side. Sadly, many people are convinced that practicing God's laws and adhering to wisdom is just the opposite. They believe wisdom takes all the fun out of life. They say wisdom is reserved for stone-faced monks and mountaintop monasteries; it certainly is not practical for life in the real world. Yet Scripture reminds us that wisdom was an integral part of this real world's very beginnings. In this sense, wisdom was created for human happiness and is the creator of happiness itself. The entire human family and the world in which we live spring forth from this truth.

WISE WAYS   What do you think of when describing a "wise" person? How is wisdom related to happiness?

Today, Lord, I realize you have given me wisdom for my own happiness. Help me to practice wisdom today.

**Read
Proverbs 8**

WISDOM CHEERS

And how happy I was with what he created—his wide world and all the human family!
Proverbs 8:31

November 9

Read
Proverbs 9

SIN'S MENU

*"Stolen water is
refreshing;
food eaten
in secret tastes
the best!"
But the men
don't realize that
her former guests
are now
in the grave.*
Proverbs 9:17-18

There are those who find delight in taking culinary
risks and those who prefer to find their thrills elsewhere. Daredevil eaters crave the delicacies of a hole-
in-the-wall or a dive café. Of course, thanks to local
health laws, there are certain inherent risks one must
recognize—for salmonella is no respecter of persons.
This proverb employs a similar backdrop whereby
people frequent a promising café filled with tempting
fare. However, the dining area is strangely empty—
eerie evidence that something has gone wrong.

Sin's "menu" is always tempting—refreshing and
secretly delightful. In the world of food, presentation is everything. Compromise is served in bite-
sized pieces—no one can stop with just one. Adultery
is garnished with petite lies carved to look like roses.
And Greed is served on tap. However, what is not on
the menu is what one must beware. Former guests
have died from their naiveté. Take note of those
whose sinful indulgences have led to ruin.

WISE WAYS   Why do you think wrongdoing can
be so appealing? What can you learn from others'
wrongdoing?

*Today, Lord, I thirst for your truth and hunger for your ways. Feed
my soul with what is right and good for me.*

November 10

Storm trackers are usually the first to sight storm activity. However, even with their advanced equipment to measure air pressure and wind, they can provide no more than a few minutes' warning for those in the storm's path to seek shelter. In the same way, stormy trials can drop in unexpectedly in all of our lives.

The distinction in this proverb is not who goes through a storm—the wicked or the godly. Both are thrust into the middle of a storm. However, the dramatic difference is the outcome. Everything the wicked owns and even the wicked people themselves are whirled away in the storm's fury. However, the godly people withstand the trial. The difference is in their foundation.

The image in this proverb is similar to a commonly televised aerial shot panned early the next morning after a destructive storm. Some houses remain unscathed, while the homes of next-door neighbors have hardly a stacked brick remaining. The godly will survive life's storms because of their Christ-centered foundation.

WISE WAYS   What storm are you facing in life right now? How would you describe your foundation?

Today, Lord, I need your strength to get through life's storms. Teach me what it means to have you as my strong foundation.

Read
Proverbs 10

STORMY WEATHER

Disaster strikes like a cyclone, whirling the wicked away, but the godly have a lasting foundation.
Proverbs 10:25

November 11

SABBATH

Read Proverbs 11

AS YOURSELF

Jesus replied, "The most important commandment is this: 'Hear, O Israel! The Lord our God is the one and only Lord. And you must love the Lord your God with all your heart, all your soul, all your mind, and all your strength.' The second is equally important: 'Love your neighbor as yourself.' No other commandment is greater than these."

Mark 12:29-31

Jesus didn't think it was enough to be kind or nice to our neighbor. He insisted on repeating his Father's standard (Leviticus 19:18)—love your neighbor as you love yourself.

The second part of the great commandment completes a triangle of love that challenges each person: love for God, love for neighbor, love for self. Each one affects the other two. None of the three is optional. All of them must be present for healthy living. Without love for God, love of self and neighbor is reduced to human effort. Without love for neighbor, love for self and for God becomes suspect (see 1 John 4:20). And without love for self, love for God and neighbor becomes impossible. All these exist for one reason—because God loved us first. God's love invites our direct response. God's love directs our response to include our neighbor. And God's love demonstrates that we are lovable (see 1 John 4:9-10).

WISE WAYS Those who learn to treat their neighbors exactly as they would like to be treated are obeying God at the deepest human level.

Lord, teach me that I can learn a lot about loving my neighbor by letting you help me love myself the right way.

November 12

Proverbs' consistent message revolves around recognizing the power of our words. For example, encouragement can make a difference in the lives of those around us. Oftentimes, we meet needy people consumed with troubles. We feel we can do nothing to lift their burdens—we may say a prayer, if that, and go on our way. However, Scripture exhorts us to a ministry of encouragement.

Our words of hope and support may be the very balm a worrier needs to get through a particular problem. From strangers on the street, to store clerks, to good friends and family members, encouragement should be the theme of all our conversation and interaction. Compliment strangers. Find something good to say. When you notice trainees in a store, affirm them. If a friend is struggling, offer your prayers. There is enough worry weighing down the world for everyone to have a share. Believers can make it their mission to make sure encouragement is as equally abundant.

WISE WAYS   How can you specifically encourage at least two people today?

Today, Lord, help me be sensitive to what I say. Let my words be encouraging to those around me.

**Read
Proverbs 12**

TIMELY RELIEF

Worry weighs a person down; an encouraging word cheers a person up.
Proverbs 12:25

November 13

**Read
Proverbs 13**

HOT PURSUIT!

*Trouble chases
sinners, while
blessings chase the
righteous!*

Proverbs 13:21

Laughter helps learning. Studies show that motivational speakers who use humor in their presentations have a more attentive audience. Accordingly, Proverbs often uses humor in its teachings. Here, we see an exaggerated portrayal of how God uses persistency to make his point. "Trouble" is like a guard dog, nipping at the heels of the sinful. However, "blessing" is a faithful companion who follows after the godly.

God overwhelms the righteous with his favor—so much so that it appears as if they can't get away from his goodness even if they tried! Blessings and curses are God's means for teaching us a lesson. Curses pursue those who are sinful—they can't get away with their crimes. However, blessings are always on the heels of the righteous person. So, if we are having a hard time discerning the wicked from the righteous, look around. Is a person constantly surrounded by troubles? Or hardly able to keep up with the outpouring of God's blessings?

WISE WAYS   How do you recognize a blessed person? In what ways is God blessing you right now?

Today, Lord, I am grateful that your blessings are my faithful companion. Thank you for all you have done for me.

November 14

At any given time, hundreds of thousands of people in our society are teetering on the edge of rage. And it's not who you might expect. They are young mothers who grow impatient on the freeway. They are wallflower employees who silently grow disgruntled, and quiet back-row students plotting revenge. They are apparently religious people who suddenly snap. News reports frequently detail how otherwise ordinary people in otherwise ordinary circumstances suddenly explode into extraordinary rage. And the mistakes they make are legion—verbal abuse, physical abuse, even murder. Anger can be deadly.

The Bible recognizes anger's lethal potential and says we must control it. "Understanding" is the by-product of someone who has learned to control his or her temper. We begin to understand that we actually never "lose" our temper; we "choose" it. No one can "make" us mad. We choose our response on our own accord. Asking God for great understanding will help us think about our course of action.

WISE WAYS When has a hasty temper led to a lapse in your judgment? What does it take to control your temper?

Today, Lord, forgive me for "choosing" to lose my temper. Give me great understanding for how to control anger.

**Read
Proverbs 14**

RELIEF

Those who control their anger have great understanding; those with a hasty temper will make mistakes.

Proverbs 14:29

November 15

**Read
Proverbs 15**

PRECISION

*Everyone enjoys a
fitting reply; it is
wonderful to say the
right thing at the
right time!*

Proverbs 15:23

Ann Landers, the popular advice columnist, has nothing on Proverbs—the ultimate daily column. Her millions of readers, however, have proven this truth: everyone loves to give advice. By her own testimony, she receives a sizable volume of letters from people who are not seeking advice. They are giving it. And doing so in abundance. Apparently for every printed reply to a problem, her readers offer their own version. Even so, her daily task is to attempt to say the right thing at the right time.

Though it is unlikely that we will ever see our words read by millions, this proverb reminds us of the value of a well-said word. We must ask God's help in choosing our timing as well as our words. Many people feel they often don't know what to say when a friend is hurting or in need of advice. However, God extols us to say the right thing at the right time—and promises his help in doing so. We won't do it perfectly every time, but we will get better the more we do it.

WISE WAYS How do you feel about giving advice? How do you determine what to say to a friend in need?

Today, Lord, give me the right things to say at the right times. May you be pleased in all I say.

November 16

The mission of the believer is not too different from that of history's most noted conquerors. We must be determined. Forceful. Inspired. Yet we do not set our sights on triumphing over nations. Our foe is our nature—the sinful nature that is used to getting what it wants. Our weapons of war are patience and self-control. Learning to be patient is the mark of maturity. For example, a baby cries until it gets what is needed. It is impossible for a baby to understand or appreciate the principle of delayed gratification. However, a mature adult learns to control his or her desires and practice patience.

Self-control allows us to disarm natural urges. Delayed gratification means waiting for sex until marriage. Patience allows us to discipline our children in love, never in anger. Power conquers cities; patience conquers sin. We need not set sail for new horizons seeking the ultimate conquest. We can merely look into the nearest mirror. It is better to conquer oneself than to conquer an entire city.

WISE WAYS In what ways are you developing greater patience? How do you demonstrate self-control?

Today, Lord, I will fight my greatest foe—myself. Make me victorious and self-controlled today.

Read Proverbs 16

STRATEGIC VICTORY

It is better to be patient than powerful; it is better to have self-control than to conquer a city.

Proverbs 16:32

November 17

ATTENTION

*Sensible people keep
their eyes glued on
wisdom, but a fool's
eyes wander to the
ends of the earth.*

Proverbs 17:24

Horse-drawn carriage rides in big cities mean big
business. After a delightful meal downtown, many
tourists and even locals enjoy a lazy trip around the
city sites. However, the setting itself is usually not so
serene. Taxis screech to a halt. Buses lumber along
with booming diesel engines. Pedestrians by the
hundreds flood city walkways. Yet the animals seem
to hardly notice the thoroughfare, blinded to the
left and right by leather patches. Steadily they trod,
centered on the road ahead.

Focus. That's the difference between a fool and a
sensible person. Fools are flighty. They may set their
sights on one job or relationship for a while, but
then their all-consuming efforts quickly dissipate.
Easily distracted, they are soon on to the next thing.
The ability to focus on what is truly important is
essential to success. Like the carriage horse, we must
fix our eyes on Christ—the central point of our lives.
He will safely guide us to success.

WISE WAYS How are you easily distracted from
your goals? What does it mean to you to fix your eyes
on Christ?

*Today, Lord, bring your wisdom into focus. And guide my steps to
success.*

November 18

Weeds are killers. Mowing seems like twice the chore due to the excessive amounts of weeds that seem to spring up almost overnight. A lovely lawn is the result of steamrolling this persistent plant life with a fine grade mower . . . at least for the moment. It isn't long, however, until nature's nuisance sprouts forth from unscathed roots with a vengeance. The secret to weed killing is at the root-level.

In the same way, we are often tempted to cut our bad habits at the lip-level—foul language, criticism. We swear off swearing and promise "not an idle word" from our lips. Soon, however, the roots of sinful behavior that are firmly implanted in our hearts sprout new growth and work their way up to become visible again. Jesus gets to the root of the issue: evil words come from an evil heart. It is not enough to merely cut bad habits at the lip-level. We need a heart transformation—pulling up weeds of ungodliness by the roots and planting goodness in their place. Only then are we prepared to give account for our words.

WISE WAYS   How is your speech affected by knowing that Christ holds you accountable for your words?

Today, Lord, cleanse my heart and affect my speech. May I be accountable to you for each word.

Read Proverbs 18

HARVEST

A good person produces good words from a good heart, and an evil person produces evil words from an evil heart. And I tell you this; that you must give an account on judgment day of every idle word you speak.
Matthew 12:35-36

November 19

Read
Proverbs 19

IN PUBLIC

*Children who
mistreat their father
or chase away their
mother are a public
disgrace and an
embarrassment.*

Proverbs 19:26

Role-reversal is a favorite game of children who love
to mimic the role of mother or father. However,
fantasy often has the opportunity to become reality
when the children become adults with an equal or
even superior position of authority. Maybe the adult
children become wealthier, more educated, and/or
more physically able than their parents. Many adult
children find a special pleasure in mistreating
parents—especially those who were raised feeling they
were mistreated themselves.

At first, revenge seems sweet. Yet it comes with a
price. Sure, it's embarrassing for the parents to have
their child disgrace them. However, this proverb says it
is better to be embarrassed than to become an embarrassment. Additionally, the disgraceful behavior is a
public concern because it reflects poorly on Christ
himself. Supposedly Christian people who mistreat
their own parents demonstrate a dichotomy that is hard
for others to understand. If this is the way Christians
treat those who are the very closest to them, then the
world wants nothing to do with their message. Their
actions are much more convincing than their words.

WISE WAYS What challenges do you experience
in your relationship with your parents or those in
authority?

*Today, Lord, don't let me be an embarrassment to you. Help me
treat my family in a way that honors you.*

November 20

There is a molecular universe that is unseen to the naked human eye. We're talking small. Without the benefit of scientific instruments, it would be impossible to describe the appearance of an atom. We wouldn't have a clue about the detail of a proton or neutron.

Likewise, there are components of the human spirit that have never been seen with the human eye. Does anyone other than our Creator know exactly what a motive looks like? Impossible! For motives are imbedded deep within our spirit, hidden behind good intentions and false pretenses. Only God can penetrate human defenses and expose a person's wrong motive—hidden or otherwise. The bottom line of this proverb is this—we're transparent. There's no point in keeping things from God. There's no sense in lying to him. With his penetrating gaze, he can see right through us. Like the multiples of volumes that have been created on the molecular universe, God has us all figured out.

WISE WAYS How do you deal with wrong motives? Why is it helpful to know God searches your spirit?

Today, Lord, search my spirit freely. May my motives be pure and pleasing to you.

Read Proverbs 20

EXPOSED!

The LORD'S searchlight penetrates the human spirit, exposing every hidden motive.
Proverbs 20:27

November 21

MOUTH
CONTROL

*If you keep your
mouth shut,
you will stay
out of trouble.*
Proverbs 21:23

Once again, this proverb willingly plays the role of
"Master of the Obvious." However, this simple piece
of advice, though touted in various forms, is rarely
practiced. Foot-in-mouth disease is a worldwide
epidemic. We regularly spill secrets. We speak
volumes about what we don't really know. We say the
first thing that comes to mind with fluent precision
but little forethought about its implications.

Instead of implementing the proverb's "quit while
ahead" philosophy, we often open our mouths wider
in an attempt to talk our way out of trouble. In short,
the advice is simple, but following the advice is something else altogether. However, the whole of Scripture
helps put the principle into practice. Wait on the
Lord. Pray for wisdom. Meditate on God's Word. If
we feel we must do something in the heat of the
moment, there are many things to keep us busy as we
practice keeping our mouths shut.

WISE WAYS When is it most difficult for you to
keep your mouth shut? Why is that?

*Today, Lord, I am thankful for the times you have saved me from
trouble by helping me stay quiet.*

November 22

His image cannot be found in the yellow pages or spread on the backs of phone books. He will likely never tout a slogan on a billboard or bus. Don't look for him to star in his own commercial. However, he is the most powerful personal injury lawyer on the planet. He is the Lord. Don't mess with him.

The Bible makes it clear from cover to cover that he is especially interested in the poor and needy. Although biblical history is full of injustice against the afflicted, God's message is still the same. He is their defender and will cause their foes to come to ruin. In contrast, our culture is generally complacent about the poor. They are often considered easy prey for robbery or exploitation in more than one sense. They are robbed of their dignity. They are exploited for their lack of resources. Yet God reserves special honor for them. How we ought to do the same!

WISE WAYS   What do you think God's interest in the poor reveals about his character? What does your interest in the needy say about you?

Today, Lord, make me sensitive to the poor and needy. Show me how I can share your special burden for them.

Read
Proverbs 22

DIVINE DEFENDER

Do not rob the poor because they are poor or exploit the needy in court. For the LORD is their defender. He will injure anyone who injures them.

Proverbs 22:22-23

November 23

**Read
Proverbs 23**

✳

DEAD-END
SOLUTIONS

*Don't let the sparkle
and smooth taste of
wine deceive you. For
in the end it bites like
a poisonous serpent;
it stings like a viper.*

Proverbs 23:31-32

A piece of eraser easily serves as a missing earring back. Bubble gum can substitute for glue in a pinch. And some say duct tape can fix anything. Quick fixes do wonders for the time being, yet they rarely have anything to offer in the long run. Alcohol and drug abuse are popular quick-fix solutions to life's problems. However, as this proverb points out, in the end they prove more than useless—they are deadly. People often actually wind up in greater trouble than when they first started.

Alcohol abuse is initially appealing as a means for escape—especially for people who have lost the ability to see an alternate solution. However, over time, alcohol leads a person to become progressively worse in order to "feel better." The Bible calls it deception. We may try a number of ways to deal with our problems, but "in the end" they fail to provide relief. A true solution is one that both gets us through problems and makes us better people.

WISE WAYS When are you tempted to take a shortcut or escape from your problems?

Today, Lord, forgive me for trying to solve my problems without your help. Help me to turn to you for solutions.

November 24

Initially, this proverb may read like a specific message for a specific audience: an entrepreneur buying her first home. However, the proverb is actually illustrating a universal principle about proper order. Just as a new business entrepreneur would "build up" to the purchase of a new home, certain things must be done in sequence for greater success. If someone bought a house and then began to balance a start-up business, he or she would risk the possibility of losing both.

The applications of this principle are found in more than just investments and business matters. For example, there must be love before marriage. And ideally marriage comes before children. Getting these steps out of order can be devastating. The Bible teaches the importance of having order to show us something about God's character. It shows us that he is a loving God—intricately involved and interested in our lives. What we do and how we do it matters to God.

WISE WAYS Why is sequence important to success? In what ways do you tend to "get ahead" of God's plan for you?

Today, Lord, I may be tempted to get ahead of you. Slow me down. Teach me the meaning of an orderly life.

**Read
Proverbs 24**

WISE ORDER

Develop your business first before building your house.

Proverbs 24:27

November 25

**Read
Proverbs 25**

WORTHWHILE REWARD

God blesses the people who patiently endure testing. Afterward they will receive the crown of life that God has promised to those who love him.

James 1:12

In Greek, the term used here for "crown" refers to a ceremonial victory wreath in athletics or the military. Like a weary marathon runner who patiently endures muscle-testing mile upon mile, so we must commit ourselves to completing the course. In the end, the prize will be worth the effort.

Temptation and testing is part of life. However, we cannot allow that to dissuade us. Like a wounded warrior battling the temptation to surrender to the enemy, we must be steadfast. For no matter how severe the trial, the outcomes that await us are far more significant: God's blessing, eternal life, and God's promise.

Temptation comes to us in earthly forms like materialism, sex, money, and power. They provide temporary satisfaction. In contrast, God rewards those who endure temptation with eternal benefits. He provides a winner's medal that never tarnishes and a living victory wreath that never shrivels or dies. Although earthly testing is difficult, the reward is heavenly—heaven itself!

WISE WAYS   What is difficult about temptation? Why does God reward endurance?

Today, Lord, I may be tempted and tested. Help me decide beforehand, right now, to endure and not give in.

November 26

This proverb is not about bad luck or little-known laws of nature. Known by some as "what goes around comes around," this biblical boomerang actually describes the way God has structured natural consequences for breaking his commands. Whatever we do to harm others will ultimately harm us. Whatever we do to seek revenge against an enemy will eventually become our own downfall. For example, hatred toward others causes self-inflicted wounds.

People who are consumed with hatred stress out and worry. Sometimes their feelings are so intense that they can't sleep or eat. Hatred is a trap we set for others, yet we get hung up in it ourselves. Like a scene in a slapstick comedy, our entangled foot dangles us upside-down out on a limb. Meanwhile, our "victim" passes by unharmed. Yet it is no laughing matter. Revenge is a dangerous game, best left to the professional—God himself.

WISE WAYS   When have you experienced the truth of this proverb? Why are people tempted to take matters into their own hands?

Today, Lord, others may try to hurt me. Remind me of your truth when I want revenge.

Read Proverbs 26

BOOMERANG

If you set a trap for others, you will get caught in it yourself. If you roll a boulder down on others, it will roll back and crush you.

Proverbs 26:27

November 27

Read
Proverbs 27

INTERNAL IMAGE

*As a face is reflected
in water, so the heart
reflects the person.*
Proverbs 27:19

Science has discovered a new way of looking at things. There is a mirror on the market that provides the most accurate reflection yet. Instead of gazing upon a reversed image seen in a typical mirror, this new technological advancement allows people to see themselves the same way the rest of the world does. People who have used it claim to prefer the new image. This "true reflection" makes a person skinnier, younger, and a number of other improvements.

The best mirror still doesn't show the real person, however. Our hearts represent the true person we are on the inside. If we want to see our whole being the way the rest of the world does, we must peer inside our hearts and face what is there. We may be startled by what we see. We may squint to see anything good at all. Fortunately, we are works in progress. God works in us to gradually mold and shape each heart to one day perfectly reflect the image of Jesus Christ.

WISE WAYS What does the condition of your heart say about your character? How can you reflect more of Christ's character?

Today, Lord, mold my heart to reflect more of the character of Christ.

November 28

It is possible to use flattery to gain many friendships, perks, and opportunities. However, the gain may be temporary at best. At the end of a friendship paved with flattery, friends may find they really have nothing in common. At the end of a workday, puffed full of empty compliments from manipulative employees, a supervisor may feel used instead of affirmed.

This proverb is not saying that people don't appreciate flattery. In reality, they do. In general, people love to have their ego stroked. And yet the Bible teaches that people value truthfulness, couched in love, much more. Being frank is not the same as being rude. Being frank with a friend means telling a person our honest, objective evaluation of a situation or issue. Flattery means telling a person only what he or she wants to hear. According to this proverb, the bottom line is being truthful instead of insincere.

WISE WAYS Why do you think people appreciate frankness more than flattery? When are you tempted to use flattery to get what you want?

Today, Lord, I will follow your guidance and speak the truth in love.

Read
Proverbs 28

VALUED TRUTH

In the end, people appreciate frankness more than flattery.
Proverbs 28:23

November 29

Read
Proverbs 29

✳

TRUE SAFETY

Fearing people is a dangerous trap, but to trust the LORD means safety.
Proverbs 29:25

A phobia is defined as an irrational fear that controls a person's daily life. Arachnophobia is the fear of spiders. Claustrophobia is the fear of being confined in small spaces.

The Bible describes what it is like to have an irrational fear of other people. It is a trap—a paralyzing situation where we are no longer in control of our lives. It is one thing to have appropriate concern for a person's opinion. It is quite another to cower before it. The fear of disappointing people can lead churches to abandon new visions for ministry. Leaders may compromise their own convictions due to an irrational fear of hurting someone's feelings. Believers may remain stunted in their spiritual growth, afraid of living out their faith at work or at home. Imagine an animal that deliberately runs into a trap, thinking it will find safety there. Of course, it finds the very opposite. In the same way, we cannot find safety through our attempts to please others. We must please God and trust him alone—then we find true safety.

WISE WAYS What must you do in order to be free from the fear of other people's opinion?

Today, Lord, I will trust in you. Teach me what it means to find security in you alone.

November 30

In the manner of "Which came first: the chicken or the egg?" this proverb makes an important distinction about the sequence of natural causes. Beating cream yields butter. Beaten noses yield blood. Anger yields quarrels. Which comes first: anger or a quarrel?

This proverb indicates that anger is the precursor to quarrels. It is the common denominator in most quarrelsome relationships. Fighting is a symptom of anger. Well-intentioned parents may bring an end to the fighting between quarreling children. Sending them to their rooms brings temporary peace. Meanwhile, the anger remains seething just below the surface. Eventually, anger that is not properly dealt with will give birth to more quarrels. As a result, we must deal with anger on a deeper level to fully address our concerns. Human relationships—marriages, friendships, and families—hinge on cause and effect dynamics. We must get to the root cause of a problem in order to deal with its effects.

WISE WAYS Why is anger an issue for many people? How do you appropriately deal with anger?

Today, Lord, teach me how to handle my emotions so I can enjoy the relationships I have with others.

**Read
Proverbs 30**

CONNECTIONS

As the beating of cream yields butter, and a blow to the nose causes bleeding, so anger causes quarrels.
Proverbs 30:33

DECEMBER

December 1

Read
Proverbs 1

KEEP LISTENING

*But all who
listen to me
will live in peace
and safety,
unafraid of harm.*
Proverbs 1:33

Who among us would not desire a life of peace and safety, one without fear of harm? To have that, is it true that all we must do is listen to God? Is it reasonable to conclude that if we are not experiencing peace and safety, if we are living with fear, we are not listening to God? Can it really be that simple? If so, how then should we interpret James 1:2, which says, "Whenever trouble comes your way, let it be an opportunity for joy?" And what about I Peter 1:6, which says, "There is wonderful joy ahead, even though it is necessary for you to endure many trials for a while"? Trouble? Trials? Peace? Safety? How can all these come in the same package?

It is important to note that the passages in James and I Peter go on to say that trials produce perseverance and maturity, and that suffering proves our faith. Through the eyes of a mature faith, we can begin to realize that in the midst of the temporary turmoil and strife of this life, we can know God's eternal peace and safety. We need not be concerned about harm that may come to these earthly bodies of ours, because we know what God ultimately has in store for us.

WISE WAYS What message is God trying to get you to hear as you go through difficult circumstances?

Today, Lord, may I welcome with praise whatever comes my way, because I know you will use these circumstances to make me into what you want me to be.

December 2

SABBATH

One of the greatest misunderstandings of people throughout the ages is thinking that their religious efforts will make God look favorably upon them when they die and face him for judgment. Christianity is the world's only religion that doesn't make this claim. It was that very misunderstanding among the Pharisees of the New Testament that Jesus so roundly condemned. Jesus' message was that God's acceptance of us is his act of love and mercy, not the result of our conforming to certain standards of a religious creed. His love for us is a gift to be humbly received by coming to him through his son, Jesus.

Why, then, does this verse in James seem to say that the *true* religion is caring for orphans and widows? Isn't he asking us to act a certain way to obtain his favor? Certainly, God wants us to care for orphans and widows, but he is not asking us to do this in order to earn his favor. Instead, he is simply stating that if we truly love him, we will love and serve the most needy among us with selfless humility. Rather, our good deeds are the natural outpouring of our gratitude to God for his gift of love to us.

WISE WAYS Can you distinguish between a kindness done to earn favor and one done out of love?

Today, Lord, may my attitude be one of humility, and may I accept and love others as you have loved me.

**Read
Proverbs 2**

GRATEFUL
EFFORTS

Pure and lasting religion in the sight of God our Father means that we must care for orphans and widows in their troubles, and refuse to let the world corrupt us.

James 1:27

December 3

**Read
Proverbs 3**

HEART
CONTRAST

*The LORD mocks at
mockers, but he
shows favor to the
humble.*

Proverbs 3:34

The Lord mocking mockers and favoring the humble is
just one variation of a theme often repeated in the
Bible; namely, God's primary interest is in the attitudes of the heart. Mockers can be characterized in one
of two ways, and both are the result of an improper
image of self. One is blatant pride that says, "I am
better than others." The other is a sense of worthless-
ness that says, "I try to hide by degrading others."

Pride prevents people from seeking God because
it makes them think they don't need him. Feeling
worthless prevents people from seeking God because
it makes them think they can't measure up.

Humility, on the other hand, allows a realistic
perspective. Humility recognizes that we are the
pinnacle of God's creation, created by him in his
image in order to worship him. But it also recognizes
that we are sinners who turned our backs on God and
that, except for God's grace, we would be eternally
separated from him and his love. It is because of his
grace that he has permitted us to reenter his presence.
How can we not accept that second chance?

WISE WAYS   True humility recognizes not just the
depths to which you have fallen, but also the hope
inherent in God's love for you and his offer of a
second chance. Have you accepted that second chance?

*Today, Lord, may I not be a mocker separated from you, but a
humble seeker of your perfect ways.*

December 4

Today's verse was Solomon's way of stating a very familiar principle. In I Corinthians 9:24, the apostle Paul stated it in terms of running a race, and running it with the goal of obtaining the prize. In Philippians 3:14, Paul spoke of purposefully "aiming toward the mark of the high calling." Even the well-known children's fable about a tortoise and a hare is centered around the same message: Keep focused, have a definite goal, work diligently toward that goal, and don't let yourself be distracted.

Why is that advice so often repeated? Probably because it is so difficult to follow. Diligence is work—hard work. Becoming distracted is easy; it happens even when we're not looking. It is also all too easy to follow evil. It happens when we simply let down our guard, when we stop working toward our goal.

What should that goal be? Solomon answers that question, too. In Ecclesiastes 12:13, he says, "Fear God and obey his commands: for this is the duty of every person." The greater our focus on God and his Word, the less will be our tendency to get sidetracked.

WISE WAYS Are you truly focused on following your Lord, or are you easily distracted even to the point of following evil?

Today, Lord, let my mind be stayed on you. Let the words of my mouth and the meditation of my heart be acceptable in your sight.

Read
Proverbs 4

AVOIDING
DETOURS

Don't get sidetracked; keep your feet from following evil.
Proverbs 4:27

December 5

**Read
Proverbs 5**

✳

BIG PICTURE

*[The evil man] will
die for lack of self-
control; he will be
lost because of his
incredible folly.*

Proverbs 5:23

The primary thrust of Proverbs 5 is that a man should
be faithful to his wife. But the last three verses, including verse 23, give the chapter a broader context. They
speak of evil deeds ensnaring a person, the "ropes that
catch and hold him" (v. 22). Verse 23 uses words we
might use to describe a person's relentless addiction to
drugs. We think of drug addicts as having a total lack of
self-control, and of their incredible folly in choosing
to waste their lives. In the depths of their addiction,
drug addicts also like to think that they can get their
fixes secretly, out of the view of those who love them.

Our evil ways are like that, too. We are all addicted
to sin from birth, because our mother (and father)
were addicts. We were born addicted to sin, and we
choose with incredible folly to continue our addiction
with our evil ways. And despite our attempts to deny
or hide them, our evil ways are in full view of the
Lord. He knows our sin. He also knows that our
addiction is beyond self-correction. That is why he
gave us Jesus—to save us from our incredible folly,
and to restore us to our faithfulness to him.

WISE WAYS   How have you dealt with your addiction to sin? Though your evil ways are in full view of
your Savior, he extends his hand to help you up
every time you fall.

*Today, Lord, I confess my addiction to sin, and accept your extended
hand to lift me from my evil ways.*

December 6

If we are to believe the cultural message of the late twentieth and early twenty-first centuries, sexual acts of any kind are simply alternative lifestyles. Current logic also says that the Old Testament is not applicable to modern living, so this advice in Proverbs can be safely ignored. Further, according to this logic, even Jesus said in his Sermon on the Mount, "Stop judging others, and you will not be judged" (Matthew 7:1). So does all this mean that we must accept these "alternatives" without condemnation because all choices are equally moral? Viewed through the eyes of political correctness, it does. But this line of thinking is just one more example of man's attempts to rationalize behavior that God clearly condemns.

Today's proverb says that the adulterous man is a fool. According to the descriptions in Proverbs, a fool is not someone who lacks intellectual ability, but one who chooses to rationalize wrong behavior. The fool casts off the fear of God, thinking and acting as if he could safely disregard God's righteousness. Remember this: God's principles are eternal. They are never out of date.

WISE WAYS   Have you become so hardened that you have cast off the fear of God? In what ways do you attempt to rationalize your sin?

Today, Lord, may I be truly sensitive to your urgings, and not so foolish that I ignore you. Help me to see my sin as sin, and not to rationalize it.

**Read
Proverbs 6**

✳

SELF-
DEMOLITION

The man who commits adultery is an utter fool, for he destroys his own soul.
Proverbs 6:32

December 7

Read
Proverbs 7

DANGER SIGNS

[The immoral woman's] house is the road to the grave. Her bedroom is the den of death.

Proverbs 7:27

Today's verse is a familiar warning to the reader of Proverbs. Stay away from sexual sin because it is one of the mileage markers on the road to spiritual death. Sexual sin, like lying, never shows up alone in a person's life. You cannot participate in it without participating in many other forms of sin. Adultery is usually accompanied by lies and deceit. It is also a selfish act that involves the breaking of your marriage vows, and a disregard for the well-being of your children.

But this knowledge can also lead to a misunderstanding. Because warnings against sexual sin are so frequent in Scripture, Christians often treat sex and sexuality as if they are particularly offensive to God, rather than a wonderful gift from him when used as he intended. It is only when the gift is used as God did not intend that it becomes sin. But that is also true of all of God's gifts. God is a generous God who bestows upon us many precious gifts, but using any of them inappropriately is sin, and "the wages of [any] sin is death" (Romans 6:23).

WISE WAYS   Think about those who trivialize a particular sin because they think others are more serious. What does that tell you about their understanding of the holiness of God?

Today, Lord, help me to confess my every sin, no matter how small, that I may be holy as you are holy.

December 8

Confusing and incomprehensible as the Bible sometimes seems, one simple message is woven through its
pages—the message of life. In Genesis, we read that
God created the world, and that he created people in
his own image to walk with and worship him. But they
sinned, and at that very moment, they died spiritually.
They broke their relationship with God and were
forever separated from him. Physical death soon
followed. God could have turned his back on his
creation to let it self-destruct. But the glorious message
of the Bible is that he didn't—because he loved us too
much. That is why the Bible doesn't end after the first
few chapters of Genesis. It goes on to record the history
of God's relationship with men and women and his
offering us a restored relationship with him.

Today's proverb speaks of this restored relationship by saying that whoever finds God's wisdom finds
life and the Lord's approval. How do we find that
wisdom? God's wisdom is found in a person—Jesus
Christ, who is "the wonderful wisdom of God"
(1 Corinthians 1:24). In Christ, we have God's
wisdom. In him, we have life!

WISE WAYS Nothing is more futile than life
without God; no life is more fulfilling than the one
you find in Christ. Consider an example from your
own life of how you know this to be true.

*Today, Lord, I acknowledge my sin has separated me from you, but I
thank you that through Jesus, you have provided me a second chance.*

**Read
Proverbs 8**

YOU HAVE
BEEN APPROVED

*Whoever finds me
finds life and wins
approval from the
Lord.*

Proverbs 8:35

December 9

Read Proverbs 9

✴

THE FRAMEWORK OF LOVE

Jesus replied, "The most important commandment is this: 'Hear, O Israel! The Lord our God is the one and only Lord. And you must love the Lord your God with all your heart, all your soul, all your mind, and all your strength.' The second is equally important: 'Love your neighbor as yourself.' No other commandment is greater than these."

Mark 12:29-31

Our twelve encounters with this central proverb have only scratched its surface. The better we understand this great commandment, the more it challenges us. No other proverb gives us a challenge more applicable every single day.

As a thought for further meditation, consider that this proverb implies or describes ten types of love: (1) God's love for us; (2) God's love for our neighbor; (3) our heart-love for God; (4) our soul-love for God; (5) our mind-love for God; (6) our strength-love for God; (7) our love for our neighbor; (8) our love for ourselves; (9) our neighbor's love for God; and (10) our neighbor's love for us. Meditating on these will require considerable exposure to the rest of Scripture.

Consider also exactly how this great two-part commandment summarizes the Ten Commandments in Exodus 20:1-17. Remember that an increased understanding of the deep things of God will broaden your responsibility to apply them in your life.

WISE WAYS   What lessons have you learned from digging deeply into Jesus' words? How should they change your life?

Today, Lord, renew my commitment to be a doer of your Word, applying this great commandment throughout my life.

December 10

Laziness is its own self-condemnation. Laziness brings poverty (Proverbs 10:4). The homes of the lazy fall into disrepair (Ecclesiastes 10:18). But today's verse is not just directed at the lazy. It is a warning to others. Lazy people are an aggravation to those who must deal with them, like smoke in the eyes or a fingernail scratching a chalkboard.

Employers hire workers to work. An employee who is lazy, who doesn't do his job, causes frustration to set in. The natural response of the employer is to fire lazy workers because they don't do what they were hired to do. If the natural and justifiable response of the employer is to fire a lazy employee, how much more understandable is God's response to our sin.

Sin is living, acting, and thinking in ways not intended by God when he created us. As sinners, we should expect nothing less than expulsion from God's presence. What is surprising is that despite God's "irritation" with us, he pursues us with the purpose of bringing us back to him. That knowledge is a lesson for us. Though some people may irritate us to the point of distraction, we must still love them and pursue them to bring them into God's very presence.

WISE WAYS How would you describe your work ethic? Are you a joy or a pain to your employer? How do you treat those who irritate you?

Today, Lord, may I be patient with those around me and love them as you have loved me.

Read
Proverbs 10

ON THE JOB

Lazy people are a pain to their employer. They are like smoke in the eyes or vinegar that sets the teeth on edge.
Proverbs 10:26

December 11

Read
Proverbs 11

✳

STILL TRUE

*It is possible to give
freely and become
more wealthy, but
those who are stingy
will lose everything.*

Proverbs 11:24

Those who would argue against the truth and reliability of the Bible might use this verse (and many others in Proverbs) to support their view because everyone knows of real situations that contradict what the verse seems to say. We can all name people who are greedy and stingy but also have great wealth. And we can name very generous people who live in or on the edge of poverty. Those who approach the Bible with the preconceived notion that it is unreliable deny themselves the greater opportunity to know God and discover the deeper meaning of these truths.

If we believe the Bible contains many historical inaccuracies and inconsistencies, it becomes a meaningless book. Then, if we read it at all, we tend to look for shallow interpretations that support our notion of its fallibility. But if we accept Jesus' own testimony that the Scriptures are reliable, and we are willing (with the help of the Holy Spirit) to search out its deeper meanings, we will find Scripture to be utterly truthful, consistent, infallible, and very relevant to our personal lives. To understand that truth is to understand true wealth.

WISE WAYS To give freely requires an open hand; to hear God speak through his Word requires an open mind. How do you read the Bible? In what ways do you seek to discover its truths?

Today, Lord, as I read your Word, may I not doubt, but come expecting to find in it the depths of your truth.

December 12

Young people, in particular, find it very difficult to distinguish between evaluating their friendships on the basis of advice those friends offer and evaluating advice on the basis of those friendships. Their desire for friendship and acceptance often overrules their awareness of bad advice. Unfortunately, those who are not true friends don't hesitate to use their "friendship" as a condition to get someone to go along with a bad plan.

Conversations about friendship ought to be frequent during a child's earliest years. Culture tends to cheapen the relationship to the point of being synonymous with acquaintance. Young people list among their friends people whom they barely know. A child who has learned the high value of the word "friend" will be less likely to trust as friends those who have not really proven themselves trustworthy.

Both genuine friendship and good advice stand the test of time. Neither occurs instantly. Both are to be treasured.

WISE WAYS Those who learn what it means to be a true friend have also learned to recognize one. Who would you name as your true friends? Why? Do you consider yourself a true friend?

Today, Lord, I thank you for my friendships. Thank you for being my ultimate friend. Help me be the right kind of friend to others.

**Read
Proverbs 12**

TRUE FRIENDS

The godly give good advice to their friends; the wicked lead them astray.
Proverbs 12:26

December 13

LOVING DISCIPLINE

If you refuse to discipline your children, it proves you don't love them; if you love your children, you will be prompt to discipline them.

Proverbs 13:24

Unfortunately, discussions about child discipline in our times have been reduced to arguments over spanking. Even more tragically, while people have debated spanking, parents have been cowed into forms of child-rearing that have been as abusive by default as child-rearing that has misused corporal punishment.

Parents often decide on a form of discipline long before they have actually met their children. Parental concepts of discipline must take into account the character of their own real children. Otherwise, these parents may be poorly prepared for the differences between children who are either very soft-hearted and respond positively to "light" discipline and children who are strong-willed and require a stronger-willed set of parents. Real discipline must fit the child. Real discipline conveys love to the child. When promptly applied, real discipline produces lifelong positive results.

WISE WAYS   Discipline is not only tough love; it's real love. If you have children, how are you disciplining them? What could you do better?

Today, Lord, remind me of the benefits I have received through discipline. Help me not to withhold these from my own children.

December 14

We're a generation of high rollers: high cholesterol, high blood pressure, high anxiety, and high levels of stress. While science pushes back the battle lines of real diseases, we continue to suffer devastating losses from self-inflicted illnesses. This proverb offers an unexpected insight. A "relaxed attitude" does have an amazing impact on longevity, but how does jealousy affect life?

Jealousy implies strong feelings (some translations say "passion") about what others have, what we think they have, or what we think we deserve. If we have very narrow expectations about life, and those are disappointed, what follows is the temptation to become resentful, angry, and unhappy. By way of contrast, this proverb implies a certain degree of acceptance and contentment.

This proverb doesn't argue for laziness and lack of goal-setting. It simply states the fact that unhealthy desires and a jealous outlook will seriously undermine our ability to enjoy life. We will allow what we don't have to rot away what we do have. We will shorten our lives even if we don't shorten our years.

WISE WAYS The commandment about coveting (Exodus 20:17) anticipates the contrasting results described by this proverb. Would you describe yourself as someone with a relaxed attitude, or as someone who is jealous? Why?

Today, Lord, make me aware of the differences between healthy and proper desires, and those that rob and rot my contentment.

**Read
Proverbs 14**

A KEY TO
CONTENTMENT

*A relaxed attitude
lengthens life;
jealousy rots it
away.*
Proverbs 14:30

December 15

**Read
Proverbs 15**

GOOD FEAR

*Fear of the LORD
teaches a person to
be wise; humility
precedes honor.*

Proverbs 15:33

Throughout this year as we have sought to grow in
wisdom, we have inevitably deepened our understanding of the fear of the Lord. Proverbs begins
with counsel: "Let those who are wise listen to these
proverbs and become even wiser. And let those who
understand receive guidance by exploring the depth
of meaning in these proverbs, parables, wise sayings,
and riddles. Fear of the LORD is the beginning of
knowledge" (1:5-7). The decision to pursue wisdom
is itself a wise decision, and all true wisdom and
knowledge rest on our understanding of God.

Fear of the Lord directs our use of wisdom. Fear of
the Lord reminds us that understanding and knowledge are gifts to be used for the benefit of others.
Fear of the Lord never allows us to forget who God is,
and that we aren't God. Fear of the Lord fosters the
right kind of humility. The finest honors we receive
in life are wasted if they aren't preceded by humility
and if they don't proceed from our use of wisdom to
make a difference in people's lives.

WISE WAYS   What have you learned about wisdom
and the fear of the Lord? How has this knowledge
made a difference in your life this past year?

*Today, Lord, allow me to see ways in which I can use my skills and
understanding to help others.*

December 16

The fact that the words *prayer* and *pray* do not appear in the book of Proverbs might lead some to think that wisdom doesn't include prayer. They would be wrong. Probably no book in the Bible describes the balance between faith and wise action like the book of James. The two go hand in hand. Faith always makes its presence known externally.

The entire book of Proverbs could be prefaced by this statement: "Once you have prayed, keep praying and do any number of the following wise actions, depending on the circumstances you face." The fear of the Lord mentioned in the first chapter of Proverbs is a fear developed and expressed in the laboratory of prayer.

A person who is growing in wisdom prays earnestly. Wisdom provides many lessons to direct and sharpen the way we pray. That is why James can confidently write that the prayer of a wise (righteous) person accomplishes results. Righteous prayer doesn't seek its own answers, but God's will.

WISE WAYS   How would you describe your prayers? Are you consistently seeking God's will? In what ways are you seeing "wonderful results"?

Today, Lord, I declare my renewed desire to see your will be done in my life, and in the lives of others I will mention, even as it is done in heaven.

Read
Proverbs 16

WISE PRAYER

The earnest prayer of a righteous person has great power and wonderful results.
James 5:16

December 17

NUGGETS

*A truly wise person
uses few words;
a person with
understanding is
even-tempered.*

Proverbs 17:27

Much can be said with few words. A picture may express a thousand words, and a wise proverb leads to a thousand applications.

A wise person chooses his words carefully, and uses no more of them than necessary. As other proverbs clearly remind us, the degree of foolishness usually rises to keep pace with the number of words we use. The greater the quantity of words, the less likely we are to find the quality in them.

The person with understanding can be even-tempered because he or she knows more than the immediate circumstance. Uneven temper comes from being too influenced by the moment. Even-temperedness doesn't mean that the person approaches everything the same way; rather it means that the person has an understanding that directs him to respond to each situation with the appropriate temper (response). When Jesus was angry, he was displaying a profound even-tempered reaction to dishonoring evil in God's house. We would do well to seek to become even-tempered people of few words!

WISE WAYS   Silent wisdom is most effective when it produces a few, well-chosen words. How much do you talk? How much do you listen? How do you respond to the events in your life?

Today, Lord, make the few things I say really count for you.

December 18

What better meditation could we have on the meaning of this proverb than the words of Jesus? "I command you to love each other in the same way that I love you. And here is how to measure it—the greatest love is shown when people lay down their lives for their friends. You are my friends if you obey me. I no longer call you servants, because a master doesn't confide in his servants. Now you are my friends, since I have told you everything the Father told me" (John 15:12-15).

Jesus demonstrated the greatest love of a friend. He laid down his life for us. As wonderful and close as brothers can be, there is a place for friendship that is even closer. Part of this comes from the fact that brothers aren't chosen, but friends are. A brother (or sister) who chooses to be a friend is as close as humans can be. The only relationship closer is the one Jesus defined as his alone—a friend whose death would ransom and save his friends in a way no one else could do, and which they could never do for themselves. What a friend we have in Jesus!

WISE WAYS Do you consider Jesus to be your very best friend? How can you show him how much you love him? How can you be his friend?

Today, Lord, I thank you for your sacrificial gift; for giving me the immeasurable honor of your friendship.

**Read
Proverbs 18**

WHAT A FRIEND WE HAVE!

There are "friends" who destroy each other, but a real friend sticks closer than a brother.
Proverbs 18:24

December 19

COSTLY BODY
LANGUAGE

*If you stop listening
to instruction,
my child,
you have turned
your back on
knowledge.*
Proverbs 19:27

Body language speaks loudly! Fingers in ears, an empty stare into space, or a turned back communicate an unwillingness to listen. Those actions are often meant to convey a rejection of the person speaking, but this proverb makes it clear that the real harm occurs to the one who turns away.

Instruction describes the means; knowledge describes the ends. The instruction lasts for a limited time; knowledge stays for a long time. If the instruction gets rejected, the knowledge won't be available when it is needed.

The child in this proverb is receiving a priceless piece of counsel. Children who have been trained to listen well have been given a life skill they will use every day of their lives. The instruction may or may not be good ("friends" are always ready with "instruction"), but failure to pay attention will prevent the opportunity to reject or accept the instruction. And it will greatly limit the young person's growth in wisdom and knowledge. There are few successful adults who don't wonder how much more they could have accomplished if they had listened to wise mentors earlier and better.

WISE WAYS How easily do you listen to and accept instruction? Consider a time when you listened, learned, and were the better for it.

Today, Lord, help me remember I am your child. I can't afford to stop listening to your instructions every day.

December 20

Middle age offers a unique time for reflection. This proverb sounds like someone wrote it in the central days of life. Middle-agers can look in both directions. They look back on earlier life; they look forward to their senior years. They have enough experience to realize past mistakes and can reasonably expect enough time to make important corrections.

Obviously, what amazes middle-agers about youth is the raw, seemingly unlimited energy they exude. It's tiring to even think about it. Mid-lifers also wonder when they might exhibit the kind of quiet wisdom and experience that seems so obvious in their seasoned elders.

So, what is the splendor and glory of the in-between years? As mentioned above, it is the incomplete perspective that includes two kinds of opportunity: a chance to acknowledge that the energy of youth is not inexhaustible and a chance to make significant adjustments in life as the autumn years approach. An acceptance of both these opportunities marks the wisdom and beauty of middle age.

WISE WAYS What season of life are you in right now? How can you use the gifts of this time for God's glory?

Today, Lord, help me live my age. Help me to be grateful for the years you have given and hopeful of years of service and obedience in the future. I also anticipate heaven!

Read
Proverbs 20

LOOKING
BOTH WAYS

*The glory of
the young
is their strength;
the gray hair
of experience
is the splendor
of the old.*

Proverbs 20:29

December 21

Read
Proverbs 21

✳

LIMITED
FREE WILL

*Human plans,
no matter how wise
or well advised,
cannot stand
against the LORD.*
Proverbs 21:30

Human will empowers us to accomplish great good or great evil. An individual or group can plan an act of terrorism that shocks the world. Meanwhile, other individuals can choose to act with such selfless aban-don that the world cries with wonder and honor. Are we to conclude from such events that the world is on its own, that humanity's plans succeed or fail by chance or brilliance without God's interference?

As horrific as some acts seem, do they not create an impression of how bad things might become if all limits and all checks on human will were removed? The answer to the question, "If God loves and is all power-ful why doesn't he stop people from doing evil?" must be that God does love and is all powerful and stops acts of evil all the time. Every day. We can't see most of his work, except when he foils some evil plan of ours.

We are eager to question God when evil breaks out but reluctant to praise God when good breaks out. Given the evidence from Scripture and history, is it not more amazing that good is ever done than that some people succeed in expressing their sinful character?

WISE WAYS   How would you answer someone who asked you, "If God is loving and all powerful, why is there so much evil in the world?" Practice your answer—you'll probably need it.

Today, Lord, help me to be aware of your watchfulness over the world. Help me to always submit my plans and intentions to you.

December 22

What are the distinguishing characteristics of the people this proverb describes as "angry, short-tempered people"? They live in a constant state of anger that is capable of almost instant and unexpected escalation to rage. Two types of people stay away from this kind of person: those who are under attack by them and those who are wise.

So, why is the warning necessary? Because angry, short-tempered people work hard to recruit allies. There often occurs an almost eerie process in which friends of angry, short-tempered people take on the same characteristics out of an instinct for self-preservation. The old "If-you-can't-beat-them-you-might-as-well-join-them" principle seems to take over. The results, this proverb points out, can endanger the soul.

Because attraction and attachment to angry, short-tempered people is difficult to understand or figure out, this word of wisdom usually has to be practiced before its value is recognized. The distance of keeping away allows for better perspective.

WISE WAYS Are there angry, short-tempered people in your life? If they are part of your daily living (family, employer, coworker), in what ways can you keep from learning to be like them?

Today, Lord, help me be aware of the clues I get from my surroundings. Don't let me pick up bad habits from those I'm with, and keep me from influencing them badly.

**Read
Proverbs 22**

CONTAGIOUS ANGER

Keep away from angry, short-tempered people, or you will learn to be like them and endanger your soul.

Proverbs 22:24-25

December 23

**Read
Proverbs 23**

JUST LISTEN

*God blesses the one
who reads this
prophecy to the
church, and he
blesses all who listen
to it and obey what it
says. For the time is
near when these
things will happen.*

Revelation 1:3

Two blessings and three conditions are included in this proverb. God promises to bless those who read the prophecy to the church. God also promises to bless those who listen and obey what it says. The conditions are clear and the blessings are worth pursuing.

Particularly when it comes to the book of Revelation, Christians seem far more interested in listening to others offer their interpretation of John's great vision than in actually reading the book themselves. But no blessing is offered in this proverb for those who interpret the vision. The listening seems to refer to an attitude of attentiveness to commands that will then be obeyed. Our overattention to descriptions in Revelation often blunt our interest in the prescriptions of Revelation.

The final phrase of this proverb, written nineteen hundred years ago, points to Jesus' towering words: "You also must be ready all the time. For the Son of Man will come when least expected" (Matthew 24:44). Listen and obey—be ready.

WISE WAYS If Jesus were to return today, are you ready to go with him? Why or why not?

If you come today, Lord, I'm ready! I know I don't expect it, but I'm ready to be surprised!

December 24

Long before someone invented the alarm, people invented the snooze. In fact, the snooze button is a grudging attempt to satisfy those who turn off their alarms and go back to sleep. Snooze buttons blunt the sheer effectiveness of cold-turkey wake-up buzzers.

This proverb highlights our tendency to describe laziness in diminutive terms—a little extra sleep, a little more slumber. In reality, those terms describe a bad habit. A little of this and a little of that leads to a life of inattention and poor preparation. When the alarm finally rings loud enough, the person wakes up to an overwhelming condition—poverty.

Neither scarcity nor poverty is an armed robber. There's nothing left to steal. But these experiences tend to demoralize people and rob them of the desire to reverse their habit. The warning of this proverb comes early in the process. The best time to break the tendency to be lazy occurs when it's still "a little" laziness. Fill your life with reasons to get up. Anticipate using tomorrow well. When the alarm goes off, get up! God has given you another day!

WISE WAYS How would you describe your attitude in the morning? Dread? Frustration? How can you learn to delight in another day to work for God and see what he can do through you?

Today, Lord, allow me to plan tomorrow in such a way that I will be eager to get up and be useful for you in the morning.

**Read
Proverbs 24**

YOU SNOOZE, YOU LOSE

*A little extra sleep,
a little more slumber,
a little folding of
the hands to rest—
and poverty will
pounce on you
like a bandit;
scarcity will
attack you like
an armed robber.*
Proverbs 24:33-34

December 25

**Read
Proverbs 25**

EASY TARGET

*A person without
self-control is as
defenseless as a city
with broken-down
walls.*
Proverbs 25:28

Ancient cities depended on their walls. Tall parapets and towers, built from massive blocks of stone, provided a measure of security. Those inside the city controlled access by means of narrow, fortified gates. Once the walls were breached, attacks could come from any direction. The terror of defenselessness that underlies this proverb is difficult for us to feel; it's ancient history. Perhaps a current concern like disease would give us a better sense of the crucial insight of this wise saying. A person without self-control is as helpless as a body whose autoimmune system has completely collapsed.

Self-control, like strong walls and healthy immune systems, doesn't mean that challenges or attacks won't come. It does mean that the person has established a thoughtful way to respond to pressure or attack. Without self-control, every challenge (even unintended ones) tends to be seen as a life-threatening attack. A person without self-control becomes exhausted from battling in all directions, often against imagined opposition.

WISE WAYS   How well is the fruit of the Spirit of self-control growing in your life? In what areas do you need to improve?

Today, Lord, I too need self-control. I invite your Holy Spirit in me to create in me the kind of self-control that pleases you.

December 26

Lying tends to be our first line of defense. The most damning evidence presented by our original ancestors that they had accepted their fallen condition was their attempt to lie to God. The shame they felt after eating the forbidden fruit indicated that their consciences had been awakened. They hid from God for the same reason. Up until God asked his questions, Adam and Eve could have repented. Instead, they lied. Every time we lie, we confirm that ancient family trait.

This proverb points out that lying fosters or reveals that we "hate" those to whom we lie. When we lie to people we love, we are treating them with hatred. Because successful lying creates powerful guilt, and because we want to avoid guilt, we tend to develop hatred toward those who accept our lies under the false excuse that they are gullible. Hatred toward a victim of our lies indicates that we have seriously succumbed to our own lies. To adapt an old saying, "We have lied to the enemy, and he is us."

WISE WAYS   In what ways do lying and hate go together in your own life? Where do you need to learn to be truthful?

Today, Lord, help me remember that lying includes an expression of hatred toward you. Help me abhor and resist it for that reason.

Read
Proverbs 26

DEADLY LIES

A lying tongue hates its victims, and flattery causes ruin.
Proverbs 26:28

December 27

Read
Proverbs 27

PRAISE
GAUNTLET

*Fire tests the purity
of silver and gold,
but a person
is tested by
being praised.*
Proverbs 27:21

How do we respond to praise? Do we say, "It was really nothing," or, "Anyone could have done that"? What if we feel like saying, "You know? You're right. I am the best!" Praise does turn out to be a significant test.

God designed us to respond positively to praise. We enjoy being encouraged. We relish affirmation. In fact, a central motivation for Christians is the hope that we will eventually hear God say to us, "Well done, my good and faithful servant" (Matthew 25:14-30).

This proverb offers a hint on how to respond to praise. Like fire, praise melts and purifies what is valuable while burning up what is impure. It can bring to the surface things that aren't good. For example, "Great job with that presentation! It made me rethink some assumptions I was making. But one illustration you used distracted me from your main point. Why not come up with a different one that drives home your helpful idea?" Wise praise includes a little heat.

Those receiving it shouldn't take superficial praise or flattery too seriously. It's a fire that hasn't gotten hot enough to purify.

WISE WAYS   How do you respond to praise? Can you tell the difference between genuine, sincere praise and flattery? How do you respond when people give helpful critiques as well?

Today, Lord, help me to express gratitude to those who make it a point to give me helpful praise.

December 28

The contrasts included in many proverbs offer startling insights about life. They are not mathematical equations about life, but truthful observations that guide life. More often than not, these proverbs help us look at practical issues from God's perspective.

Greed might be defined as the human tendency to create a god out of our desires. Untamed greed is an idol that must be served and satisfied. Greed abhors humility, generosity, and compassion. Greed tends to attack anything or anyone that dares to come between it and possible satisfaction. Greed does lead to fighting. And it is never satisfied.

Trusting God turns greed on its head, however. It replaces our desires with God's desires. We are trusting God when we say, "I desire to see your will done, Lord, more than my will." Trusting God does lead to prosperity. It leads to confident living. It results in a full life, measured not against what everyone else has, but by the contentment that God has supplied what we need and will continue to do so. Eventually, trusting God leads to the ultimate prosperity—eternal life.

WISE WAYS   In what areas of your life has greed come in and taken up residence? How can you learn to trust in the Lord in those areas?

Lord, allow me at least one very clear opportunity to practice trusting you as I go about my routine today.

**Read
Proverbs 28**

TRUST
INVESTMENT

*Greed causes
fighting;
trusting the LORD
leads to prosperity.*
Proverbs 28:25

December 29

Read
Proverbs 29

SUPREME COURT

*Many seek
the ruler's favor,
but justice comes
from the LORD.*
Proverbs 29:26

The system of justice in the fallen world often operates on the principle of the highest clout. To paraphrase this proverb, "If you have the king's favor, you've got nothing to worry about." In a sense, people understand an underlying principle in the universe. There is someone at the top. There is someone beyond whom there is no further appeal. The problem isn't so much that people want to appeal to a higher power to settle the issues of life. The problem is that people don't go high enough!

This proverb does not say that lower forms of authority and justice never operate. Nor does this proverb attempt to dissuade people from seeking the king's favor. It does, however, remind us that even the ruler receives his authority from God. This truth reminds us that depending on anyone other than God for ultimate justice is a hopeless effort. Eventually, we must trust that an all-wise, all-knowing, and absolutely just and holy God will settle the loose ends that keep tripping us up in life.

WISE WAYS Have you placed your hope and confidence completely in the Lord? Are there any areas of your life where you are holding back?

Today, Lord, as this year winds down, I trust that you have been pleased with my efforts to grow in wisdom. Thank you for all the lessons along the way.

December 30

One of the most popular and least expensive forms of advertising is the practice of announcing that the product is "new and improved!" Detergents promise to clean cleaner, brighten brighter, and whiten whiter. The enthusiasm of the claims is rarely proven by the results in the laundry.

How appropriate to bring the year to a close with this last blessing from Scripture! The washing to which this proverb refers cannot be improved and it is ever new. It is described more specifically in Revelation 7:14: "Then he said to me, 'These are the ones coming out of the great tribulation. They washed their robes in the blood of the Lamb and made them white.' " Jesus is God's detergent, the only one capable of washing us clean from our sin. Jesus used three single word titles to describe how he provides a spiritual cleansing to our lives. "I am the way, the truth, and the life. No one can come to the Father except through me" (John 14:6). The Way, Truth, Life—now there is a detergent that can wash you whiter than snow!

WISE WAYS In what ways is Jesus your "way"? Your "truth"? Your "life"?

Today, Heavenly Father, allow me to live as someone trusting fully in the One who washed me of my sin and gave me a new life—Jesus my Lord.

**Read
Proverbs 30**

WISE
DETERGENT

Blessed are those who wash their robes so they can enter through the gates of the city and eat the fruit from the tree of life.

Revelation 22:14

December 31

**Read
Proverbs 31**

WHAT DOES
LAST

*Charm is deceptive,
and beauty does not
last; but a woman
who fears the LORD
will be greatly
praised.*
Proverbs 31:30

The last day of the year marks a turning point in time. It counts down earthly life. It reminds us, like a birthday, that we have accumulated another year of experiences and memories in exchange for 365 precious days that cannot be retrieved. We often use the last day of the year for reflection, resolutions, and reaffirmation of our purposes in life.

The book of Proverbs ends the same way the king ended Ecclesiastes. Solomon's closing thoughts in that book were, "Here is my final conclusion: Fear God and obey his commands, for this is the duty of every person. God will judge us for everything we do, including every secret thing, whether good or bad" (Ecclesiastes 12:13-14). The woman in today's proverb represents everyone. Like her, we are challenged to fear the Lord.

The fear of the Lord begins and ends the book of Proverbs. It is that state of humble awe in which we remind ourselves every day of God's greatness, grace, and holiness. It is that state of mind in which we passionately pursue wisdom. The outcome will be God's praise.

WISE WAYS   The year's end marks the beginning of a new year, and another round of opportunities to grow in wisdom and the fear of the Lord. What can you do in the coming year to become more wise and to live more wisely?

Today, Lord, thank you again for the taste and texture of wisdom that has been such a healthy spiritual diet for me this year.

SCRIPTURE INDEX

Proverbs 25:21-22, *9/25*

Proverbs 25:27, *10/25*

Proverbs 25:28, *12/25*

Proverbs 26:1, *1/26*

Proverbs 26:11, *2/26*

Proverbs 26:12, *3/26*

Proverbs 26:17, *4/26*

Proverbs 26:18-19, *5/26*

Proverbs 26:20, *6/26*

Proverbs 26:21, *7/26*

Proverbs 26:23, *9/26*

Proverbs 26:24-25, *10/26*

Proverbs 26:27, *11/26*

Proverbs 26:28, *12/26*

Proverbs 27:1, *1/27*

Proverbs 27:2, *2/27*

Proverbs 27:3, *3/27*

Proverbs 27:4, *4/27*

Proverbs 27:6, *6/27*

Proverbs 27:10, *7/27*

Proverbs 27:14, *8/27*

Proverbs 27:17, *9/27*

Proverbs 27:18, *10/27*

Proverbs 27:19, *11/27*

Proverbs 27:21, *12/27*

Proverbs 28:5, *2/28*

Proverbs 28:7, *3/28*

Proverbs 28:9, *4/28*

Proverbs 28:10, *5/28*

Proverbs 28:13, *6/28*

Proverbs 28:14, *7/28*

Proverbs 28:20, *8/28*

Proverbs 28:21, *9/28*

Proverbs 28:23, *11/28*

Proverbs 28:25, *12/28*

Proverbs 29:6, *1/29*

Proverbs 29:15, *3/29*

Proverbs 29:17, *5/29*

Proverbs 29:18, *6/29*

Proverbs 29:20, *8/29*

Proverbs 29:21, *9/29*

Proverbs 29:22, *10/29*

Proverbs 29:25, *11/29*

Proverbs 29:26, *12/29*

Proverbs 30:1-3, *1/30*

Proverbs 30:4, *1/30*

Proverbs 30:5, *3/30*

Proverbs 30:6, *4/30*

Proverbs 30:7-8, *5/30*

Proverbs 30:10, *6/30*

Proverbs 30:15-16, 18-
19, 21-23, *1/9*

Proverbs 30:17, *7/30*

Proverbs 30:20, *8/30*

Proverbs 30:32, *10/30*

Proverbs 30:33, *11/30*

Proverbs 31:8-9, *1/31*

Proverbs 31:10-12, *2/14,
3/31*

Proverbs 31:20, *5/31*

Proverbs 31:25, *7/31*

Proverbs 31:26, *8/31*

Proverbs 31:27, *2/14*

Proverbs 31:28-29, *10/31*

Proverbs 31:30, *12/31*

Ecclesiastes 10:18, *12/10*

Ecclesiastes 12:13, *12/4*

Ecclesiastes 12:13-14, *12/31*

Isaiah 2:5, *4/13*

Isaiah 59:2, *4/28*

Isaiah 66:2, *9/1*

Jeremiah 2:12-13, *9/28*

Jeremiah 29:13, *6/10*

Daniel 9:14, *5/2*

Hosea 6:6, *2/15*

Micah 6:6-8, *2/15*

Micah 6:8, *4/11*

Matthew 5:1-12, *4/6*

Matthew 5:3, *1/28*

Matthew 5:4, *2/25*

Matthew 5:5, *3/25*

Matthew 5:6, *4/22*

Matthew 5:7, *5/27*

Matthew 5:8, *6/24*

Matthew 5:9, *4/26, 7/22*

Matthew 5:10, *8/26*

Matthew 5:11-12, *9/23*

Matthew 5:14-16, *6/3*

Matthew 5:21-22, *7/20*

Matthew 5:43-44, *1/7,
9/25*

Matthew 6:2, *7/29*

Matthew 6:9, *4/22*

Matthew 6:14-15, *4/1*

Matthew 6:19-21, *10/7*

Matthew 6:21, *6/10*

Matthew 6:24, *3/11, 9/17*

Matthew 7:1, *12/6*

Matthew 7:1-2, *4/15*

Matthew 7:12, *1/31, 2/4,
5/27*

Matthew 7:20, *5/6*